Collecting Metal Shoulder Titles

To Barbara

Ray Westlake

Collecting Metal Shoulder Titles

Second Edition

LEO
COOPER

LONDON

First published in Great Britain in 1980 by
Frederick Warne (Publishers)Ltd
Reprinted in this Second Edition 1996 by Leo Cooper
an imprint of Pen & Sword Books Limited
47 Church Street, Barnsley, South Yorkshire S70 2AS

*For up-to-date information on other titles
produced under the Pen & Sword imprint,
please telephone or write to:*

Pen & Sword Books Limited
FREEPOST
47 Church Street
Barnsley
South Yorkshire
S70 2BR

Telephone (24 hours): 01226 734555

ISBN 0-85052-524-1

British Library Cataloguing in Publication Data

**Printed by Redwood Books Ltd
Trowbridge, Wiltshire.**

Contents

ACKNOWLEDGEMENTS

I would like to thank all those friends and fellow collectors without whose help this book would not have been possible. Thanks must also go to the curators of the many Regimental Museums who have provided information and the opportunity to inspect unit scrap books and photograph albums.

ABBREVIATIONS

Admin. Bn. Administrative Battalion
Bn. Battalion
C.B. Cadet Battalion
C.C.N. *Catalogue of Clothing and Necessaries*
Coy Company
H.A.C. Honourable Artillery Company
HQ Headquarters
K.D. Khaki Drill
L.I. Light Infantry
O.T.C. Officer Training Corps
R.A. Royal Artillery
R.F.A. Royal Field Artillery
R.G.A. Royal Garrison Artillery
R.H.A. Royal Horse Artillery
R.S.M. Regimental Sergeant Major
R.V.C. Rifle Volunteer Corps
R.Vs. Rifle Volunteers
S.D. Service Dress
Sqn Squadron
T. Territorial
T.A.V.R. Territorial Army and Volunteer Reserve
T.F. Territorial Force
V. Volunteer
V.B. Volunteer Battalion
w.m. white metal
Yeom Yeomanry

Introduction

Metal shoulder titles were introduced shortly after 1881 and were at first only worn on officers' tropical uniforms. Khaki drill uniforms were issued in India in 1885 and it was on this dress that titles were first used by all ranks. Home service and other forms of dress at first had the title of the regiment stitched into the shoulder straps, metal titles being issued by 1907. Embroidered titles were used on the service dress that was introduced in 1902; these were retained until 1907 when the *Priced Vocabulary of Clothing and Necessaries* for that year stated that embroidered titles would be replaced by metal. By 1908 metal titles were being worn throughout the British Army and the following quotation from *Clothing Regulations* indicates how and on what forms of dress they were worn: 'Metal shoulder titles will be worn on both shoulder straps of garments for which they are authorized. The lower edge of the title (or shoulder badge if authorized in lieu) will be $\frac{1}{2}$ inch above the seam joining the shoulder strap to the sleeve. In cases where a badge (i.e. bugle, grenade, etc) is authorized in addition to the title, the lower edge of the title will be worn $\frac{1}{4}$ inch above the seam.' The *Regulations* go on to say that: 'Titles, etc, will be worn on the shoulder straps of tunics, S.D., and K.D. jackets, and greatcoats.' Embroidered titles, similar to those worn on service dress between 1902 and 1907, were taken into use by the Brigade of Guards in 1914 and were worn on service dress throughout the Great War.

Battle dress was introduced in March, 1938, and by 1943 coloured, embroidered shoulder titles were being worn by practically every regiment and corps on the blouse. Cavalry regiments, however, were later to change to metal. Battle dress was to last, in one form or another, for almost a quarter of a century, becoming obsolete for the Regular Army in 1961.

Only the Cavalry, Brigade of Guards, members of the Light Division and some elements of the T.A.V.R. wear metal titles on the No 2 Service Dress which was introduced in 1961. Titles are now also worn on the white tropical uniform and by some units in full dress, shirtsleeve order and on the barrack jersey.

Titles listed are in brass, unless otherwise stated, and have been described as follows; titles in two or more tiers have been indicated by vertical strokes, i.e. that for the 10th Bn, The King's Liverpool Regiment, which is T over 10 over SCOTTISH over LIVERPOOL, appears in the text as T | 10 | SCOTTISH | LIVERPOOL. An oblique stroke indicates that it appears as such on the badge. The number in italics after the description of the badge refers to the illustration.

THE HOBBY

The shoulder title appears to have done more to frustrate the collector than almost any other form of insignia. Complication is encountered when non-military items are acquired and specimens just bearing straight initials cannot be identified, or, worse still, can be applied to more than one unit. Two examples that come to mind are the titles LSC and EDC. The former was in my collection as an unidentified item for some time before I saw it being worn by the London Salvage Company of the London Fire Brigade. It would, of course, have been much more pleasing if it has turned out to be the London Scottish Cyclists or perhaps the Lovat Scouts Cadets. The other title, EDC, was once offered to me as an item reputedly once worn by the Essex and Devon Cyclists. There is, of course, no such unit; the title was, in fact, worn on the winter coats supplied to roundsmen of the Express Dairy Company. Other non-military titles that turn up regularly are those worn by the Red Cross. The vast majority of Red Cross titles were much smaller in size and non-voided but many were simply smaller versions of county titles and it is just not possible to say whether or not a small CORNWALL or NORFOLK is a Red Cross item or a smaller version, possibly for officers, of a regimental title.

Another problem encountered by the collector of British (UK) titles is titles worn by overseas countries. Often items worn by, say, Canadian, Indian or South African units, can be wrongly included in a UK-only collection. Two examples are the titles DUKE's, which could mistakenly be included with titles worn by the Duke of Cornwall's or Duke of Wellington's Regiments, and the large w.m. title DLI, which could quite easily find a home with items of the Durham Light Infantry. The former is, in fact, worn by a South African regiment, The Duke of Edinburgh's Own Rifles, and the latter by the Durban Light Infantry, also of South Africa. It is recommended that a list be kept of overseas units that are encountered in books and articles. This, together with a reference to any titles shown, will prove of great assistance in eliminating any titles that are not wanted as part of a collection.

The first thing to be considered when starting any collection is what to include; the problem is basically the same as that incurred by collectors of cap badges. If titles only are to be collected it must be decided whether or not all variations are to be included and if so should this also include minor differences in sizes and metals. Other aspects to be considered are whether or not to include items worn by service battalions, volunteers, territorials, cadets etc or just to collect regular patterns.

The most popular form of collecting is the specialist collection. This usually includes all items of insignia, and sometimes medals, belonging to one particular regiment or group of regiments, or perhaps military bodies formed within a particular county. One other form of collecting which usually proves most satisfying is to collect just one example of cap badge, button, collar badge and shoulder title of as many regiments and corps as can be managed financially.

One of the most rewarding aspects of collecting is correspondence with other collectors, and the passing of information can be just as pleasing as acquiring actual items. Describing badges in print, when a photo or rubbing is not available, can sometimes be quite difficult and will often require detailed heraldic descriptions. This problem is not encountered in shoulder title collecting but one golden rule must be observed at all times when describing titles: always state the exact wording of the item and if possible include any full stops and other punctuation marks. It should also be made quite clear, when describing titles that include bugles or other devices that are worn in pairs, which way the badge is facing. It is usually accepted among collectors that when looking at a light infantry title and the mouthpiece of the bugle is on the right it will be described as facing left.

Titles have also been worn on items of uniform other than the shoulder strap. During the South African War of 1899–1902 a wide-brimmed head-dress known as the slouch hat was introduced. It soon became the custom to wear the hat with the left side turned up and fixed to the main body. Several methods of fixing the brim to the hat were used. Some units had special badges made, while others used those already in general use. In many cases the shoulder title was considered the most convenient method and it soon became widely used as the slouch hat badge. Shoulder titles were also used by some units on the field service cap of 1894–1902.

DATING

It is well known among collectors that, despite such official publications as *Dress Regulations, Clothing Regulations,* etc, dating military insignia is by no means an exact science. Although such items as cap badges can be put into neat groups, i.e. King's Crown, Queen's Crown, etc, it is now understood that these changes did not occur overnight. One pattern of title was often worn by one battalion of a regiment serving at home while another, serving abroad, was wearing something completely different. Regiments serving overseas for many years frequently had badges made up in local bazaars, the end product often bearing little or no resemblance to that listed in regulations and catalogues. Drafts from the home battalion were often sent overseas which resulted in group photos being taken of the same regiment wearing two or more patterns of title simultaneously. Regulation or sealed patterns were also ignored when titles were made up at the whim of the Commanding Officers.

Two important sources of information, however, are *Clothing Regulations* and the *Priced Vocabulary of Clothing and Necessaries,* both publications printing lists of titles to be worn. Usually the lists included in the *P.V.C.N.,* with very few exceptions, state the exact wording on the title. Several copies issued around 1923, however, did include lists which in most cases bore no resemblance to the actual titles.

From time to time lists of changes in titles worn have appeared in Army Orders and have been of immense help in establishing when a new pattern was introduced. It should be noted, however, that an order is usually preceded by a note saying that 'existing stocks of the old titles will be used up'.

Introduction to New Edition

Published in 1980, *Collecting Metal Shoulder Titles* recorded for the first time the metal titles worn throughout the British Army by units of the Regular, Militia, Yeomanry, Volunteer, Territorial and Cadet forces. As a back-up to the shoulder title records, dates of formation, amalgamation, disbandment and changes in designation for all regiments were also provided.

This new addition incorporates with the original work *Supplements 1* and 2, together with listings of new titles discovered or introduced since.

Sincere thanks to John Gaylor, Norman Litchfield, Mr N Pallot, John Pimlott and Barry Sutton for help with this edition.

1
Cavalry

Metal shoulder titles were worn before 1885 on officers' tropical uniforms, embroidered titles being worn on all other forms of dress. Khaki drill was introduced for all ranks in 1885 and one-piece metal titles were worn. In the 1900 *Priced Vocabulary of Clothing and Necessaries* separate numerals and letters were listed for wear by cavalry regiments, the letters being D *(1)*, H *(2)*, L *(3)* and the one-piece DG *(4)*. By 1907 the one-piece RD, was listed for the 1st Royal Dragoons and one-piece numerals for regiments numbered between 10 and 21 were being worn, although not listed in the *P.V.C.N.* Also by 1907 metal titles had replaced embroidered ones on the full dress tunics and the *P.V.C.N.* for that year states that metal titles would now be worn on service dress.

Two- or three-piece titles, which were worn numeral above initials, continued until 1913 when the *P.V.C.N.* lists the more familiar one-piece horizontal title.

Only one pattern of the single letters D, H and L seems to have been used, although cast brass versions do exist. The double letters, DG and RD, however, did appear in several variations; the RD patterns have been listed under the Royal Dragoons, the Dragoon Guard titles so far noted are *5, 6* and *7*.

Shoulder titles worn by amalgamated regiments have been included with those of the senior regiment.

The Life Guards

1660 Two regiments raised which later became known as 1st and 2nd Life Guards.

1922 Amalgamated as The Life Guards (1st and 2nd). Subtitle soon omitted.

Shoulder titles: LG (8) which also served as the field service cap badge and is now worn in gold anodised. Two other versions have been worn (9, 10), the latter being an officers' pattern. No special titles distinguishing the two Regiments have been found. It is possible, however, that the separate numbers, '1' and '2', may have been worn above the title.

The Royal Horse Guards (The Blues)

1661 Raised.

1969 Amalgamated with The Royal Dragoons (1st Dragoons) to form The Blues and Royals (Royal Horse Guards and 1st Dragoons).

Shoulder titles: RHG (11) which was later issued in gold anodised. A smaller version was worn by officers (12). BLUES & ROYALS (13) in gold anodised. A badge commemorating the capture of the Standard of the French 105th Infantry Regiment at Waterloo in 1815 is worn above the titles. The badge, which is worn in pairs, is an eagle standing on a tablet inscribed '105' with a laurel wreath on its breast. The eagle is in gold anodised while the wreath and number are in silver (14).

Household Battalion

1916 This battalion, which served as infantry, was formed from personnel of the Reserve Regiment of the Household Cavalry.

1918 Disbanded.

Shoulder title: HB (15).

1st King's Dragoon Guards

1685 Raised.

1959 Amalgamated with The Queen's Bays (2nd Dragoon Guards) to form 1st The Queen's Dragoon Guards.

Shoulder titles: K | D.G (16) for officers and K | DG (17) for other ranks. Two other titles (18, 19) were made and worn overseas; both are in cast brass. These were superseded in 1913 by 1DG, (20, 21), which themselves were replaced by KDG.

(*22, 23, 24*), in 1921. The first two titles are officers' patterns, while the latter is the other ranks' issue. Other versions were *25*, which is made from cast brass and was worn overseas, *26* and K.D.G (*27*), which was worn by other ranks. QDG (*28*).

The Queen's Bays (2nd Dragoon Guards)

1685 Raised.
1959 Amalgamated with 1st King's Dragoon Guards.
Shoulder titles: 2DG (*29*) was worn until 1921. The post-1921 titles were BAYS, the smaller patterns being worn by officers, the R.S.M. and by all members of the band, while the larger type was worn by all other ranks. Both large and small titles appeared both with a gap at the bottom of the 'A' and without: *30, 31* and *32*, which is in cast brass, *33, 34* and *35*.

3rd Carabiniers (Prince of Wales's Dragoon Guards)

1685 Raised.
1922 Amalgamated with The Carabiniers (6th Dragoon Guards) to form 3rd/6th Dragoon Guards.
1928 Redesignated 3rd Carabiniers (Prince of Wales's Dragoon Guards).
1971 Amalgamated with The Royal Scots Greys (2nd Dragoons) to form The Royal Scots Dragoon Guards (Carabiniers and Greys).
Shoulder titles: 3.DG (*36*): 3DG (*37, 38*) are officers' patterns while *39, 40, 41, 42* and *43* are other ranks'. A smaller version (*44*), which is in gold anodised, was introduced in the 1960s. The title 3RD KDG (*45*) remains a mystery, the Regiment never being known as King's.
3/6DG (*46, 47*) was worn between 1922 and 1928, the smaller pattern being for officers.
ROYAL SCOTS | DRAGOON GDS (*48*) in gold anodised.

4th Royal Irish Dragoon Guards

1685 Raised.
1922 Amalgamated with 7th Dragoon Guards (Princess Royal's) to form 4th/7th Dragoon Guards.
1936 Redesignated 4th/7th Royal Dragoon Guards.
Shoulder titles: 4DG (*49, 50, 51, 52*).
4/7DG (*53, 54*) and 4/7D.G (*55*): 4/7RDG (*56, 57*). The smaller titles were worn by officers, the R.S.M. and the Bandmaster. *57* is now worn in gold anodised.

5th Royal Inniskilling Dragoon Guards

1685 Raised.
1922 Amalgamated with The Inniskillings (6th Dragoons) to form the 5th/6th Dragoons.
1927 Redesignated 5th Inniskilling Dragoon Guards.
1935 Became 5th Royal Inniskilling Dragoon Guards.

Shoulder titles: 5DG *(58. 59)*. The first title to be worn after amalgamation was
v.vI | D *(60)* which was listed in the *P.V.C.N.* for 1926. *Clothing Regulations*
for 1936 gives the titles as castle | DG, which were worn with the flags flying to the
rear *(61. 62)*. The castle, which is in w.m., has also appeared with both windows
and the door closed *(63)*. A smaller version is now worn in gold and silver
anodised *(64, 65)*. v | horse | DG *(66)* was worn prior to 1900, possibly by
officers only.

The Carabiniers (6th Dragoon Guards)

1685 Raised.
1922 Amalgamated with 3rd Dragoon Guards.
Shoulder titles: 6DG *(67)*, changing to CARABINIERS *(68)* in 1920.

7th Dragoon Guards (Princess Royal's)

1688 Raised.
1922 Amalgamated with 4th Royal Irish Dragoon Guards.
Shoulder titles: 7DG *(69. 70)*.

The Royal Dragoons (1st Dragoons)

1661 Raised.
1969 Amalgamated with The Royal Horse Guards.
Shoulder titles: Before 1913 the title RD *(71. 72)* was worn with a 'I' separate
above; one-piece versions also exist *(73. 74)*, the latter being made from cast
brass and worn overseas. Between 1913 and 1921 the titles were 1RD *(75.
76)*. A further change took place in 1921 when ROYALS *(77)* was introduced.
These were worn in brass by other ranks and in bronze by officers. Smaller
versions *(78)* were issued in 1952, followed by one in gold anodised in the 1960s.

The Royal Scots Greys (2nd Dragoons)

1678 Raised.
1971 Amalgamated with 3rd Carabiniers.
Shoulder titles: 2D *(79)*, changing to GREYS *(80)* in 1920. A smaller version
(81) was introduced in 1952 which changed to gold anodised in the late 1960s.
Officers wore RSG *(82)* and R.S.G *(83)*.

3rd The King's Own Hussars

1685 Raised.
1958 Amalgamated with 7th Queen's Own Hussars to form The
      Queen's Own Hussars.
Shoulder titles: 3H *(84)*. Officers' titles were 111KOH, which was replaced by
3KOH *(85, 86)* and 3.K.O.H *(87)*, the latter being in cast brass.
QOH *(88)*.

4th Queen's Own Hussars

1685 Raised.
1958 Amalgamated with 8th King's Royal Irish Hussars to form
The Queen's Royal Irish Hussars.
Shoulder titles: 4H (*89*). Officers wore IV│QOH (*90*), which is in cast brass, and
4QOH (*91, 92*), which were worn until amalgamation.
QRIH (*93*) is now worn in gold anodised.

5th Royal Irish Lancers

1689 Raised.
1799 Disbanded.
1858 Reformed.
1922 Amalgamated with 16th The Queen's Lancers.
Shoulder titles: 5L (*94*) and 5.L (*95, 96*).

The Inniskillings (6th Dragoons)

1689 Raised.
1922 Amalgamated with 5th Dragoon Guards.
Shoulder titles: 6D (*97*), which was replaced by INNISKILLING (*98, 99*) in 1920,
the latter being the officers' pattern. Another title, 6│INS.D (*100*), which is made
from cast brass, was worn by officers overseas before 1914.

7th Queen's Own Hussars

1690 Raised.
1958 Amalgamated with 3rd King's Own Hussars.
Shoulder titles: 7H (*101, 102*).

8th King's Royal Irish Hussars

1693 Raised.
1958 Amalgamated with 4th Queen's Own Hussars.
Shoulder titles: VIIIH (*103*) for officers and R.S.M., 8H (*104, 105*) for other ranks.

9th Queen's Royal Lancers

1715 Raised.
1960 Amalgamated with 12th Royal Lancers (Prince of Wales's)
to form 9th/12th Royal Lancers (Prince of Wales's).
Shoulder titles: 9L (*106*) is the title listed in *Clothing Regulations* and the
Vocabulary of Clothing and Necessaries and was the issue pattern. However,
recruits were obliged to buy IXL (*107*). Other versions of this title exist: *108*
and *109*, which are in cast brass; *110*, which has been made from three
separate letters; *111*, which has extra long lugs ($\frac{1}{2}$in) for fitting to the shoulder
chains; *112* and *113*.
IX/XIIL (*114*) is now worn in gold anodised.

10th Royal Hussars (Prince of Wales's Own)

1715 Raised.

1969 Amalgamated with 11th Hussars (Prince Albert's Own) to form The Royal Hussars (Prince of Wales's Own).

Shoulder titles: 10H (*115*) was the title listed in *Clothing Regulations* and the *Vocabulary of Clothing and Necessaries* until 1952 but it would seem that XRH was favoured by the Regiment. Variations of the title are *116*, which is the earlier pattern, *117* and *118*. An anodised version (*119*) was introduced in the 1960s.

ROYAL | HUSSARS (*120*), which is in gold anodised.

11th Hussars (Prince Albert's Own)

1715 Raised.

1969 Amalgamated with 10th Royal Hussars

Shoulder titles: 11H (*121*) is the only title to be listed in *Clothing Regulations* but two Roman numeral versions exist, both in cast brass (*122, 123*). The latter is fitted with extra long lugs ($\frac{1}{2}$in) for wear on shoulder chains.

12th Royal Lancers (Prince of Wales's)

1715 Raised.

1960 Amalgamated with 9th Queen's Royal Lancers.

Shoulder titles: 12L (*124*) is listed in *Clothing Regulations*. However, recruits were obliged to buy XIIRL. The longer version (*125*) was worn by officers, the R.S.M. and the Bandmaster while the shorter pattern (*126*) was worn by all ranks below.

13th Hussars

1715 Raised.

1922 Amalgamated with 18th Hussars (Queen Mary's Own) to form 13th/18th Hussars.

1935 Redesignated 13th/18th Royal Hussars (Queen Mary's Own).

Shoulder titles: 13H (*127, 128, 129*); 13/18H (*130, 131*), the smaller title being worn by officers and the R.S.M. After 1935 the officers' titles were changed to include the letter 'R'. The new titles first appeared as 13/18RH (*132*) but later changed to XIII/XVIIIRH (*133*). A larger version of *132* also exists (*134*). *131* is now worn in gold anodised by other ranks.

14th King's Hussars

1715 Raised.

1922 Amalgamated with the 20th Hussars to form the 14th/20th Hussars.

1936 Redesignated 14th/20th King's Hussars.

Shoulder titles: 14H (*135, 136, 137*); the latter, in cast brass, was worn overseas. All these patterns were worn by other ranks. Four versions of the officers' title, which included Roman numerals, were worn: XIV.H (*138, 139*); XIVH (*140, 141*). Two unofficial titles were also worn by officers: XIV.KH (*142*), which is in cast brass, and XIV│H (*143*).

14/20H (*144, 145*), the latter being worn by officers. Another title, XIV/XXKH (*146*), was worn by officers after 1936. An anodised version of *145* is now worn.

15th The King's Hussars

1759 Raised.
1922 Amalgamated with 19th Royal Hussars to form 15th/19th Hussars.
1934 Redesignated 15th/19th The King's Royal Hussars.

Shoulder titles: 15.H (*147*) and 15H (*148*) for other ranks. Five versions of the officers' title have been noted: XVKH (*149, 150, 151*), XV.K.H (*152*) and XV.KH (*153*). Two other titles exist: XVH (*154*) and XV│KH (*155*), the latter being hand-cut.

The post-amalgamation title for other ranks was 15/19H (*156*), the officers having a smaller pattern (*157, 158*), until after 1934 when XV.XIX.KRH (*159*) was adopted. Officers' titles were later changed to XV.XIX.H (*160, 161*), the latter now being worn in silver anodised.

16th The Queen's Lancers

1759 Raised.
1922 Amalgamated with 5th Royal Irish Lancers to form 16th/5th Lancers.
1954 Redesignated 16th/5th The Queen's Royal Lancers.

Shoulder titles: 16QL (*162*), 16.QL (*163*) and 1.6.Q.L (*164*) were the first one-piece titles to be worn. These were replaced, before 1913, by 16L (*165*).

16/5L (*166*) for all ranks below Bandmaster and *167* for ranks above. An anodised version is now worn (*168*).

17th Lancers (Duke of Cambridge's Own)

1759 Raised.
1922 Amalgamated with 21st Lancers to form 17th/21st Lancers.

Shoulder titles: 17L (*169, 170, 171*).

17/21L (*172*) for officers and the R.S.M.; *173* for all ranks below.

18th Royal Hussars (Queen Mary's Own)

1858 Raised.
1922 Amalgamated with 13th Hussars.

Shoulder titles: 18H (*174, 175*), the latter being the officers' pattern.

19th Royal Hussars (Queen Alexandra's Own)

1858 Raised.
1922 Amalgamated with 15th The King's Royal Hussars.

Shoulder titles: 19H (*176*). Officers' titles were XIXH (*177*) superseded by XIXRH (*178*) after 1908.

20th Hussars

1858 Raised.

1922 Amalgamated with 14th King's Hussars

Shoulder titles: 20H (*179*). Three versions of the officers' title XHX have been noted: *180*, *181* and *182*, the last two being in cast brass. Another cast brass title was XX│H (*183*).

21st Lancers (Empress of India's)

1858 Raised as 3rd Bengal European Light Cavalry.

1861 Redesignated 21st Hussars.

1897 Redesignated 21st Lancers.

1922 Amalgamated with 17th Lancers.

Shoulder titles: The pre-1897 title was in Roman numerals XXI, placed upon the letter H (*184*). A smaller version of this title also exists. After 1897 the shoulder titles changed to 21L (*185*, *186*) for other ranks and XXIL (*187*, *188*) for officers.

22nd Dragoons

1940 Raised.

1948 Disbanded.

Shoulder titles: 22.D (*189*) for other ranks and XXIID (*190*) for officers.

23rd Hussars

1940 Raised.

1948 Disbanded.

Shoulder title: 23.H (*191*).

24th Lancers

1940 Raised.

1948 Disbanded.

Shoulder title: 24L.

25th Dragoons

1941 Raised.

1948 Disbanded.

Shoulder title: 25D (*192*).

26th Hussars

1941 Raised.

1948 Disbanded.

Shoulder titles: XXVIH for officers and 26H (*193*) for other ranks.

27th Lancers

1941 Raised.
1948 Disbanded.
Shoulder title: 27L (*194*).

Royal Tank Regiment

16 Feb 1916 Formed as Tank Detachment of Machine Gun Corps.

Mar 1916 Became Armoured Car Section of Motor Machine Gun Service.

May 1916 Became Heavy Section, M.G.C.

Nov 1916 Redesignated Heavy Branch.

Jul 1917 Withdrawn from M.G.C. to form the Tank Corps.

Oct 1923 Redesignated Royal Tank Corps.

Apr 1939 Redesignated Royal Tank Regiment.

Shoulder titles: TC (*195*); RTC (*196*); RTR (*197*). TANKS (*198*) was worn unofficially between 1916–20.

Royal Armoured Corps

Formed in April, 1939, from the Royal Tank Regiment and Cavalry Regiments of the Line that had been mechanized. Later several Territorial Army Battalions were added, together with Yeomanry Regiments still serving in a mounted role. In 1944 the R.A.C. absorbed the Reconnaissance Corps. The R.A.C. is an administrative and training body only, its badges and titles being worn by staff and recruits.

Shoulder titles: RAC (*199, 200, 201*), the smaller title being an officers' pattern.

2
Yeomanry

The Yeomanry Cavalry, as it was styled until 1901, was created during the latter part of the 18th Century and served as the mounted element of the Volunteer system.

A force known as the Imperial Yeomanry was created from volunteers of the existing yeomanry regiments in December, 1899, almost 200 companies being formed for service in the South African War. The entire Yeomanry was redesignated Imperial Yeomanry in April, 1901, a term that survived until the creation of the Territorial Force in 1908 when the force was titled, simply, Yeomanry.

Shoulder titles fall more or less into three groups: the pre-1900 or Yeomanry Cavalry group, the Imperial Yeomanry group, 1900–1908, and the post-1908 Territorial group. Very few titles have been noted for the first group, these being those that normally include the letters 'YC'. Titles for the second, however, which contain the letters 'IY', are much more frequent, some specimens also serving as the slouch-hat badge. Regulations for the Territorial Force stated that titles for yeomanry regiments should contain the name of the regiment surmounted by the letters 'T | Y'. This type of three-tier title was adopted by almost all the yeomanry regiments and survived until the end of the 1st World War. It is during this period, 1908–1919, that most confusion as to what was worn arises, as it would seem from inspection of actual uniforms and photos of the period that titles other than regulation were being worn simultaneously with those that were permitted. Most of the unofficial titles were usually made up from straight initials and were often very similar to the pre-1908 patterns but minus the letter 'I'. Three-tier titles were also issued in two pieces, i.e. the T | Y worn separately above the name of the regiment. *Regulations for the Territorial Force, 1908*, state that white metal titles will be worn on full dress tunics; regiments permitted to wear gold lace, however, are allowed to wear brass or gilding metal.

After the 1st World War the 'T' was dropped from the titles, the new patterns being, simply, 'Y' over the name of the unit. This type of title was often issued and worn with the 'Y' separate.

On conversion to other arms, regulations directed that shoulder titles of the parent unit should be worn with the letter 'Y' worn above. This was not strictly adhered to and in most cases the old yeomanry title was retained.

The order of precedence of yeomanry regiments was laid down in a list issued by the War Office in 1885. The order used here is based on that list.

North Irish Horse

1900 Raised as The North Irish Horse.
1902 Redesignated North of Ireland Yeomanry.
1908 Redesignated North Irish Horse.
1967 Became 'D' (North Irish Horse) Sqn, The Royal Yeomanry Regiment.

Shoulder titles: NIH; IY│NORTH OF IRELAND (202). N.I.H (203) was introduced after 1939 and is now worn with a silver maple leaf below. The leaf is worn in commemoration of the Regiment's association with Canadian infantry during the Italian campaign of 1944.

South Irish Horse

1900 Raised as The South Irish Horse.
1902 Redesignated South of Ireland Yeomanry.
1908 Redesignated South Irish Horse.
1922 Disbanded.

Shoulder titles: SIY; SIH.

1st King Edward's Horse (The King's Overseas Dominions Regiment)

1901 Raised as the 4th County of London Imperial Yeomanry (King's Colonials).
1905 Redesignated The King's Colonials Imperial Yeomanry.
1910 Redesignated King Edward's Horse (The King's Overseas Dominions Regiment).
1914 Numbered 1st.
1924 Disbanded.

Shoulder titles: KC; KEH│K.O.D.R (204).

2nd King Edward's Horse (The King's Overseas Dominions Regiment)

1914 Raised.
1917 Absorbed into the Tank Corps.

Shoulder title: 2│KEH (205).

Royal Wiltshire Yeomanry (Prince of Wales's Own)

1794 Raised.
1967 Became 'A' Sqn, The Royal Yeomanry Regiment and 'B' Coy, The Royal Wiltshire Territorials.
Shoulder titles: RWIY; T│Y│ROYAL WILTS (206); Y│R.WILTS (207); R.W.Y (208), which is listed in the *P.V.C.N.* for 1950; a smaller version also exists (209).

Warwickshire Yeomanry

1794 Raised.
1956 Amalgamated with The Queen's Own Worcestershire Hussars to form The Queen's Own Warwickshire and Worcestershire Yeomanry.
Shoulder titles: WARWICK.IMP.YEO (210); T│Y│WARWICK; Y│WARWICK (211); a smaller version was worn by officers: WY (212); WKY (213).

Queen's Own Warwickshire and Worcestershire Yeomanry

1956 Formed by the amalgamation of The Warwickshire Yeomanry and The Queen's Own Worcestershire Hussars.
1971 Became 'A' Sqn, The Mercian Yeomanry.
Shoulder title: WWY (214), latter issued in gold anodised.

Yorkshire Hussars (Alexandra, Princess of Wales's Own)

1794 Raised.
1956 Amalgamated with The Queen's Own Yorkshire Dragoons and The East Riding of Yorkshire Yeomanry to form The Queen's Own Yorkshire Yeomanry.
Shoulder titles: YHIY; T│Y│YORKS HUSSARS; Y│YORKS HUSSARS (215). YH was introduced in 1952 (216, 217), the latter being the officers' pattern.

Queen's Own Yorkshire Yeomanry

1956 Formed from the amalgamation of The Yorkshire Hussars, The Queen's Own Yorkshire Dragoons and The East Riding of Yorkshire Yeomanry.
1971 Became 'Y' Sqn, The Queen's Own Yeomanry.
Shoulder title: A fox in full cry worn in pairs (218, 219). The titles are in gold anodised.

Sherwood Rangers Yeomanry

1794 Raised.
1967 Became 'B' Sqn, The Royal Yeomanry Regiment.
Shoulder titles: SRIY; T│Y│SHERWOOD RANGERS (220); Y│SHERWOOD RANGERS (221). SRY was introduced in 1952, 222 for officers and 223 for other ranks.

Staffordshire Yeomanry (Queen's Own Royal Regiment)

1794 Raised.
1971 Became 'B' Sqn, The Queen's Own Mercian Yeomanry.
Shoulder titles: SIY; T | Y | STAFFORD (224); Y | STAFFORD (225).

Shropshire Yeomanry

1795 Raised.
1940 Converted as 75 (Shropshire Yeomanry) Medium Regiment, Royal Artillery.
1947 Transferred to Royal Armoured Corps as The Shropshire Yeomanry.
1971 Became 'C' (Shropshire Yeomanry) Sqn, The Queen's Own Mercian Yeomanry.
Shoulder titles: SIY; T | Y | SHROPSHIRE (226); Y | SHROPSHIRE (227). SY was introduced in 1947.

Ayrshire Yeomanry (Earl of Carrick's Own)

1803 Raised.
1940 Converted to 151 Field Regiment Royal Artillery.
1947 Transferred to Royal Armoured Corps as The Ayrshire Yeomanry.
1971 Became 'A' (Ayrshire Yeomanry) Sqn, The Queen's Own Yeomanry.
Shoulder titles: AIY (228); T | Y | AYRSHIRE (229); Y | AYRSHIRE (230); AY (231).

Cheshire Yeomanry (Earl of Chester's)

1803 Raised.
1945 Transferred to Royal Signals.
1947 Transferred to Royal Armoured Corps.
1971 Became 'C' (Cheshire Yeomanry) Sqn, The Queen's Own Yeomanry.
Shoulder titles: ECYC (232) which is in w.m.; ECIY (233); T | Y | CHESHIRE (234); Y | CHESHIRE (235) and (236).

Queen's Own Yorkshire Dragoons

1803 Raised.
1942 Converted to 9th Bn, The King's Own Yorkshire Light Infantry.
1947 Transferred to Royal Armoured Corps as The Yorkshire Dragoons.
1956 Amalgamated with The Yorkshire Hussars and The East Riding of Yorkshire Yeomanry.
Shoulder titles: T | Y | YORKSHIRE DRAGOONS; YORKS DRAGNS (237), which is listed in the 1920 *P.V.C.N.*; YD.

Leicestershire Yeomanry (Prince Albert's Own)

1803 Raised.

1939 Converted as 153 Field Regiment, Royal Artillery.

1947 Transferred to Royal Armoured Corps as The Leicestershire Yeomanry.

1957 Amalgamated with The Derbyshire Yeomanry to form The Leicestershire and Derbyshire (Prince Albert's Own) Yeomanry.

Shoulder titles: LIY; T|Y|LEICESTER; Y|LEICESTER; LEICESTERSHIRE| P.A.O|YEOMANRY (238) introduced in 1953; LY (239).

Leicestershire and Derbyshire (Prince Albert's Own) Yeomanry

1957 Formed from the amalgamation of The Leicestershire Yeomanry (Prince Albert's Own) and The Derbyshire Yeomanry.

1971 Became a squadron of 7th (V) Bn, The Royal Anglian Regiment.

Shoulder title: LDY (240).

North Somerset and Bristol Yeomanry

1803 Raised.

1943 Converted to 4 Air Formation Signals.

1947 Transferred to Royal Armoured Corps as The North Somerset Yeomanry.

1956 Amalgamated with 44th/50th Royal Tank Regiment to form The North Somerset Yeomanry/44th R.T.R.

1965 Redesignated The North Somerset and Bristol Yeomanry.

1967 Became 'A' Coy, The Somerset Yeomanry and Light Infantry (T).

Shoulder title: NSIY; T|Y|N. SOMERSET; Y|N. SOMERSET; NSY; NSY/44RTR (241) in w.m.

Duke of Lancaster's Own Yeomanry

1819 Raised.

1940 Converted to 77 Medium Regiment, Royal Artillery.

1947 Transferred to Royal Armoured Corps as the Duke of Lancaster's Own Yeomanry.

Shoulder titles: T|Y|D OF LANCASTERS (242). Y|D OF LANCASTERS was the first title to be used after the 1st World War but it was soon replaced by Y|D of L's OWN (243) which is listed in the *P.V.C.N.* for 1920. Y|LANCASTER was introduced before 1953, as DLCY (244) was introduced that year and is listed as replacing it. A smaller version (245) was later issued which also appeared in gold anodised. Another title, DLO (246), also exists.

Lanarkshire Yeomanry

1819 Raised.

1939 Converted to 155 Field Regiment, Royal Artillery.

1947 Transferred to Royal Armoured Corps as The Lanarkshire Yeomanry.

1956 Amalgamated with The Queen's Own Royal Glasgow Yeomanry and the 1st/2nd Lothians and Border Horse to form The Queen's Own Lowland Yeomanry.

Shoulder titles: T | Y | LANARK (247); Y | LANARK (248), shown in the P.V.C.N. for 1920; Y | LANARKSHIRE (249).

Queen's Own Lowland Yeomanry

1956 Formed by the amalgamation of The Lanarkshire Yeomanry, The Queen's Royal Glasgow Yeomanry and the 1st/2nd Lothians and Border Horse.

Shoulder title: QOLY (250).

Northumberland Hussars

1819 Raised.

1940 Converted to 102 Light Anti-Aircraft/Anti-Tank Regiment, Royal Artillery.

1947 Transferred to Royal Armoured Corps as The Northumberland Hussars.

1971 Became 'NH' Sqn, The Queen's Own Yeomanry.

Shoulder titles: NHIY, T | Y | NORTHUMBERLAND (251); Y | NORTHUMBERLAND.H; NHY. NH in brass (252) was introduced in 1953, changing to chrome shortly after. Officers wore a smaller version in silver (253).

South Nottinghamshire Hussars

1826 Raised.

1920 Converted to 107 Brigade, Royal Field Artillery.

1967 Redesignated South Nottinghamshire Hussars Yeomanry (RHA).

1971 Became 'B' Battery, 3rd (V) Bn, The Worcestershire and Sherwood Foresters.

Shoulder titles: T | Y | SNH; Y | SNH.

Denbighshire Yeomanry (Hussars)

1830 Raised.

1920 Converted to 243 and 244 Batteries of 61 Medium Brigade R.G.A.

1956 Amalgamated with 384 Light Regiment, Royal Artillery to form 372 (Flintshire and Denbighshire Yeomanry) Light Regiment, Royal Artillery.

1967 Redesignated The Flintshire and Denbighshire Yeomanry, Royal Artillery.

1971 Became 'B' Coy, 3rd (V) Bn, Royal Welch Fusiliers.
Shoulder titles: DHIY *(254)*; T│Y│DENBIGH *(255)*; Y│DENBIGH.

Westmorland and Cumberland Yeomanry

1830 Raised.
1920 Converted to 369 and 370 Batteries of 93 (Westmorland and
Cumberland Yeomanry) Brigade R.F.A.
1967 Became 'B' (Westmorland and Cumberland Yeomanry) Coy,
4th (T) Bn, The Border Regiment.
Shoulder titles: WCIY *(256)*; T│Y│W AND C *(257)*; Y│W AND C *(258)*.

Pembroke Yeomanry (Castlemartin)

1830 Raised.
1920 Converted to 102 (Pembroke and Cardigan) Brigade R.F.A.
1961 Transferred to Royal Armoured Corps as The Pembroke
Yeomanry.
1967 Became 'A' Coy, (Pembroke Yeomanry), 4th (T) Bn, The
Welch Regiment.
Shoulder titles: PYC; PIY *(259)* also worn in w.m.; T│Y│PEMBROKE *(260)*;
Y│PEMBROKE; PY *(261)* in gold anodised, which was introduced after 1961.

Royal East Kent (The Duke of Connaught's Own) (Mounted Rifles)

1830 Raised.
1920 Merged with the West Kent Yeomanry and convered to 385
and 386 Batteries of 97 (Kent Yeomanry) Army Brigade R.F.A.
1961 Amalgamated with 3rd/4th County of London Yeomanry to
form The Kent and County of London Yeomanry (Sharpshooters).
Shoulder titles: T│Y│ROYAL EAST KENT *(262)*; Y│ROYAL EAST KENT.; REKY *(263)*;
KY *(264)*.

Kent and County of London Yeomanry (Sharpshooters)

1961 Formed by the amalgamation of the Kent Yeomanry and the
3rd/4th County of London Yeomanry (Sharpshooters).
1967 Became 'C' (Kent and County of London) Sqn, The Royal
Yeomanry Regiment.
Shoulder title: KCLY *(265)* which was also issued in gold anodised.

Hampshire Carabiniers

1830 Raised.
1887 Title 'Carabiniers' added.
1922 Converted to 95 (Hampshire Yeomanry) Army Brigade
R.F.A.

1967 Became 'C' Coy, The Hampshire and Isle of Wight Territorials.

Shoulder titles: HIY; HANTS│CARABINIERS (266, 267). Another version which has the top tier curved upwards also exists. HANTS│T│CARABINIERS (268) was introduced after 1908.

Royal Bucks Hussars

1830 Raised.

1920 Converted to 393 and 394 Batteries of 99 Brigade R.F.A.

1967 Became 'P' (Royal Bucks Yeomanry) Battery, The Buckinghamshire Regiment, Royal Artillery.

Shoulder titles: RBH (269, 270). RBY (271) is an officers' title.

Derbyshire Yeomanry

1830 Raised.

1920 Became 24th (Derbyshire Yeomanry) Armoured Car Coy, The Tank Corps.

1939 Transferred to Royal Armoured Corps as The Derbyshire Yeomanry.

1957 Amalgamated with The Leicestershire Yeomanry.

Shoulder titles: DIY; T│Y│DERBYSHIRE; Y│DERBYSHIRE (272). D.Y (273) was an officers' title which was introduced for all ranks in 1951; a larger version also exists.

Queen's Own Dorset Yeomanry

1830 Raised.

1920 Converted to 375 and 376 Batteries of 94 Brigade R.F.A.

1967 Became 'A' Coy, The Dorset Territorials.

Shoulder titles: QO│DORSET│IY (274). T│Y│DORSET and, later, Y│DORSET were worn on service dress, while QO│DORSET│Y (275) was worn on the blue patrol tunic in w.m.

Royal Gloucestershire Hussars

1830 Raised.

1920 Became 21st (Gloucestershire Yeomanry) Armoured Car Coy, The Tank Corps.

1939 Transferred to Royal Armoured Corps as The Royal Gloucestershire Hussars Yeomanry.

1971 Became 'HQ', 'A' and 'C' Sqns of The Wessex Yeomanry.

Shoulder titles: T│Y│RGH; Y│RGH (276). RGH alone (277) was worn after 1950.

Hertfordshire Yeomanry

1830 Raised.

1920 Converted to 86th (Herts Yeomanry) Brigade R.F.A.

1961 Amalgamated with 305 (Bedfordshire Yeomanry) Light Regiment, Royal Artillery to form 286 (Hertfordshire and Bedfordshire Yeomanry) Field Regiment, Royal Artillery.

1967 Became 201st (Hertfordshire and Bedfordshire Yeomanry) Medium Battery of 100th (Eastern) Medium Regiment, Royal Artillery and 2nd and 3rd Companies of the Bedfordshire and Hertfordshire Regiment (T).

Shoulder titles: HIY; T|Y|HERTS (*278*); Y|HERTS (*279*). HY was also worn and can be seen in 1st World War photographs.

Berkshire Yeomanry (Dragoons) (Hungerford)

1831 Raised.
1920 Converted to 395 and 396 Batteries of 99 Brigade R.F.A.
1961 Amalgamated with the 2nd County of London Yeomanry (Westminster Dragoons) to form the Berkshire and Westminster Dragoons.

Shoulder titles: BERKS.I.Y (*280*); T|Y|BERKS (*281*); Y|BERKS (*282*).

Berkshire and Westminster Dragoons

1961 Formed by the amalgamation of the Berkshire Yeomanry and the 2nd County of London Yeomanry (Westminster Dragoons)
1967 Became 'HQ' (Berkshire and Westminster Dragoons) Sqn. The Royal Yeomanry Regiment.

Shoulder title: B&WDGNS (*283*).

1st County of London Yeomanry (Middlesex, Duke of Cambridge's Hussars)

1831 Raised as the Uxbridge Yeomanry.
1838 Redesignated 'Middlesex'.
1884 Subtitle 'Hussars' added.
1908 Designated 1st County of London Yeomanry (Middlesex, Duke of Cambridge's Hussars).
1920 Converted as 2nd Cavalry Divisional Signals, Royal Corps of Signals (Middlesex Yeomanry).

Shoulder titles: MIDDLESEX|HUSSARS, the top tier being curved upwards and the bottom tier down; MH (*284*); T|Y|MIDDLESEX; Y|MIDDLESEX.

Note Three other titles exist that were possibly worn by the Middlesex Yeomanry: T|Y|COUNTY OF LONDON (*285*), T|Y|LONDON (*286*) and Y|LONDON (*287*). The last title is listed in the 1920 *P.V.C.N.* as being worn by the 1st, 2nd and 3rd County of London Yeomanrys. During the 1st World War the lower tier of the shoulder titles worn by the 9th to 28th Bns of the London Regiment changed from COUNTY OF LONDON to LONDON. If the same rule is applied to the County of London Yeomanry it would seem that the titles worn were *285* 1908-c1916, *286* c1916-1919 and *287* 1919, possibly by all three units.

Royal 1st Devon Yeomanry

1831 Raised.
1920 Amalgamated with The Royal North Devon Yeomanry as the 96th Brigade R.F.A. (Royal Devon Yeomanry).
1967 Became 'A' Sqn, The Devonshire Territorials.
Shoulder titles: R1│DIY; R1D│IY (288) and RID│IY (289); in this title the figure '1' has been cast as a capital 'I'; R1s.t.DY (290); RDY (291) which was worn in brass by other ranks and silver by officers.

Duke of York's Own Loyal Suffolk Hussars

1831 Raised.
1921 Converted to 411 and 412 Batteries of 103 (Suffolk and Norfolk Yeomanry) Brigade R.F.A.
1967 Became 202nd (Suffolk and Norfolk) Medium Battery of 100th (Eastern) Medium Regiment, Royal Artillery and 'A' and 'D' (Suffolk and Norfolk) Coys of The Suffolk and Cambridgeshire Regiment.
Shoulder titles: The intertwined letters LSH (292); T│Y│SUFFOLK (293); Y│SUFFOLK (294); LSH.

Royal North Devon (Hussars) Yeomanry

1831 Raised.
1920 Amalgamated with The Royal 1st Devon Yeomanry.
Shoulder titles: NDIY; NDH (295) in bronze; RNDH (296), which was worn by officers in w.m.

Queen's Own Worcestershire Hussars

1831 Raised.
1920 Converted to 397 and 398 Batteries of 100 (Worcestershire and Oxfordshire Yeomanry) Army Brigade R.F.A.
1950 Transferred to Royal Armoured Corps as The Queen's Own Worcestershire Hussars.
1956 Amalgamated with The Warwickshire Yeomanry.
Shoulder titles: IY│WORCESTER (297); T│Y│WORCESTERSHIRE (298); ʸY│WORCESTERSHIRE. QOWH was introduced in 1951.

West Kent Yeomanry (Queen's Own)

1831 Raised.
1920 Amalgamated with The Royal East Kent Yeomanry.
Shoulder titles: WKIY (299) in both brass and w.m.; T│Y│WEST KENT (300); Y│WEST KENT (301); WKY (302).

West Somerset Yeomanry

1831 Raised.

1920 Converted to 373 and 374 Batteries of 94 (Somerset and Dorset Yeomanry) Brigade R.F.A.

1967 Became 'B' Coy. The Somerset Yeomanry and Light Infantry (T).

Shoulder Titles: WSYC; WSIY (303); T|Y|W. SOMERSET (304); Y|W. SOMERSET (305); 1/1stW.S.Y (306) which was worn 1914–18.

Queen's Own Oxfordshire Hussars

1931 Raised.

1922 Converted to 399 and 400 Batteries of 100 (Worcestershire and Oxfordshire Yeomanry) Brigade R.F.A.

1967 Became 'A' Coy. The Oxfordshire Territorials.

Shoulder titles: QOOH|IY; T|Y|OXFORD; QOOH (307) which is in both brass and w.m.

Montgomeryshire Yeomanry

1831 Raised.

1920 Became two companies of the 7th Bn. Royal Welch Fusiliers.

Shoulder titles: MYC (308); MIY; T|Y|MONTGOMERY (309); Y|MONTGOMERY (310).

1st/2nd Lothians and Border Horse

1846 Raised as East Lothian Troop.

1848 Amalgamated with the Berwickshire Troop (raised 1845).

1877 Designated Lothians and Berwickshire Yeomanry.

1908 Redesignated Lothians and Border Horse.

1920 Became 19th (Lothians and Border) Armoured Car Coy. The Tank Corps.

1939 Transferred to Royal Armoured Corps as 1st Lothians and Border Yeomanry.

1947 Amalgamated with 2nd Lothians and Border (formed 1939) as 1st/2nd Lothians and Border.

1956 Amalgamated with The Lanarkshire Yeomanry and The Royal Glasgow Yeomanry.

Shoulder titles: L&B (311) which was worn before 1908; T|Y|L.&B. HORSE (312); Y|L.&B. HORSE.

Queen's Own Royal Glasgow Yeomanry

1848 Raised.

1920 Converted as 101 (Queen's Own Royal Glasgow Yeomanry) Army Brigade R.F.A.

1947 Transferred to Royal Armoured Corps as The Queen's Own Royal Glasgow Yeomanry.

1956 Amalgamated with The Lanarkshire Yeomanry and The Lothians and Border Horse.

Shoulder titles: QOR | GIY *(313)*; QOR | GY; T | Y | Q.O.R. GLASGOW *(314)*; Y | Q.O.R. GLASGOW; QORGY *(315)* which was introduced in 1953.

Lancashire Hussars

1848 Raised.
1920 Converted to 106 (Lancashire Yeomanry) Army Brigade R.F.A.
Shoulder titles: T | Y | LANCASHIRE HUSSARS *(316)*; Y | LANC.H; LHY *(317)*

Surrey Yeomanry (Queen Mary's Regiment)

1901 Raised.
1920 Converted to 391 and 392 Batteries of 98 (Surrey and Sussex Yeomanry) Army Brigade R.F.A.
1947 Redesignated 298 Field Regiment, Royal Artillery (Surrey Yeomanry).
1967 Transferred to Royal Armoured Corps as The Surrey Yeomanry.
1971 Became 'D' Battery of the 6th (V) Bn, The Queen's Regiment.
Shoulder titles: IY | SURREY; T | Y | SURREY *(318)*; Y | SURREY *(319)*; S&Sx.YEO *(320)* which was worn between 1920 and 1947.

Fife and Forfar Yeomanry

1901 Raised.
1922 Became the 20th (Fife and Forfar) Armoured Car Coy, The Tank Corps.
1939 Transferred to Royal Armoured Corps as The Fife and Forfar Yeomanry.
1956 Amalgamated with The Scottish Horse to form The Fife and Forfar Yeomanry/Scottish Horse.
Shoulder titles: F&FIY *(321)*; T | Y | FIFE & FORFAR *(322)*; Y | FIFE & FORFAR *(323)*; F & FY, which is curved, a straight version in a border *(324)* being introduced in 1951; F&F.

Fife and Forfar Yeomanry/Scottish Horse

1956 Formed by the amalgamation of The Fife and Forfar Yeomanry and The Scottish Horse.
Shoulder title: FFY/SH *(325)* in w.m.

Norfolk Yeomanry (The King's Own Royal Regiment)

1901 Raised.
1920 Converted to 108 (Norfolk Yeomanry) Brigade R.F.A.
1923 Amalgamated with the Suffolk Yeomanry as 108 (Suffolk and Norfolk Yeomanry) Brigade R.F.A.
Shoulder titles: KORR *(326, 327)*.

Sussex Yeomanry

1901 Raised.
1920 Converted to 389 and 390 Batteries of 98 (Surrey and Sussex Yeomanry) Army Brigade R.F.A.
1947 Became 344 (Sussex Yeomanry) Light Anti-Aircraft/ Searchlight Regiment, Royal Artillery.
1967 Became 200th (Sussex Yeomanry) Medium Battery, 100th (Eastern) Medium Regiment, Royal Artillery.
Shoulder titles: IY│SUSSEX; T│Y│SUSSEX (328); Y│SUSSEX (329); S&SX. YEO (320) which was worn between 1920 and 1947.

Cadets: The 1st Cadet Regiment, Sussex Yeomanry was recognized in 1914 as the Brighton Brigade, Sussex Cadets, being redesignated in 1916. The Regiment consisted of three battalions, the 1st and 3rd being disbanded in 1920 with the 2nd following in 1921.
Shoulder title: CADETS│Y│SUSSEX (330).

Glamorgan Yeomanry

1901 Raised.
1920 Converted to 324 Battery of 81 Brigade R.F.A.
1967 Became 211 (South Wales) Light Air Defence Battery of 104 L.A.D. Regiment.
Shoulder titles: GIY (331); T│Y│GLAMORGAN (332); Y│GLAMORGAN (333).

Lincolnshire Yeomanry

1901 Raised.
1920 Disbanded.
Shoulder titles: T│Y│LINCOLN (334); Y│LINCOLN.

City of London Yeomanry (Rough Riders).

1901 Raised.
1922 Converted as 'C' Battery of 11th (Honourable Artillery Company and City of London Yeomanry) Brigade, Royal Horse Artillery.
1947 Transferred to Royal Armoured Corps as The City of London Yeomanry.
1961 Amalgamated with The Inns of Court Regiment.
Shoulder titles: ROUGH│IY│RIDERS (335); ROUGH│RIDERS (336); T│Y│CITY OF LONDON (337); Y│CITY OF LONDON (338). After 1922 the titles changed to Y│RHA (339, 340) for other ranks and CITY OF LONDON│Y│RHA (341) for officers. CITY OF LONDON│YEOMANRY was introduced in 1952, the title, which is oval in shape, exists in two sizes. RR also exists in two sizes.

Westminster Dragoons (2nd County of London Regiment)

1901 Raised.
1922 Became 22nd Armoured Car Coy. The Tank Corps.
1939 Became 102 Officer Cadet Training Unit.
1940 Transferred to Royal Armoured Corps as The Westminster Dragoons.
1961 Amalgamated with The Berkshire Yeomanry.

Shoulder titles: IY | WESTMINSTER DRAGOONS (342); WD (343); 2 | WD (344), which was worn by 2/2nd County of London Yeomanry which was formed in 1914 and disbanded by 1916. WDGNS (345) was introduced in 1951. See also note under 1st County of London Yeomanry.

3rd/4th County of London Yeomanry (Sharpshooters)

1901 Raised.
1920 Became 23rd Armoured Car Coy. The Tank Corps.
1938 Transferred to Royal Armoured Corps as 23rd Cavalry Armoured Car Regiment.
1939 Redesignated 3rd County of London Yeomanry (Sharpshooters).
1944 Amalgamated with the 4th County of London Yeomanry (Sharpshooters) to form the 3rd/4th.
1961 Amalgamated with The Kent Yeomanry.

Shoulder titles: SS; SSY; FIRST | SHARPSHOOTERS, worn 1939 to 1944; SHARPSHOOTERS (346), introduced in 1952. See also note under 1st County of London Yeomanry.

Bedfordshire Yeomanry

1901 Raised.
1920 Converted as 105 (Bedfordshire Yeomanry) Army Brigade R.F.A.
1961 Amalgamated with The Hertfordshire Yeomanry.

Shoulder titles: BIY (347); T | T | BEDFORD; Y | BEDFORD.

Essex Yeomanry

1901 Raised.
1920 Converted to 104 Brigade R.F.A.
1967 Redesignated The Essex Yeomanry (R.H.A.) Royal Artillery.

Shoulder titles: The intertwined letters EY were worn between 1905 and 1908; T | Y | ESSEX (348); Y | ESSEX. E Y (349) and E.Y (350) were introduced in 1951.

Northamptonshire Yeomanry

1902 Raised.
1920 Converted to 25th Armoured Car Coy. The Tank Corps.
1939 Transferred to Royal Armoured Corps at The Northamptonshire Yeomanry.

1956 Became 'D' (Northampton Yeomanry) Sqn. The Inns of Court Regiment.
1961 Withdrawn and converted to 250 (NY) Field Sqn. Royal Engineers.
1967 Became 'A' Coy. The Northamptonshire Regiment (T).
Shoulder titles: NIY (*351*); T│Y│NORTHAMPTON (*352*); Y│NORTHAMPTON (*353*); NY (*354*) in gold anodised.

East Riding Yeomanry

1902 Raised.
1920 Converted to 26th Armoured Car Coy. The Tank Corps.
1939 Transferred to Royal Armoured Corps as The East Riding Yeomanry.
1956 Amalgamated with The Yorkshire Hussars and The Yorkshire Dragoons.
Shoulder titles: ERYIY (*355*); T│Y│E. RIDING (*356*); Y│E. RIDING; ERY, introduced in 1952.

Lovat Scouts

1903 Raised.
1949 Converted to 677 Regiment, Royal Artillery (Lovat Scouts).
1967 Became Orkney and Zetland (Lovat Scouts) Battery, The Highland Regiment RA and 'A' (Lovat Scouts) Coy, 3rd (T) Bn. The Queen's Own Highlanders.
Shoulder titles: LS (*357*); Y│LS.

Scottish Horse

1903 Raised.
1940 Converted to 79 Medium Regiment, Royal Artillery.
1947 Transferred to Royal Armoured Corps as The Scottish Horse.
1956 Amalgamated with The Fife and Forfar Yeomanry.
Shoulder titles: SCOTTISH│HORSE with leaves (*358*) was worn by other ranks, the officers having a plain version (*359*). Another pattern was *360*.

Welsh Horse

1914 Raised.
1917 Amalgamated with The Montgomeryshire Yeomanry.
Shoulder title: WELSH HORSE (*361*) which is in bronze.

4th County of London Yeomanry (Sharpshooters)

1939 Raised.
1944 Amalgamated with the 3rd County of London Yeomanry.
Shoulder titles: 4CLY (*362*); 4CLY│"SHARPSHOOTERS" (*363*).

Royal Yeomanry

1967 Formed as The Royal Yeomanry Regiment and consisting of:
HQ (Berkshire and Westminster Dragoons) Sqn.
A (Royal Wiltshire Yeomanry) Sqn.
B (Sherwood Rangers Yeomanry) Sqn.
C (Kent and County of London Yeomanry) Sqn.
D (North Irish Horse) Sqn.
1971 Redesignated The Royal Yeomanry.
Shoulder titles: RYR (*364*), replaced in 1971 by ROYAL|YEOMANRY (*365*), both in gold anodised.

Queen's Own Yeomanry

1971 Formed and consisting of:
NH Sqn The Northumberland Hussars.
Y Sqn The Queen's Own Yorkshire Yeomanry.
A Sqn The Ayrshire Yeomanry.
C Sqn The Cheshire Yeomanry.
Shoulder titles: QOY in gold anodised. 'Y' Sqn wear the figure of a fox in full cry (*218, 219*), also in gold anodised.

Queen's Own Mercian Yeomanry

1971 Formed and consisting of:
A Sqn The Queen's Own Warwickshire and Worcestershire Yeomanry.
B Sqn The Staffordshire Yeomanry.
C Sqn The Shropshire Yeomanry.
Shoulder title: QOMY.

Wessex Yeomanry

1971 Formed and consisting of:
HQ Sqn Royal Gloucestershire Hussars.
A Sqn Royal Gloucestershire Hussars.
B Sqn Royal Wiltshire Yeomanry.
C Sqn Royal Gloucestershire Hussars.
D Sqn Royal Devon Yeomanry.
Shoulder title: WESSEX|YEOMANRY in gold anodised.

3
Arms and Services

Army Air Corps

1942 Formed; containing the Glider Pilot Regiment and the Parachute Regiment.

1944 The Special Air Service also included.

1946 S.A.S. disbanded.

1949 Parachute Regiment became part of the infantry of the line.

1950 Glider Pilot Regiment formed as a separate regiment. Army Air Corps disbanded.

1957 Reformed, incorporating the Glider Pilot Regiment.

Shoulder title: AAC (366) in gold anodised.

Army Catering Corps

1941 Formed.

Shoulder titles: ACC (367, 368, 369), the latter also being issued in gold anodised. 370 is an officers' pattern.

Army Physical Training Corps

1860 Formed as the Army Gymnastic Staff, became the Army Physical Training Staff.

1940 Redesignated Army Physical Training Corps.

Shoulder titles: A.P.T.S. (371, 372); APTC (373, 374); AP.T.C (375) which is in cast brass.

Corps of Military Accountants

1919 Formed.

1927 Disbanded.

Shoulder title: CMA (376).

General Service Corps

1942 Formed.

Shoulder title: GSC (377).

Intelligence Corps

1940 Formed.

Shoulder title: INT. CORPS (378) which has also been issued in gold anodised.

Labour Corps

1917 Formed.
1919 Disbanded.
Shoulder titles: LC (379, 380).

Machine Gun Corps

1915 Formed by Royal Warrant dated 22 October, 1915, the Machine Gun Corps consisted of three branches: Cavalry, Infantry and the Motor Machine Gun Service. The Heavy Branch, which became The Tank Corps in July, 1917, was formed in November, 1916.
1922 Corps disbanded.
Shoulder titles: At first all four branches wore the title MGC (381) with the addition of the relevant letter, 'C' (382), 'I' (383), 'H' (384) or 'M' (385) below. One-piece titles were also worn, (386), and by 1922 the MGC title was being worn alone by the Cavalry and Infantry and the Motor section had been issued with MMG (387). Other titles, which were privately made and quite unofficial, were IX|MGC (388), which was worn by the 9th Battalion, HS|MGC, HEAVY SECTION|MGC and ARMOURED|MOTORS (389) which was worn by Motor Machine Gun Batteries formed in India.

Another unit within the Machine Gun Corps was the Ist Armoured Motor Battery. It was formed in 1915 from M.G.C. and Army Service Corps personnel and saw service in East Africa.
Shoulder title: 1|AMB (390).

Military Provost Staff Corps

1901 Formed as the Military Prison Staff Corps.
1906 Redesignated Military Provost Staff Corps.
Shoulder title: MPSC (391).

National Defence Company

1916 Formed as the Royal Defence Corps.
1936 Redesignated National Defence Company.
1939 Companies were merged into battalions and linked with infantry of the line regiments. The new battalions were usually numbered 30th with the sub-title (Home Defence).
Shoulder titles: R.D.C (392); N.D.C (393).

Non-Combatant Corps

1915 Non-Combatant Corps formed and served throughout the 1st World War.
1939 Reformed as the Non-Combatant Labour Corps.
1940 Redesignated Non-Combatant Corps. Disbanded after 1945.
Shoulder titles: N.C.C. (394); NCLC. The former also exists without the full stops. Both titles were also used as cap badges.

Royal Army Chaplains' Department

1796 Official formation date of the Army Chaplains' Department.
1919 Became the Royal Army Chaplains' Department.
Shoulder titles: ACD (395); CHAPLAIN (396) which is in cast brass.

Royal Army Dental Corps

1921 Formed as the Army Dental Corps.
1946 Became the Royal Army Dental Corps.
Shoulder titles: A.D.CORPS (397); RADC (398, 399), the latter being an officers' pattern.

Royal Army Educational Corps

1920 Formed as the Army Educational Corps.
1946 Became the Royal Army Educational Corps.
Shoulder titles: A.E.C (400); RAEC (401, 402, 403, 404), the latter being an officers' pattern.

Royal Army Medical Corps

Regulars

1873 The Army Medical Department formed, consisting of officers only.
1884 Redesignated Army Medical Staff.

1855 The Medical Staff Corps formed, consisting of other ranks only.
1898 The A.M.S. and the M.S.C. amalgamated as the Royal Army Medical Corps.

Shoulder titles: AMS; MSC (405). The post-1898 RAMC title has been worn in three sizes, 406 on service dress until 1939, 407 on tropical uniforms, being replaced in the 1960s by 408. The latter is now worn in gold anodised. Another pattern (409) is made from cast brass.

Militia

Regular pattern titles were worn with the addition of the letter 'M' worn separate below.

Volunteers

The South London Volunteers Medical Staff Corps formed part of the Home District, London Companies, and wore the title SL | MSC (410). The Army List for January, 1908 shows over forty volunteer units of the R.A.M.C. So far only the following metal titles have been noted, all in w.m.:
2 | V | RAMC | LONDON (411); V | RAMC | LEICESTER & LINCOLN (412); V | RAMC | LEEDS; V | RAMC | LIVERPOOL (413); V | RAMC | MAIDSTONE; V | RAMC | DEVON; V | RAMC | SOUTH WALES; V | RAMC | SOUTH WALES BORDER.
Volunteers of the 1914–18 period wore the two-piece title V | RAMC (414).

Territorials

Royal Army Medical Corps Territorials were divided up into six sections between 1908 and 1921: Mounted Brigade Field Ambulances, Divisional Field Ambulances, General Hospitals, Sanitary Companies, Divisional Sanitary Sections and Casualty Clearing Stations. After 1921 all units wore the title T | RAMC, either in one or two pieces.

Mounted Brigade Field Ambulances

Eastern	T | RAMC | EASTN. MTD. BGDE. (*415*)
Highland	T | RAMC | HIGHLAND (*416*)
London	T | RAMC | LONDON (*417*)
Lowland	T | RAMC | LOWLAND (*418*)
North Midland	T | RAMC | N. MIDLAND (*419*)
Notts and Derby	T | RAMC | NOTTS & DERBY
South Eastern	T | RAMC | SOUTH EASTERN (*420*)
1st South Midland	T | RAMC | SOUTH MIDLAND (*421*)
2nd South Midland	T | RAMC | SOUTH MIDLAND (*421*)
South Wales	T | RAMC | HEREFORDSHIRE (*422*)
1st South Western	T | RAMC | WILTS (*423*)
2nd South Western	T | RAMC | S. WESTERN (*424*)
Welsh Border	T | RAMC | CHESHIRE
Yorkshire	T | RAMC | YORKSHIRE

Divisional Field Ambulances

1st East Anglian	T | RAMC | EAST ANGLIAN (*425*)
2nd East Anglian	T | RAMC | EAST ANGLIAN (*425*)
3rd East Anglian	T | RAMC | 3 EAST ANGLIAN
1st Highland	T | RAMC | HIGHLAND (*416*)
2nd Highland	T | RAMC | HIGHLAND (*416*)
3rd Highland	T | RAMC | HIGHLAND (*416*)
1st Home Counties	T | RAMC | HOME COUNTIES (*426*)
2nd Home Counties	T | RAMC | HOME COUNTIES (*426*)
3rd Home Counties	T | RAMC | HOME COUNTIES (*426*)
1st East Lancashire	T | RAMC | E. LANCASHIRE (*427*)
2nd East Lancashire	T | RAMC | E. LANCASHIRE (*427*)
3rd East Lancashire	T | RAMC | E. LANCASHIRE (*427*)
1st West Lancashire	T | RAMC | W. LANCASHIRE (*428*)
2nd West Lancashire	T | RAMC | W. LANCASHIRE (*428*)
3rd West Lancashire	T | RAMC | W. LANCASHIRE (*428*)
1st London (City)	T | RAMC | CITY OF LONDON (*429*)
2nd London (City)	T | RAMC | CITY OF LONDON (*429*)
3rd London (City)	T | RAMC | CITY OF LONDON (*429*)
4th London	T | RAMC | LONDON (*417*)
5th London	T | RAMC | LONDON (*417*)
6th London	T | RAMC | LONDON (*417*)
1st Lowland	T | RAMC | LOWLAND (*418*)
2nd Lowland	T | RAMC | LOWLAND (*418*)
3rd Lowland	T | RAMC | LOWLAND (*418*)

1st North Midland	T │ RAMC │ DERBYSHIRE (*430*)
2nd North Midland	T │ RAMC │ LEICESTER
3rd North Midland	T │ RAMC │ N. MIDLAND (*419*)
1st South Midland	T │ RAMC │ SOUTH MIDLAND (*421*) and
2nd South Midland	T │ RAMC │ S. MIDLAND (*431*). It is not
3rd South Midland	known which of the three units wore which title.
1st Northumbrian	T │ RAMC │ NORTHUMBRIAN (*432*)
2nd Northumbrian	T │ RAMC │ NORTHUMBRIAN (*432*)
3rd Northumbrian	T │ RAMC │ NORTHUMBRIAN (*432*)
1st West Riding	T │ RAMC │ W. RIDING (*433*)
2nd West Riding	T │ RAMC │ W. RIDING (*433*)
3rd West Riding	T │ RAMC │ W. RIDING (*433*)
1st Welsh	T │ RAMC │ MONMOUTH
2nd Welsh	T │ RAMC │ WELSH (*434*)
3rd Welsh	T │ RAMC │ WELSH (*434*)
1st Wessex	T │ RAMC │ DEVON
2nd Wessex	T │ RAMC │ DEVON
3rd Wessex	T │ RAMC │ HANTS (*435*)
	T │ RAMC │ WESSEX (*436*) was also worn.

General Hospitals

1st Eastern	T │ RAMC │ EASTERN (*437*)
2nd Eastern	T │ RAMC │ EASTERN (*437*)
1st London (City)	T │ RAMC │ CITY OF LONDON (*429*)
2nd London (City)	T │ RAMC │ CITY OF LONDON (*429*)
3rd London	T │ RAMC │ LONDON (*417*)
4th London	T │ RAMC │ LONDON (*417*)
5th London	T │ RAMC │ LONDON (*417*)
1st Northern	T │ RAMC │ NORTHERN
2nd Northern	T │ RAMC │ LEEDS
3rd Northern	T │ RAMC │ NORTHERN
	T │ NGH │ RAMC was also worn.
4th Northern	T │ RAMC │ LINCOLN
5th Northern	T │ RAMC │ LEICESTER
1st Scottish	T │ RAMC │ SCOTTISH (*438*)
2nd Scottish	T │ RAMC │ SCOTTISH (*438*)
3rd Scottish	T │ RAMC │ SCOTTISH (*438*)
4th Scottish	T │ RAMC │ SCOTTISH (*438*)
1st Southern	T │ RAMC │ SOUTHERN
2nd Southern	T │ RAMC │ BRISTOL (*439*)
3rd Southern	T │ RAMC │ OXFORD
4th Southern	T │ RAMC │ SOUTHERN
5th Southern	T │ RAMC │ HANTS (*435*)
1st Western	T │ RAMC │ LIVERPOOL
2nd Western	T │ RAMC │ MANCHESTER

Sanitary Companies

1st London (City)	T | RAMC | CITY OF LONDON (*429*)
2nd London	T | RAMC | LONDON (*417*)

Divisional Sanitary Sections

East Anglian	T | RAMC | EAST ANGLIAN (*425*)
Highland	T | RAMC | HIGHLAND (*416*)
Home Counties	T | RAMC | HOME COUNTIES (*426*)
East Lancashire	T | RAMC | E. LANCASHIRE (*427*)
West Lancashire	T | RAMC | W. LANCASHIRE (*428*)
Lowland	T | RAMC | LOWLAND (*418*)
Northumbrian	T | RAMC | NORTHUMBRIAN (*432*)
North Midland	T | RAMC | N. MIDLAND (*419*)
South Midland	T | RAMC | S. MIDLAND (*431*)
West Riding	T | RAMC | W. RIDING (*433*)
Welsh	T | RAMC | WELSH (*434*)
Wessex	T | RAMC | WESSEX (*436*)

Casualty Clearing Stations

East Anglian	T | RAMC | EAST ANGLIAN (*425*)
Highland	T | RAMC | HIGHLAND (*416*)
Home Counties	T | RAMC | HOME COUNTIES (*426*)
East Lancashire	T | RAMC | E. LANCASHIRE (*427*)
West Lancashire	T | RAMC | W. LANCASHIRE (*428*)
1st and 2nd London	T | RAMC | LONDON (*417*)
Lowland	T | RAMC | LOWLAND (*418*)
North Midland	T | RAMC | N. MIDLAND (*419*)
South Midland	T | RAMC | S. MIDLAND (*431*)
Northumbrian	T | RAMC | NORTHUMBRIAN (*432*)
West Riding	T | RAMC | W. RIDING (*433*)
Welsh	T | RAMC | WELSH (*434*)
Wessex	T | RAMC | WESSEX (*436*)

Royal Army Ordnance Corps

1875 The Ordnance Store Department formed, consisting of officers only.
1896 Redesignated Army Ordnance Department.

1877 Ordnance Store Branch formed, consisting of other ranks only.
1881 Redesignated Ordnance Store Corps.
1896 Redesignated Army Ordnance Corps.

1918 The Army Ordnance Department and the Army Ordnance Corps amalgamated as the Royal Army Ordnance Corps.

Shoulder titles: AOD; OSC (*440*); AOC (*441, 442*); RAOC, the larger pattern (*443*) was worn until shortly after the 2nd World War when replaced by *444* for other ranks and *445* for officers. The officers' pattern was issued to all ranks in the 1950s and is now worn in gold anodised.

Royal Army Pay Corps

1870 Pay Sub-Department of the Control Department formed, consisting of officers only.
1878 Designated Army Pay Department.
1905 Redesignated Army Accounts Department.
1909 Redesignated Army Pay Department.

1893 Army Pay Corps formed, consisting of other ranks only.

1920 Army Pay Department and the Army Pay Corps amalgamated as the Royal Army Pay Corps.

Shoulder titles: APD (446, 447), the latter made from cast brass; APC (448), which also served as the headdress badge between 1898 and 1900. After 1920 the titles changed to the intertwined letters RAPC. An anodised version (449) appeared in the 1960s, with one almost half-size being issued by 1975. The straight letters RAPC (450) have also been worn.

Royal Army Service Corps

Regulars

1855 The Land Transport Corps formed.
1856 Redesignated the Military Train.
1870 The Military Train was divided; the officers formed the Control Department and the men the Army Service Corps.
1881 The two units were merged as the Commissariat and Transport Corps.
1889 Redesignated the Army Service Corps.
1918 Became the Royal Army Service Corps.
1965 Became the Royal Corps of Transport.

Shoulder titles: ASC (451, 452, 453, 454); RASC, the larger pattern (455), was worn until just after the 2nd World War when 456 was introduced for other ranks and 457 for officers. The officers' title was issued to all ranks in the late 1950s.

Motor Companies

Motor Companies were first formed during the 1st World War, their shoulder title being MT | ASC (458), changing to MT (459, 460, 461).

Volunteers pre-1908

The only metal shoulder titles so far noted for the Volunteer element of the Army Service Corps are ASC | V | 1ST LOTHIAN, which was worn in three separate pieces and V | ASC | SUFFOLK; both titles are in w.m.

Volunteers 1914-18

Although almost every county in the British Isles formed Motor Volunteer units during the 1st World War only one shoulder title has so far been noted, M.V | E. YORK (462). All Motor Volunteers, who were part of the Volunteer Training Corps, were placed under the wing of the Army Service Corps in 1918 and designated A.S.C. M.T. (Volunteers). Another transport unit that was formed during the 1st World War was the National Motor Volunteers. It was also administered by the A.S.C. and the shoulder title was NM | VOLUNTEERS (463).

Territorials

Mounted Brigade Transport and Supply Columns

Eastern	T | ASC | EASTERN
Highland	T | ASC | HIGHLAND (*464*)
London	T | ASC | LONDON (*465*)
Lowland	T | ASC | LOWLAND (*466*)
North Midland	T | ASC | N MIDLAND (*467*)
1st and 2nd South Midland	T | ASC | SOUTH MIDLAND
Notts and Derby	T | ASC | NOTTS | AND | DERBY (*468*)
South Eastern	T | ASC | SOUTH EASTERN
South Wales	T | ASC | GLAMORGAN (*469*)
1st and 2nd South Western	T | ASC | S. WESTERN (*470*)
Welsh Border	T | A.S.C | W.B.M.B (*471*)
Yorkshire	T | ASC | YKS MTD BDE (*472*)
	T | ASC | YORKSHIRE (*473*)

Divisional Transport and Supply Columns

EAST ANGLIAN, containing East Anglian Divisional Company, Norfolk and Suffolk Brigade Company, East Midland Brigade Company and the Essex Brigade Company.

T \| ASC \| EAST ANGLIAN
T \| ASC \| NORFOLK & SUFFOLK
T \| ASC \| EAST MIDLAND
T \| ASC \| ESSEX (*474*)

HIGHLAND, containing 1st (HQ) Company, 2nd (Seaforth and Cameron) Brigade Company, 3rd (Gordon) Brigade Company and the 4th (Black Watch) Brigade Company.

T \| ASC \| HIGHLAND (*464*)
T \| ASC \| GORDON
T \| ASC \| BLACK WATCH (*475*)

HOME COUNTIES, containing Home Counties Divisional Company, Surrey Brigade Company, Kent Brigade Company and Middlesex Brigade Company

T \| ASC \| HOME COUNTIES (*476*)
T \| ASC \| SURREY
T \| ASC \| KENT (*477*)
T \| ASC \| MIDDLESEX (*478*)

EAST LANCASHIRE, containing East Lancashire Divisional Company, Lancashire Fusiliers Brigade Company, East Lancashire Brigade Company and the Manchester Brigade Company.

T \| ASC \| E. LANCASHIRE
T \| ASC \| MANCHESTER (*479*)

WEST LANCASHIRE, containing West Lancashire Divisional Company, North Lancashire Brigade Company, Liverpool Brigade Company and the South Lancashire Brigade Company.

T \| A.S.C \| W. LANCASHIRE (*480*)
T \| ASC \| NORTH LANCASHIRE (*481*)
T \| ASC \| N LANCASHIRE (*482*)
T \| ASC \| LIVERPOOL (*483*)
T \| ASC \| S. LANCASHIRE

1ST AND 2ND LONDON, containing eight companies.

T \| ASC \| LONDON (*465*)

LOWLAND, containing 1st (HQ) Company, 2nd Company, 3rd (Scottish

T \| ASC \| LOWLAND (*466*)

Rifle) Brigade Company and the 4th (Highland
Light Infantry) Brigade Company.

NORTH MIDLAND, containing North Midland Divisional Company, Lincoln and Leicester Brigade Company, Staffordshire Brigade Company and the Notts and Derby Brigade Company.	T | ASC | N. MIDLAND (467) T | ASC | STAFFORD T | ASC | NOTTS & DERBY T | ASC | N.M.D (484)
SOUTH MIDLAND, containing South Midland Divisional Company, Warwickshire Brigade Company, Gloucester and Worcester Brigade Company and the South Midland Brigade Company.	T | ASC | SOUTH MIDLAND T | ASC | WARWICKSHIRE T | ASC | WORCESTERSHIRE (485)
NORTHUMBRIAN, containing Northumbrian Divisional Company, Northumberland Brigade Company, York and Durham Brigade Company and the Durham Light Infantry Brigade Company.	T | ASC | NORTHUMBRIAN T | ASC | YORK & DURHAM (486) T | ASC | NORTHUMBERLAND
WEST RIDING, containing West Riding Divisional Company and the 1st, 2nd and 3rd West Riding Brigade Companies.	T | ASC | W. RIDING (487)
WELSH, containing Welsh Divisional Company, Cheshire Brigade Company, North Wales Brigade Company and the Border Brigade Company.	T | ASC | WELSH T | ASC | HEREFORDSHIRE (488) T | ASC | CHESHIRE T | ASC | NORTH. WALES (489)
WESSEX, containing Wessex Divisional Company, Devon and Cornwall Brigade Company, South Western Brigade Company and the Hampshire Brigade Company.	T | ASC | WESSEX (490) T | ASC | DEVON & CORNWALL (491) T | ASC | S. WESTERN (470) T | ASC | HANTS

After 1921 all R.A.S.C. Territorials wore the title T | RASC.

Royal Army Veterinary Corps

1858 Veterinary Medical Department formed.
1881 Redesignated Army Veterinary Department.
1903 Army Veterinary Corps formed.
1906 Amalgamated as the Army Veterinary Corps.
1918 Became the Royal Army Veterinary Corps.

Shoulder titles: AVD (492); AVC (493, 494); RAVC (495, 496).

Territorials

Mobile Veterinary Sections existed for the thirteen territorial divisions but so far
T | AVC | LONDON (497), T | AVC | WELSH (498), T | AVC | N. MIDLAND (499) and
T | AVC | NORTHUMBRIAN (500) are the only titles to have been noted. After the
reorganizations of 1921 all R.A.V.C. Territorials wore the title T | RAVC.

Royal Corps of Signals

1920 Formed from the Royal Engineers Signal Service.
Shoulder titles: ROYAL CORPS | OF | SIGNALS (*501*) changing to R. SIGNALS (*502*) in 1929. An anodised version is now worn.

Royal Corps of Transport

1965 Formed from the Royal Army Service Corps.
Shoulder title: RCT (*503*) which is now worn in gold anodised.

Royal Electrical and Mechanical Engineers

1942 Formed.
Shoulder titles: REME (*504, 505*) were replaced by *506* after 1939. Officers wore a smaller title (*507*). Two other patterns are *508* which is hand cut and *509* which is the current anodised version.

Royal Engineers

Regulars

1717 Corps of Engineers formed.
1772 Soldier Artificer Company formed at Gibraltar.
1787 Corps designated Corps of Royal Engineers, and the Corps of Royal Military Artificers formed.
1797 Gibraltar Company absorbed into Royal Military Artificers.
1812 Artificers redesignated as Royal Sappers and Miners.
1856 Both units merged as Corps of Royal Engineers.
Shoulder titles: RE (*510, 511, 512, 513*); *514*, which is an officers' pattern; *515* and *516* are made of cast brass and *517* is an anodised title.

Postal

The Postal Section of the Royal Engineers was formed in March, 1913, and continued as a separate branch until c. 1930.
Shoulder title: RE | POSTAL SECTION (*518*).

Signals

The Signal Service was formed in 1908 and remained part of the Royal Engineers until 1920 when it formed the Royal Corps of Signals.
Shoulder titles: RE | SIGNAL SERVICE (*519*), also worn with the RE separate above.

Railway Companies

Shoulder title: RE | RAILWAYS (*520*), made from cast brass.

Schools of Electric Light

There were two Schools of Electric Light, one at Plymouth and one at Portsmouth, both amalgamated in 1916.
Shoulder title: SEL (*521*), which, according to the 1936 *Clothing Regulations*, was to be worn by 'boys under instruction only'.

Inland Water Transport
Shoulder title: IWT.

Militia
Titles listed in the 1904 *Clothing Regulations* for the several units of Militia Engineers were as follows:
ANGLESEY, MONMOUTHSHIRE, FALMOUTH, HARWICH, HUMBER, MEDWAY, MILFORD HAVEN, PLYMOUTH, PORTSMOUTH, WESTERN, THAMES, NEEDLES.
All were worn with a separate RE above.
The Royal Anglesey and Royal Monmouth units were the only ones to survive the reorganizations of 1908. Their post-1908 shoulder titles were R. ANGLESEY (*522*) and R. MONMOUTH (*523*), again worn with the separate RE above.

Volunteers
Titles so far noted for the pre-1908 volunteers are as follows, all in w.m.:
1|RE|ABERDEENSHIRE; 1|RE|BEDFORDSHIRE; 1|RE|DURHAM; 1|RE|LONDON; CEV (Cheshire) (*524*); 1|RE|FLINTSHIRE; 1|RE|GLOUCESTERSHIRE; 1|RE| HAMPSHIRE; 1|RE|LANARK; 1|RE|LANCASHIRE; 1|RE|MIDDLESEX (*525*); RE| NEWCASTLE; 1|RE|SUSSEX (*526*); 1|RE|YORKSHIRE (*527*).

Engineer Volunteers were once again raised during the 1st World War and formed part of the Volunteer Training Corps.
Shoulder title: EVC (*528*).

Territorials

Divisional Engineers

East Anglian	T RE EAST ANGLIAN (*529*)
Highland	T RE HIGHLAND (*530*)
Home Counties	T RE HOME COUNTIES (*531*)
East Lancashire	T RE E. LANCASHIRE (*532*) which also exists with the lower tier non-voided (*533*).
West Lancashire	T RE W. LANCASHIRE (*534*)
1st and 2nd London	T RE LONDON (*535*)
Lowland	T RE LOWLAND (*536*)
North Midland	T RE N MIDLAND (*537*) T R.E NORTH. MIDLAND (*538*)
South Midland	T RE SOUTH MIDLAND T RE S. MIDLAND (*539*)
Northumbrian	T R.E NORTHUMBRIAN (*540*)
West Riding	T RE W. RIDING (*541*)
Welsh	T RE WELSH (*542*)
Wessex	T RE WESSEX (*543*)

Telegraph, Later Signal, Companies
(Army Troops)

London	T|RE|LONDON (*535*)
Northern	T|RE|NORTHERN (*544*)
Scottish	T|RE|SCOTLAND
Southern	T|RE|SOUTHERN (*545*)
	T|RE|WARWICKSHIRE (*546*)
Western	T|RE|WESTERN

All Territorial Signallers were transferred to the Royal Corps of Signals in 1920.

Balloon Company

London	T|RE|LONDON (*535*)

Railway Battalion

Cheshire	T|RE|CHESHIRE (*547*)

Divisional Signal Companies and Infantry Brigade Signal Sections

Generally the signallers of the above wore the title T\|SIGNAL SERVICE (*548*) or the two-piece version (*549*). However, the Cheshire Section (No. 2) of the Welsh Divisional Signal Company wore the title T\|CHES.SEC\|WELSH DIV.SIG.COY. All personnel were transferred to the Royal Corps of Signals in 1920.

Fortress Engineers

City of Aberdeen	T|RE|ABERDEEN
Cinque Ports	T|RE|CINQUE PORTS
Cornwall	T|RE|CORNWALL (*550*)
Devon	T|RE|DEVON (*551*)
Dorset	T|RE|DORSET
Wiltshire	T|RE|WILTS (*552*)
City of Dundee	T|RE|CITY OF DUNDEE (*553*)
Durham	T|RE|DURHAM
City of Edinburgh	T|RE|EDINBURGH (*554*)
Essex	T|RE|ESSEX
Glamorgan	T|RE|GLAMORGAN
Hampshire	T|RE|HANTS (*555*)
Kent	T|RE|KENT (*556*) and KFRE (*557*)
Lanarkshire	T|RE|LANARK
Renfrewshire	T|RE|RENFREWSHIRE
Sussex	T|RE|SUSSEX (*558*)
Lancashire	T|RE|LANCASHIRE
Northumberland	T|RE|NORTHUMBERLAND
East Riding	T|RE|E. RIDING (*559*)
North Riding	T|RE|N. RIDING

Electrical Engineers

London   T│RE│LONDON (535)
Tyne   T│RE│TYNE (560)
With the reorganizations of the Territorial Force in 1921 all Territorial Engineers adopted the title T│RE.

Officer Training Corps

The Engineer Companies of the Clifton College Contingent, Officer Training Corps, wore the title RE│O.T.C│CLIFTON (561)

Cadets

The 1st Company of the Kent Fortress Engineer Cadet Corps was recognized in 1911. Three other companies were formed by 1913 when the four were amalgamated as the 1st Cadet Battalion Kent (Fortress) Royal Engineers. A 2nd Battalion was formed in 1914 which was amalgamated with the 1st in 1918.
Shoulder title: C│RE│KENT (562).

The 1st Woolwich Cadet Corps was recognized in 1912 and was redesignated as the 1st County of London Royal Engineer Cadets (Woolwich) in 1918.
Shoulder title: C│RE│LONDON.

The Newcastle Modern School Cadet Corps, affiliated to the Northumbrian Divisional Engineers, was recognized in 1915.
Shoulder title: C│RE│NORTHUMBRIAN (563).

The Manchester Royal Engineers Cadet Corps was recognized in 1921.
Shoulder title: C│RE│MANCHESTER.

Royal Flying Corps

1912 Formed.
1918 Became the Royal Air Force after amalgamation with the Royal Naval Air Service.
Shoulder title: RFC (564) was worn on full dress tunics.

Territorials

The Royal Flying Corps only had one Territorial element which was formed from personnel of the Royal Aircraft Factory at Farnborough. The unit was known as the Hampshire Aircraft Parks and was disbanded after the 1st World War.
Shoulder title: T│RFC│HANTS (565).

Royal Military Police

1877 Military Mounted Police formed.
1885 Military Foot Police formed.
1926 Amalgamated as the Corps of Military Police.
1937 Field Security Police Section formed.
1940 Field Security Police transferred to the Intelligence Corps.
1946 Became the Royal Military Police.

Shoulder titles: MMP (566); MFP (567, 568). These titles also served as the headdress badge previous to 1904; CMP (569, 570) with a smaller version for officers; RMP (571) for other ranks with 572 and 573 for officers. An anodised version of the latter was introduced in 1964 for all ranks. Another title (574) was made and worn overseas. F.S.P (575).

Royal Pioneer Corps

1939 Formed as the Auxiliary Military Pioneer Corps.
1940 Redesignated Pioneer Corps.
1946 Became the Royal Pioneer Corps.

Shoulder titles: AMPC (576); PC (577); RPC (578, 579), the latter being an anodised version that was introduced in the 1960s.

Royal Regiment of Artillery

1716 Two companies of artillery formed at Woolwich.
1722 Grouped with companies from Gibraltar and Minorca as the Royal Regiment of Artillery.
1793 Royal Horse Artillery formed.
1899 Divided as the Royal Garrison Artillery and the Royal Field Artillery.
1924 Merged as Royal Artillery.

Royal Horse Artillery

Regulars

Shoulder titles: RHA (580, 581, 582, 583, 584). The last is in cast brass. 585 is an officers pattern while 586 is the current anodised title.

Territorials

Territorial elements of the Royal Horse Artillery between 1908 and 1921 were as follows:

Battery

Ayrshire	T|RHA|AYRSHIRE
Berkshire	T|RHA|BERKS (587)
Essex	T|RHA|ESSEX (588)
Glamorgan	T|RHA|GLAMORGAN (589)
Hampshire	T|RHA|HANTS (590)
Inverness-shire	T|RHA|HIGHLAND
Leicestershire	T|RHA|LEICESTER (591)

Nottinghamshire	T｜RHA｜NOTTS (*592*)
West Riding	T｜RHA｜W. RIDING (*593*)
Shropshire	T｜RHA｜SHROPSHIRE (*594*)
Somerset	T｜RHA｜SOMERSET (*595*)
Warwickshire	T｜RHA｜WARWICKSHIRE (*596*)

All the above batteries became part of the Royal Field Artillery in 1922, wearing the shoulder title T｜RFA.

Another Territorial unit was the 11th (Honourable Artillery Company and City of London Yeomanry) Brigade, R.H.A., which was formed in 1922. Although the H.A.C. batteries continued to wear their old titles, the Yeomanry Batteries adopted Y｜RHA (*339. 340*) for other ranks and CITY OF LONDON｜Y｜RHA (*341*) for officers.

Royal Artillery

Shoulder titles: RA (*597. 598. 599. 600*). The last is an officers' pattern which is now worn in gold anodised. Between 1899 and 1924 the RA title was worn by the Clerks Section only.

School of Gunnery/Artillery

The School of Gunnery, which was at Shoeburyness and later at Larkhill, wore the title S of G (*601*). The title was changed to S of A (*602*) upon redesignation as School of Artillery in 1920.

Riding Establishment

Shoulder title: RIDING｜ESTT. (*603*). This title appears in the *Priced Vocabulary of Clothing and Necessaries* for the 1907 issue only.

Royal Field Artillery

Regulars

Shoulder titles: RFA (*604. 605. 606. 607. 608. 609*). The last is in cast brass.

Militia

The Lancashire R.F.A. Militia wore, according to *Clothing Regulations*, 1904, 1｜LANC｜RFA in three separate pieces. The 2nd Battery wore the same title but with the relevant number.

Territorials

The Royal Field Artillery Territorial Force consisted of thirteen divisions. With the exception of London and Highland, all divisions were made up of four brigades, three field and one howitzer. The London Division had eight brigades, six field and two howitzer, while the Highland had two field and one howitzer with a 4th Mountain Brigade that came under the Royal Garrison Artillery. Field Brigades were made up from three batteries while the howitzer brigades consisted of two. Each brigade had its own ammunition column.

When the Territorial Force was created in 1908 one pattern of shoulder title was worn throughout a division, but as the years passed some batteries were to adopt their own individual titles. As a rule HQ batteries and ammunition columns retained their original titles.

With the reorganizations of 1921 all Royal Field Artillery units of the Territorial Army wore the title T | RFA.

Divisions

East Anglian, with batteries in Norfolk, Suffolk, Hertfordshire, Essex and Northampton	T	RFA	EAST ANGLIAN (610) T	RFA	ESSEX (611) T	RFA	SUFFOLK (612) T	RFA	HERTS T	RFA	NORTHAMPTON
Highland, with batteries in Banffshire, Forfarshire, Fifeshire, Renfrewshire and the Cities of Dundee and Aberdeen	T	RFA	HIGHLAND (613) T	RFA	ABERDEEN (614) T	RFA	CITY OF DUNDEE T	RFA	RENFREWSHIRE (615) ABERDEEN. CITY	RFA (616)
Home Counties, with batteries in Sussex and Kent	T	RFA	HOME COUNTIES (617) T	RFA	SUSSEX (618) T	RFA	KENT (619)
East Lancashire, with batteries in Lancashire and Cumberland	T	RFA	E. LANCASHIRE (620). This title also exists with the lower tier non-voided T	RFA	CUMBERLAND
West Lancashire, with batteries in Lancashire	T	RFA	W. LANCASHIRE (621)
London. The 1st Brigade was formed within the City while the 2nd to 8th were formed throughout the County of London	T	RFA	CITY OF LONDON (622) T	RFA	LONDON (623)
Lowland, with batteries in Midlothian, Ayrshire, Kirkudbright and the Cities of Edinburgh and Glasgow	T	RFA	LOWLAND (624) T	RFA	1st LOWLAND (625) T	RFA	EDINBURGH T	RFA	CITY OF GLASGOW (626)
North Midland, with batteries in Lincolnshire, Staffordshire and Derbyshire	T	RFA	NORTH. MIDLAND (627) T	RFA	LINCOLN (628) T	RFA	STAFFORD (629) T	RFA	DERBYSHIRE (630)
South Midland, with batteries in Gloucestershire, Worcestershire and Warwickshire	T	RFA	S. MIDLAND T	RFA	WORCESTERSHIRE T	RFA	GLOSTER (631) T	RFA	WARWICKSHIRE (632)
Northumbrian, with batteries in Northumberland, Durham and the East and North Ridings of Yorkshire	T	RFA	NORTHUMBRIAN (633) T	RFA.	N. RIDING (634) T	RFA	DURHAM T	RFA	E. RIDING T	RFA	NORTHUMBERLAND (635)

West Riding, all batteries in the West Riding of Yorkshire	T|RFA|W. RIDING
	T|RFA|1|W. RIDING (636)
	T|RFA|2|W. RIDING (637)
	T|RFA|3|W. RIDING (638)
	T|RFA|4|W. RIDING (639)
	T|RFA|WRDAC (640) (Divisional Ammunition Column)
Welsh, with batteries in Glamorgan, Cardiganshire, Cheshire, Flintshire and Monmouthshire	T|RFA|WELSH (641)
	T|RFA|GLAMORGAN
	T|R.F.A|CHESHIRE (642)
	T|RFA|MONMOUTHSHIRE (643)
Wessex, with batteries in Hampshire, Dorset, Wiltshire and Devon	T|RFA|WESSEX
	T|RFA|HANTS (644)
	T|RFA|DORSET (645)
	T|RFA|WILTSHIRE (646)
	T|RFA|DEVON (647)

Royal Garrison Artillery

Regulars
Shoulder titles: RGA (648, 649, 650, 651). The last is in cast brass.

Militia

List of Royal Garrison Artillery Militia units from the Army List for May, 1905	List from *Clothing Regulations* 1904 of shoulder titles to be worn. All with a separate RGA above
The Antrim	ANTRIM
The Cardigan	CARGN.
The Carmarthen	CARMN.
The Clare	CLARE
The Cork	CORK
The Cornwall and Devon Miners	C. & D.M.
The Devon	DEVON
The Donegal	DONEGAL
The Dublin City	DUBLIN
The Durham	DURHAM
The Duke of Edinburgh's Own Edinburgh	EDINBRO.
The Fife	FIFE
The Forfar and Kincardine	F. & K.
The Glamorgan	GLAMN.
The Duke of Connaught's Own Hampshire and Isle of Wight	HANTS
The Kent	KENT
The Lancashire	LANC.
The Limerick City	LIMCK.
The Londonderry	LONDY.
The Mid-Ulster	ULSTER

The Prince of Wales's Own Norfolk	NORFOLK
The Northumberland	NORTHD.
The Pembroke	PEMBKE.
The Duke of Connaught's Own Sligo	SLIGO
The South-East of Scotland	S. E. SCOTLAND
The Suffolk	SUFFOLK
The Sussex	SUSSEX
The Tipperary	TIPPY.
The Waterford	WATRFD.
The West of Scotland	W. SCOTLAND
The Wicklow	WICKW.
The Yorkshire (Duke of York's Own)	YORKS

Only two units from the above list were to survive the reorganizations of 1908, those being the batteries from Antrim and Cork, now known as Royal Garrison Reserve Artillery. The shoulder titles ANTRIM (*652*) and CORK (*653*) were retained.

Volunteers

Although over sixty units of Artillery Volunteers existed between 1880 and 1908 only the following metal shoulder titles have so far been noted, all in w.m.:
1│RA│GLAMORGAN; 2│RA│GLAMORGAN (*654*); 1│RA│GLOUCESTER (*655*); 1│RA│ BANFF (*656*); 1│RA│DURHAM (*657*); 2│RA│DURHAM; 3│RA│DURHAM (*658*); 4│RA│ DURHAM (*659*); 1│RA│LANCASHIRE; 5│RA│LANCASHIRE (*660*); 7│RA│LANCASHIRE (*661*); RA│LANCASHIRE (*662*); 1│RA│DEVONSHIRE (*663*); 2│RA│DEVONSHIRE; 1│RA│SUSSEX (*664*); 1│RA│WORCESTERSHIRE (*665*); 1│RA│ARGYLL & BUTE (*666*); RA│FIFE; RA│FORFAR (*667*); 1│RA│BERWICKSHIRE (*668*); 2│RA│MIDDLESEX; 1│RA│ CHESHIRE; 2│RA│HANTS (*669*); THE│RA│TYNEMOUTH; CAV (*670*) (Caithness); RGA│V (Royal Garrison Artillery Volunteers).

Territorials

The Territorials of the Royal Garrison Artillery appeared in monthly Army Lists under three headings: Mountain, Heavy and For Defended Ports. All R.G.A. units of the Territorial Army after the reorganizations of 1921 wore the title T│RGA.

Mountain

4th Highland (Mountain) Brigade with batteries in Bute, Argyllshire, Ross and Cromarty.
Shoulder titles: T│RGA│BUTE (*671*); T│RGA│ROSS & CROMARTY (*672*); T│RGA│ ARGYLL.

Heavy Batteries

East Anglian (Essex)	T│RGA│ESSEX
Highland (Fifeshire)	T│RGA│FIFESHIRE (*673*)
Home Counties (Kent)	T│RGA│HOME COUNTIES (*674*)
East Lancashire	T│RGA│E. LANCASHIRE
West Lancashire	T│RGA│W. LANCASHIRE (*675*)
1st and 2nd Lancashire	T│RGA│LANCASHIRE (*676*)

1st and 2nd London	T│RGA│LONDON (*677*)
Lowland (City of Edinburgh)	T│RGA│EDINBURGH and LOWLAND│HEAVY BATTERY (*678*)
North Midland (Staffordshire)	T│RGA│N MIDLAND (*679*)
South Midland (Warwickshire)	T│RGA│WARWICKSHIRE (*680*)
Northumbrian (North Riding)	T│RGA│N. RIDING (*681*)
West Riding	T│RGA│W. RIDING (*682*)
Welsh (Carnarvonshire)	T│RGA│WELSH (*683*)
Wessex (Hampshire)	T│RGA│HANTS (*684*) and T│RGA│WESSEX

Note. The East and West Lancashire Batteries were redesignated 1st and 2nd Lancashire in 1910.

For Defended Ports Batteries

Clyde	T│RGA│CLYDE
Cornwall	T│RGA│CORNWALL (*685*)
Devon	T│RGA│DEVON (*686*)
Dorset	T│RGA│DORSET (*687*)
Durham	T│RGA│DURHAM (*688*)
East Riding	T│RGA│E. RIDING (*689*)
Essex and Suffolk	T│RGA│ESSEX & SUFFOLK (*690*)
Forth	T│RGA│FORTH (*691*)
Glamorgan	T│RGA│GLAMORGAN (*692*)
Hampshire	T│RGA│HANTS (*684*)
Kent and Sussex	T│RGA│KENT & SUSSEX (*693*)
Kent	T│RGA│KENT (*694*)
Lancashire and Cheshire	T│RGA│LANCASHIRE & CHESHIRE (*695, 696*)
Orkney	T│RGA│ORKNEY
Pembroke	T│RGA│PEMBROKE
North Scottish	T│RGA│N. SCOTTISH (*697*)
Sussex	T│RGA│SUSSEX (*698*)
Tynemouth	T│RGA│TYNEMOUTH (*699*)

Note: The Kent and Sussex Batteries were divided in 1910.

Cadets

The Beccles Artillery Cadets were formed in 1906 and affiliated to the 1st Norfolk Artillery Volunteers. They were transferred to the 3rd East Anglian Brigade RFA in 1908.

Shoulder titles: I│C│RA│BECCLES (*700*) changing to I│C│RFA│BECCLES in 1908.

Cadets Norfolk Artillery were recognized in 1913 and were affiliated to the 1st East Anglian Brigade, R.F.A.

Shoulder title: CNA.

Roborough School (Eastbourne) Cadet Corps. Recognized in 1915.

Shoulder title: ROBOROUGH│C│SCHOOL (*701*).

The Brighton Brigade, Sussex Cadets, was recognized in 1914 and affiliated to the 1st Home Counties Brigade, R.F.A. They became the 1st and 2nd Cadet Regiments of the Sussex Yeomanry in 1916.
Shoulder title: CADETS | RFA | SUSSEX.

The Woolwich Cadet Corps was recognized in 1912 and affiliated to the 2nd London Brigade, R.F.A. They were redesignated the 1st County of London Royal Engineer Cadets (Woolwich) in 1918 and disbanded in 1921.
Shoulder title: WOOLWICH | CADET CORPS (702)

Small Arms School Corps

1854 School of Musketry formed.
1919 Redesignated Small Arms School, Hythe.
1926 Amalgamated with the Machine Gun School, Netheravon as the Small Arms and Machine Gun School.
1926 Redesignated Small Arms School Corps.
Shoulder titles: S of M (703); MGS (704); SAS which is larger than the Special Air Service pattern; S.A. & M.G.S (705); S.A.S.C. (706); now worn in silver anodised (707).

Special Air Service

1940 First elements formed in North Africa.
1946 Disbanded.
1947 Reformed.
Shoulder title: SAS (708).

4
Foot Guards

Grenadier Guards
1656 Raised.

The title worn until 1920 was the letters GG with a separate grenade above (709). The grenade was replaced in 1920 by the puggaree badge which is the Garter surmounted by a crown, in a voided centre, the Royal Cypher interlaced and reversed. Both King's and Queen's crown versions of the badge have been worn (710, 711), the latter also appearing in gold anodised in the 1960s. Until the 2nd World War the badge alone was worn on the full dress tunics.

Coldstream Guards
1650 Raised.

The shoulder title of the Coldstream Guards consists of the letters CG worn below a Tudor Rose (712). The title is now worn in gold anodised. The Rose alone was worn on the full dress tunics until the 2nd World War.

Scots Guards
1660 Raised.

A miniature of the regimental cap badge in bi-metal was worn on the full dress tunics until the 2nd World War (713). The service dress title was the letters SG worn below a thistle in w.m. (714). The title is now worn in gold and silver anodised.

Irish Guards
1900 Raised.

The Star of the Order of St Patrick above the letters IG was the title worn in service dress (715). An anodised version is now worn. The pre-2nd World War full dress tunic title omitted the letters.

Welsh Guards
1915 Raised.

The service dress title is leek/W.G (716) and is now worn in gold anodised. The leek alone was worn until the 2nd World War on the full dress tunic.

Guards Machine Gun Regiment

This Regiment was formed in February 1918, having begun life in 1916 as the Guards Machine Gun Battalion or Machine Gun Guards. The first shoulder title to be worn was MGG, changing to GMGR. The Regiment was disbanded in 1920.

5
Infantry Regiments

Before 1881 the Infantry of the Line consisted of 109 numbered regiments plus The Rifle Brigade. Regiments numbered 1 to 25 had 2 battalions, the 60th and The Rifle Brigade had 4, while the remainder had one each. In 1881 the Cardwell System of 1873 was carried to its logical development, Mr Cardwell being the Secretary of State for War from 1868 to 1874. The reorganizations, which were shown in General Order 41 of May, 1881, amended by General Order 70 of July, 1881, created territorial regiments which would consist of 2 regular battalions as well as militia and volunteers. As mentioned, the 1st to 25th Regiments already had 2 battalions each, thus creating no particular problems in the new system; this also applied to the 60th and the Rifle Brigade who retained their 4 battalions. This left 83 regiments that were linked in pairs to form 41 new regiments, the odd one being the 79th which remained a one-battalion regiment until 1897. It should be noted that the term 'territorial regiments' was used to localize regiments for recruiting purposes and should not be confused with regiments of the Territorial Force created in 1908.

In 1900 the following regiments were increased to 4 battalions: Northumberland Fusiliers, Royal Warwickshire, Royal Fusiliers, King's Liverpool, Lancashire Fusiliers, Worcestershire, Middlesex and Manchester. These extra battalions were all gradually disbanded, the last in 1922. The next major change was in 1948 when regular regiments were reduced to one battalion, either by amalgamation or disbandment. In the following year the Parachute Regiment became a corps of the Infantry of the Line.

Further changes were brought about in 1957 when 14 new Infantry Brigades were created, each consisting of 3 or 4 battalions. The new system required certain regiments to amalgamate and by 1960 30 regiments had been reduced to 15. By 1970 the Brigade System had disappeared, further amalgamations and disbandments had taken place and several of the new 'large regiments' had been formed. From the 69 regiments of infantry created in 1881 only 11 now remain in their original form, the present day infantry of the line consisting of 29 regiments plus the Brigade of Gurkhas.

The Militia was also affected by the reforms of 1873. Infantry battalions were attached to their local sub-district brigade depots which were made responsible for training etc. In 1881 militia battalions became part of the newly formed Territorial Regiments, being numbered on after the regulars. Under Lord Haldane's Reforms of 1908 the Militia was redesignated Special Reserve, it's main purpose being to supply reinforcement drafts for the line battalions on mobilization. The title of the force was changed back to Militia in 1921 but no infantry units were reformed after the 1st World War. Battalions existed on paper only until officially disbanded in 1953.

Very few special shoulder titles were worn by militia battalions; other ranks wore the regular pattern title with the battalion number separate above, while officers wore in addition the letter 'M' below.

VOLUNTEERS/TERRITORIALS

The Territorial Army officially dates from 1859 when the Volunteer Force was created. There were, however, several units of volunteer infantry already in existence in 1859: the Honourable Artillery Company which had been formed in 1537, the Victoria Volunteer Rifle Corps which originated as the Duke of Cumberland's Sharpshooters in 1803 and the Exeter and South Devon Volunteers which had been formed in 1852. When the call for volunteers was heard in 1859 many hundreds of units were formed, mostly of company strength. These were numbered according to their precedence within the county.

Administrative Battalions were introduced in a circular dated 24 March, 1860, their purpose being to group smaller corps together to ensure uniformity in drill etc. Larger grants were also made available for uniforms and arms. While serving within an Administrative Battalion individual corps remained independent of each other; they retained their county numbers and remained distinct and financially independent bodies. The alternative to joining an Administrtive Battalion was to consolidate or amalgamate with other corps as one battalion, which would take on the number of the senior company. During the next 20 years several Administrative Battalions were to consolidate but in 1880 consolidation was ordered for all battalions. As before, the new battalion adopted the number of the senior corps but by June renumbering from 1 upwards took place.

In 1881 the Rifle Volunteer Corps became Volunteer Battalions of regular regiments, being numbered in a separate sequence. Change in designation was gradual, each battalion being notified in General Orders. Some Rifle Volunteer Corps, although serving as a Volunteer Battalion, were never designated as such and retained their old titles until 1908.

The Territorial Force was created in 1908 and Volunteer Battalions were restyled simply as battalions, being numbered after regulars and militia. The Territorial Force became the Territorial Army in 1921 and the Territorial Army Volunteer Reserve in 1967.

Generally shoulder titles were embroidered on the full dress tunics of the volunteer period, metal being introduced for the drab service dress that appeared around 1900. As with other volunteer insignia, titles were either white metal or blackened brass; plain brass specimens do appear but these have probably had the black removed at some time.

Shoulder titles for infantry battalions of the Territorial Force usually consisted of the letter 'T' above the battalion number above the name of the regiment, which was normally that currently being worn by the regular battalions. Rifle battalions wore blackened brass titles on the full dress tunics while others wore white metal. Brass titles were worn on service dress and by battalions permitted to wear gold lace on the full-dress tunics.

Titles were also worn in two or more separate pieces. Two-piece patterns consisting of the T and number worn separately above the name are particularly common and will not be mentioned. Others made up of more than two pieces are less frequent and those recorded have been listed. For volunteer battalions of the 1st World War period see chapter 14.

SERVICE BATTALIONS

Lord Kitchener became Secretary of State for War on 6 August, 1914, and by the 7th his now famous poster calling for an additional 100,000 men was being displayed. It was decided that this expansion should not be made within the existing Regular Army or Territorial Force but instead a 'New Army' was to be created which eventually grew to over 500 battalions organized into thirty divisions. The new battalions were added to regiments of the Infantry of the Line and numbered on from their existing battalions, the full title containing the word 'Service' in brackets.

For the most part shoulder titles, if worn at all, were those of the regular battalions. However, some units did adopt special patterns and those known have been noted.

The Royal Scots (The Royal Regiment)

Regular Battalions
1633 Raised.
1751 Numbered 1st Regiment of Foot.
1881 Became The Royal Scots (Lothian Regiment).
Shoulder titles: The first title to be worn was ROYAL SCOTS (717), which was replaced by RS (718) in 1921. A larger version (719) was worn on the greatcoat with one in w.m., 720 being introduced after the 2nd World War for use on the white tropical jacket. Two other titles exist which so far have not been positively identified. The first pattern is R. SCOTS (721), which is gilt and of slightly better manufacture, which would suggest an officers' item. The second title is yet another version of RS (722), which is in w.m.

Volunteer Battalions
5th   see 7th Bn (TF).
9th   see 9th Bn (TF).

Territorial Battalions
4th & 5th   1859 Raised as the 1st Edinburgh (City) R.V.C.
1865 Absorbed other Edinburgh Corps and became the Queen's City of Edinburgh Rifle Volunteer Brigade.
1881 Joined the Royal Scots as 1st V.B., later expanded to 2nd and 3rd.
1908 Became 4th and 5th (Queen's Edinburgh Rifles) Bns (TF).
1921 Amalgamated as 4th/5th (Queen's Edinburgh) Bn.
1940 Transferred to Royal Artillery.
Shoulder titles: T│4│Q.E.R│ROYAL SCOTS (723) and T│5│Q.E.R│ROYAL SCOTS (724). T│4/5│RS (725) was the title worn after amalgamation.

6th   1860 Raised as the 16th Company of the 1st Edinburgh (City) R.V.C.
1867 Became the 3rd Edinburgh R.V.C.
1880 Renumbered 2nd.
1888 Redesignated 4th V.B. Royal Scots.
1908 Became 6th Bn (TF).
1920 Amalgamated with 8th Bn and converted to an artillery unit.
Shoulder title: T│6│ROYAL SCOTS (726).

7th   1859 Raised as the 1st Midlothian R.V.C. at Leith.

1888 Redesignated 5th V.B. Royal Scots.

1908 Became 7th Bn (TF).

1921 Amalgamated with 9th (Highlanders) Bn to form 7th/9th Bn.

Shoulder titles: 5 | v | ROYAL SCOTS in w.m.; T | 7 | ROYAL SCOTS (727). T | 7/9 | RS (728) was the title worn after amalgamation.

8th   1862 1st Admin Bn of Midlothian R.Vs formed, the senior corps being the 2nd which was formed in 1860.

1880 Bn consolidated as 2nd Midlothian R.V.C.

1888 Redesignated 6th V.B. Royal Scots, HQ Peebles.

1860 1st Admin Bn of Haddington R.Vs formed.

1880 Bn consolidated as the 1st Haddington R.V.C.

1888 Redesignated 7th V.B. Royal Scots.

1908 6th and 7th V.Bs amalgamated as 8th Bn (TF). HQ Haddington.

1920 Amalgamated with 6th Bn (TF) and converted to an artillery unit.

Shoulder title: T | 8 | ROYAL SCOTS (729).

9th   1900 Raised as Highland Bn of Queen's Edinburgh Rifle Volunteer Brigade.

1902 Became 9th (Highlanders) V.B. Royal Scots.

1908 Became 9th (Highlanders) Bn (TF).

1921 Amalgamated with 7th Bn.

Shoulder titles: 9 | v | HIGHLANDERS | RS in w.m.; T | 9 | ROYAL SCOTS (730). It will be noticed that the 'T' of the title has been altered so as to look like a 'I'. Upon the formation of 2nd and 3rd Line Battalions during the 1st World War members of the 9th Bn, who had by this time been numbered as 1st/9th, unofficially trimmed the 'Ts' of their titles. This practice was also common among battalions of other regiments.

10th   1862 1st Admin Bn of Linlithgowshire R.Vs formed, the senior corps being the 1st which was raised in 1860.

1880 Bn consolidated as 1st Linlithgowshire R.V.C. HQ Linlithgow.

1888 Redesignated 8th V.B. Royal Scots.

1908 Became 10th (Cyclist) Bn (TF).

1920 Transferred to Royal Engineers as 1st (Linlithgow) Light Bridging Company.

1921 Transferred back to The Royal Scots as 'A' Coy of the 4th/5th Bn.

Shoulder titles: T | 10 | ROYAL SCOTS (731); T | RE | ROYAL SCOTS.

Cadets

The Castle Mills Cadet Bn was recognized in April, 1918, and affiliated to the 9th (Highlanders) Bn.

Shoulder title: CASTLE MILLS | CADETS | ROYAL SCOTS.

The Queen's Royal Regiment (West Surrey)

Regular Battalions

1661 Raised.

1751 Numbered 2nd Regiment of Foot.

1881 Became The Queen's (Royal West Surrey Regiment).

1959 Amalgamated with The East Surrey Regiment to form The Queen's Royal Surrey Regiment (see chapter 6).

Shoulder titles: W. SURREY (732) was the title worn until c1900 when it was replaced by QUEEN'S (733). A straight version exists (734), but no information can be found as to when it was worn. A cast brass title THE QUEEN'S | REGT (735) was worn by officers on the tropical jacket c1900. QUEEN'S | 2 | R.W.S (736) was worn by the 2nd Bn until 1898.

Volunteer Battalions

1st   see 4th Bn (TF).

2nd   see 5th Bn (TF).

Territorial Battalions

4th   1859 Raised as 2nd Surrey R.V.C. at Croydon.

       1883 Redesignated 1st V.B. Queen's Regiment.

       1908 Became 4th Bn (TF).

       1940 Transferred to Royal Artillery.

Shoulder titles: 1 | V | QUEEN'S in w.m.; T | 4 | QUEEN'S (737).

5th   1860 3rd Admin Bn of Surrey R.Vs formed at Dorking, the senior corps being the 5th which was formed in 1859.

       1880 Bn consolidated as 4th Surrey R.V.C.

       1883 Redesignated 2nd V.B. Queen's Regiment.

       1908 Became 5th Bn (TF). HQ Guildford.

Shoulder titles: 2 | V | QUEEN'S in w.m.; T | 5 | QUEEN'S (738).

Cadets

The Cadet Corps of the 3rd Volunteer Bn was formed from boys at Streatham Grammar School.

Shoulder title: CC | 3 | V | QUEEN'S in w.m.

The 1st Cadet Bn was recognized in 1911 but was transferred to the London Regiment by the end of the same year. A new 1st C.B. was added in 1915. Both battalions were affiliated to the 4th Bn (TF), and had their HQ in Southwark.

Shoulder titles: 1 | C | QUEEN'S (739); 1 | CB | QUEEN'S (740).

The 2nd Cadet Bn was at Peckham and was recognized in 1919 and affiliated to the 5th Bn (TF).
Shoulder title: 2│C│QUEEN'S.

Affiliated to the 4th Bn (TF), the 3rd C.B. was recognized in 1919.
Shoulder title: 3│C│QUEEN'S.

The 4th C.B. was also recognized in 1919 but the Territorial Force withdrew its recognition in 1921.
Shoulder title: C│4│QUEEN'S.

Cadet Companies affiliated to the 5th Bn (TF) wore the title C│5│QUEEN'S (*741*).

The Whitgift School at Croydon was affiliated to the 1st V.B. They became part of the Junior Division O.T.C. in 1908.
Shoulder title: WHITGIFT│CADET CORPS (*742*).

The Buffs (Royal East Kent Regiment)

Regular Battalions
1572 Raised.
1751 Numbered 3rd Regiment of Foot.
1881 Became The Buff's (East Kent) Regiment.
1935 Redesignated The Buffs (Royal East Kent Regiment).
1961 Amalgamated with The Queen's Own Royal West Kent Regiment to form The Queen's Own Buffs, The Royal Kent Regiment (see chapter 6).
Shoulder titles: The first worn by the Regiment was THE. BUFFS (*743*) which was introduced in 1898. This was replaced in 1902 by BUFFS (*744, 745, 746*), the latter two being officers' patterns. Another version (*747*) was made and worn in India just prior to the 1st World War. The title is made from cast brass.

Volunteer Battalions pre-1908
2nd   see 5th Bn (TF).

Volunteer Battalions 1918
The East Kent Volunteer Fencibles formed the 1st to 4th Volunteer Bns in 1918.
Shoulder title: E.K.V.F.│CINQUE PORTS (*748*).

Territorial Battalions
4th   1860 1st Admin Bn of Cinque Ports R.Vs formed at Canterbury.
1861 Renumbered 2nd.
1874 Amalgamated with 4th Admin Bn of Kent R.Vs (formed 1860) to form 5th Kent (East Kent) R.V.C.
1880 Renumbered 2nd.

1883 Redesignated 1st V.B. Buffs.
1908 Became 4th Bn (TF). HQ Dover.
Shoulder title: T│4│BUFFS (749).

5th   1861 5th Admin Bn of Kent R.Vs formed at Cranbrook.
1880 Bn consolidated as 5th Kent (The Weald of Kent) R.V.C.
1883 Redesignated 2nd (The Weald of Kent) V.B. Buffs.
1908 Became 5th (The Weald of Kent) Bn (TF).
1921 Absorbed into 4th Bn.
Shoulder titles: 2.V.B.E KENT (750) in w.m.; T│5│BUFFS (751).

Buffs Palestinian Battalion
This battalion was recruited from Palestinian Jews and Arabs in
September 1940.
Shoulder title: BUFFS│PALESTINIAN (752).

The King's Own Royal Regiment (Lancaster)
Regular Battalions
1680 Raised.
1751 Numbered 4th Regiment of Foot.
1881 Became The King's Own (Royal Lancaster Regiment).
1959 Amalgamated with The Border Regiment to form The King's
Own Royal Border Regiment (see chapter 6).
Shoulder titles: Five titles have been worn by the Regiment's regular bns,
R:LANC: (753) in 1883, which was replaced by R. LANC. R in 1893, LANCASTER
(754) in 1899, R. LANCASTER in 1902 and KING'S OWN (755. 756) in 1905.
Another title, which is illustrated in a Gaunt's Catalogue that was printed c1904,
was ~~THE KING'S OWN~~ and is in fact the cap badge minus the lion. No evidence
can be found as to when, if at all, this pattern was worn.

Territorial Battalions
4th   1862 5th Admin Bn of Lancashire R.Vs formed, the senior corps
being the 10th which was formed in 1859.
1875 Bn consolidated as 10th Lancashire R.V.C. with HQ at
Ulverston.
1883 Redesignated 1st V.B. King's Own.
1900 Expanded into two battalions, 1st and 2nd, the latter being at
Lancaster.
1908 1st V.B. became 4th Bn (TF).
1938 Transferred to Royal Artillery.
Shoulder title: T│4│KING'S OWN (757).

5th   1900 Formed from part of the 1st V.B. as 2nd V.B. at Lancaster.
1908 Became 5th Bn (TF).
1942 Transferred to Royal Armoured Corps.
Shoulder title: T│5│KING'S OWN (758).
T│KING'S OWN was issued to both bns in 1920 for wear on the greatcoat.

The Royal Northumberland Fusiliers

Regular Battalions

        1674 Raised.
        1751 Numbered 5th Regiment of Foot.
        1881 Became The Northumberland Fusiliers.
        1935 Redesignated The Royal Northumberland Fusiliers.
        1968 Became 1st Bn The Royal Regiment of Fusiliers (see chapter 6).
Shoulder titles: The first title to be issued to other ranks was NF (759), which was worn with a separate grenade above. The one piece pattern, N grenade F (760), which had the figure of St George and the motto QUO FATA VOCANT on the ball of the grenade, was introduced c1910 and had replaced 759 by 1913. Two variants of the title exist, one having a slightly more pointed flame to the grenade (761), and the other with the motto misspelt as QUO FASA VOCANT. N grenade F, but with a plain ball to the grenade, was worn by officers until 1913 when a similar title bearing the Motto and St George in silver was adopted (762, 763). Other ranks' titles have only been noted with the St George facing to the right; officers' patterns, however, were worn in pairs. After 1935, when the Regiment became Royal, a scroll inscribed ROYAL was added to the titles (764, 765, 766). Other ranks' titles were reduced in size during the 1960s (767).

Volunteer Battalions 1918

        The Newcastle-upon-Tyne Volunteer Training Corps formed part
        of the 2nd Volunteer Bn in 1918.
Shoulder title: NEWCASTLE | VTC | UPON-TYNE (768) in w.m.

Territorial Battalions

4th   1860 1st Admin Bn of Northumberland R.Vs formed at Alnwick.
        1880 Bn consolidated as 1st Northumberland R.V.C.
        1883 Redesignated 1st V.B. Northumberland Fusiliers.
        1908 Became 4th and 7th Bns (TF). HQ Hexham.
        1941 4th Bn transferred to Reconnaissance Corps.
Shoulder titles: T | 4 | grenade | NF; also two-piece T | 4 over grenade | NF.

5th   1861 2nd Admin Bn of Northumberland R.Vs formed at Walker,
        the senior corps being the 1st which was formed in 1860.
        1865 Bn consolidated as the 8th Northumberland R.V.C.
        1880 Renumbered 2nd.
        1883 Redesignated 2nd V.B. Northumberland Fusiliers.
        1908 Became 5th Bn (TF).
        1940 Transferred to Royal Artillery.
Shoulder titles: T | 5 | grenade | NF (769); also two-piece T | 5 over grenade | NF.

6th   1859 1st Newcastle-upon-Tyne R:V.C. formed.
        1883 Redesignated 3rd V.B. Northumberland Fusiliers.
        1908 Became 6th Bn (TF).
        1938 Transferred to Royal Tank Regiment.
Shoulder titles: T | 6 | grenade | NF (770); also two-piece T | 6 over grenade | NF.

7th   1908 Formed HQ at Alnwick.
Shoulder titles: T | 7 | grenade | NF (771); also two-piece T | 7 over grenade | NF.

Service Battalions
20th   1914 Raised with the sub-title (1st Tyneside Scottish).
             1918 Disbanded.

21st   1914 Raised with the sub-title (2nd Tyneside Scottish).
             1918 Disbanded.

22nd   1914 Raised with the sub-title (3rd Tyneside Scottish).
             1919 Disbanded.

23rd   1915 Raised with the sub-title (4th Tyneside Scottish).
             1919 Disbanded.
Shoulder titles: Officers of the four battalions wore a three-piece title consisting of, at the top, a solid tablet inscribed TYNESIDE, at the bottom a tablet inscribed SCOTTISH and in the centre a grenade bearing the usual motto and St George. The tablets are in gilt while the grenade is in silver. Men of the 1st Bn wore a similar title but with the top and bottom parts in brass and with the numeral 1 in w.m. replacing the grenade. The 2nd, 3rd and 4th Bns wore the same title but with the relevant number in brass (772, 773, 774, 775, 776).
TS (777) was worn by all battalions on the greatcoat.

24th   1914 Raised with the sub-title (1st Tyneside Irish).
             1917 Amalgamated with 27th Bn as 24th/27th (Tyneside Irish).
             1918 Disbanded.

25th   1914 Raised with the sub-title (2nd Tyneside Irish).
             1919 Disbanded.

26th   1914 Raised with the sub-title (3rd Tyneside Irish).
             1918 Disbanded.

27th   1915 Raised with the sub-title (4th Tyneside Irish).
             1917 Amalgamated with 24th Bn.
Shoulder titles: All four battalions wore what at first appears to be a cap badge on the shoulder. The badge, which is basically that of the Connaught Rangers, consisted of a crowned harp upon a scroll inscribed TYNESIDE IRISH (778). These badges were worn in conjunction with the battalion number, worn above, and the regular pattern title NF below.

Reserve battalions were formed for both the Tyneside Scottish and Irish. The 29th (Tyneside Scottish) and the 30th (Tyneside Irish) Bns were formed in 1915 but were transferred to the Training Reserve in 1916 as their 84th and 85th Bns respectively. The 33rd (Tyneside Scottish) and 34th (Tyneside Irish) were also formed. They were raised in June, 1916, but were both absorbed into the 20th Reserve Brigade by September of the same year.

No special titles have been noted for the 29th and 33rd (Tyneside Scottish) Bns although photographs do show the usual titles being worn without the numerals. Another photograph shows a member of the 30th (Tyneside Irish) Bn wearing the three-piece title.

Royal Warwickshire Regiment

Regular Battalions

> 1673 Raised.
> 1751 Numbered 6th Regiment of Foot.
> 1881 Became The Royal Warwickshire Regiment.
> 1963 Redesignated The Royal Warwickshire Fusiliers.
> 1968 Became 2nd Bn, The Royal Regiment of Fusiliers (see chapter 6).

Shoulder titles: The semicircular title WARWICK (779) was worn until 1902 when it was replaced by RWARWICKSHIRE (780, 781), the latter being worn by officers. The title issued after 1963, when the Regiment was designated as Fusiliers, was RWARF (782) which was in gold anodised. It would seem from photographs, however, that members of the band and the mascot handler wore the RWARWICKSHIRE title (780) with the anodised collar badge above.

Volunteer Battalions pre-1908

2nd   see 7th Bn (TF).

Volunteer Battalions 1918

> Five battalions of Warwickshire Volunteers were raised in 1914 and transferred to the Regiment in 1918 as 1st to 4th Volunteer Bns.

Shoulder titles: 1│VOL│WARWICKS, 2│VOL│WARWICKS and 3│VOL│WARWICKS (783). None have been recorded for the 4th and 5th Bns.

Territorial Battalions

5th   1859 1st, 3rd and 6th Warwickshire R.V.C. raised in Birmingham.
>   1860 Amalgamated as 1st.
>   1883 Redesignated 1st V.B. Royal Warwickshire Regiment.
>   1908 Became 5th and 6th Bns (TF).
>   1936 Transferred to Royal Engineers.

Shoulder title: T│5│RWARWICKSHIRE (784).

6th   1908 Formed from part of 1st V.B. HQ Birmingham.
>   1936 Transferred to Royal Artillery.

Shoulder title: T│6│RWARWICKSHIRE (785).

7th   1860 2nd Admin Bn of Warwickshire R.Vs formed in Coventry, the senior corps being the 2nd which was formed in 1859.
>   1861 Renumbered 1st.
>   1880 Bn consolidated as 2nd Warwickshire R.V.C.
>   1883 Redesignated 2nd V.B. Royal Warwickshire Regiment.
>   1908 Became 7th Bn (TF).

Shoulder titles: 2VWARWICK which is w.m. and curved; T│7│RWARWICKSHIRE (786).

8th   1908 Formed with HQ at Aston Manor, Birmingham.
Shoulder title: T│8│RWARWICKSHIRE (787).

Service Battalions

14th	1914	Raised with the sub-title (1st Birmingham).
	1919	Disbanded.
15th	1914	Raised with the sub-title (2nd Birmingham).
	1918	Disbanded.
16th	1914	Raised with the sub-title (3rd Birmingham).
	1919	Disbanded.

Shoulder titles: 1│BIRMMBATT│RWARWICKSHIRE (*788*); 2│BIRMMBATT│RWAR-WICKSHIRE (*789*) and 3│BIRMMBATT│RWARWICKSHIRE.

Royal Fusiliers (City of London Regiment)

Regular Battalions

1685	Raised.
1751	Numbered 7th Regiment of Foot.
1881	Became The Royal Fusiliers (City of London Regiment).
1968	Became 3rd Bn, The Royal Regiment of Fusiliers (see chapter 6).

Shoulder titles: RF worn with a separate grenade above (*790*). Other versions were *791* and *792*, which was adapted from the RE title of the Royal Engineers. By the end of the 1st World War one-piece titles were being worn, of which three versions have been noted: R grenade F (*793, 794, 795*). The ball of the grenade has a Tudor Rose inside the Garter surmounted by a coronet. A smaller version of the RF title (*796*) was introduced for wear by officers after the 2nd World War.

Another title, which so far remains unidentified, is grenade│RF (*797*), the grenade being that of the post-war R grenade F patterns. The only information available on this title is that they are gilt, which would suggest an officers' item, and that all specimens noted by collectors are in mint condition, suggesting that the titles were made and perhaps never issued.

Militia Battalions

5th	1797	Raised as 3rd Middlesex or Westminster Militia.
	1881	Became 3rd Bn Royal Fusiliers.
	1898	Redesignated 5th Bn.
	1953	Disbanded.
6th	1853	Raised as Royal South or 4th Middlesex Militia.
	1881	Became 5th Bn Royal Fusiliers.
	1898	Redesignated 7th Bn.
	1921	Redesignated 6th Bn.
	1953	Disbanded.
7th	1559	Raised as The City of London Militia.
	1794	Divided into two regiments, The East and West Middlesex Militia.
	1820	Amalgamated as The Royal London Militia.
	1881	Became 4th Bn Royal Fusiliers.
	1898	Redesignated 6th Bn.
	1921	Redesignated 7th Bn.
	1953	Disbanded.

Shoulder title: R grenade F (*798*), the rose in w.m.

Volunteer Battalions

4th   1860 Raised as 2nd Tower Hamlets R.V.C.

1867 Amalgamated with other corps to form The Tower Hamlets Rifle Volunteer Brigade.

1881 Became a volunteer bn of The Rifle Brigade.

1904 Transferred to The Royal Fusiliers as 4th V.B.

1908 Became 4th (City of London) Bn, the London Regiment.

Shoulder titles: Two titles have been recorded, both in v.m., 4 | VB | RF, which appears in the 1904 Gaunt catalogue, and 4 | V | grenade | RF which was being worn just prior to the transfer to the Territorial Force in 1908.

Territorial Battalions

The 1st, 2nd, 3rd and 4th City of London Bns of the London Regiment were part of the Corps of the Royal Fusiliers but their lineage and shoulder titles have been covered in chapter 7.

However, on the break-up of The London Regiment in 1937, the 1st, 2nd and 3rd Bns were transferred to the Royal Fusiliers as 8th, 9th and 10th Bns respectively. The 4th were converted to an artillery roll.

Shoulder titles: The regular pattern *(794)* in w.m. was worn on the full dress uniforms.

Service Battalions

23rd   1914 Raised with the sub-title (1st Sportsman's).

1919 Disbanded.

Shoulder titles: Two titles have been noted: 1 | SPORTSMANS | RF *(799)* and 23 | R grenade F *(800)*, the grenade having a plain ball.

24th   1914 Raised with the sub-title (2nd Sportsman's).

1919 Disbanded.

Shoulder title: 2 | SPORTSMANS | RF *(801)*.

Cadets

The 1st Cadet Bn was recognized in 1911. HQ Pond St, Hampstead.

Shoulder titles: 1 | CADETS | CITY OF LONDON *(802, 803)*. Other titles worn by cadets affiliated to the Regiment were C | RF | CITY OF LONDON *(804)*, grenade | CRF *(805)*, which was also worn with the grenade separate, and C | RF | ST PANCRAS *(806)*.

The King's Regiment (Liverpool)

Regular Battalions

1685 Raised.

1751 Numbered 8th Regiment of Foot.

1881 Became The King's (Liverpool Regiment).

1958 Amalgamated with The Manchester Regiment to form The King's Regiment (Manchester & Liverpool) (see chapter 6).

Shoulder titles: The first metal title to be worn by the Regiment was LIVERPOOL *(807)*, which was replaced before 1902 by KING'S *(808)*, the former being retained on the greatcoat until 1907. Two other titles have been worn, Lpool.R (*809*), which was worn during the Boer War, and KING'S (*810*), which was worn by officers of the 1st Bn while serving in India c1903.

Volunteer Battalions pre-1908

5th   see 8th Bn (TF).

6th   see 9th Bn (TF).

7th   1860 Raised as 2nd Isle of Man R.V.C. at Douglas.

           1880 Renumbered 1st.

           1888 Redesignated 7th (Isle of Man) V.B. King's Regiment.

           1908 Bn did not transfer to Territorial Force, serving under Volunteer Act of 1863 until disbandment in 1920.

           1915 Formed a Service Company. See The Cheshire Regiment.

Shoulder title: V│I.O.M (*811*).

Volunteer Battalions 1918

           The 5th, 6th and 8th Bns of The Lancashire Volunteer Regiment became 1st, 2nd and 3rd Volunteer Bns of The King's Regiment in 1918. The battalions were also known as 1st, 2nd and 3rd Liverpool Volunteer Guard.

Shoulder titles: LIVERPOOL│1│VOLUNTEER GUARD (*812*). The 2nd and 3rd had similar titles but with the relevant numbers.

Territorial Battalions

5th   1860 1st Admin Bn of Lancashire R.Vs formed in Liverpool, the senior corps being the 1st, which was formed in 1859.

           1861 Bn consolidated as 1st Lancashire R.V.C.

           1888 Redesignated 1st V.B. King's Regiment.

           1908 Became 5th Bn (TF).

Shoulder titles: T│5│KING'S (*813, 814*). For a short time officers wore 5│KING'S (*815*).

6th   1860 2nd Admin Bn of Lancashire R.Vs formed in Liverpool, the senior corps being the 5th which was formed in 1859.

           1862 Bn consolidated as 5th Lancashire R.V.C.

           1888 Redesignated 2nd V.B. King's Regiment.

           1908 Became 6th (Rifle) Bn (TF).

           1936 Transferred to Royal Engineers.

Shoulder titles: The first title worn was T│6│LIVERPOOL (*816*), later replaced by T│6│KING'S (*817*).

7th   1860 15th Lancashire R.V.C. formed in Liverpool.

           1888 Redesignated 4th V.B. King's Regiment.

           1908 Became 7th Bn (TF).

           1938 Transferred to Royal Tank Corps.

Shoulder titles: T│7│KING'S (*818, 819*).

8th 1860 64th Lancashire R.V.C. formed in Liverpool.
1880 Renumbered 18th.
1888 Redesignated 5th (Irish) V.B. King's Regiment.
1908 Became 8th (Irish) Bn (TF).
1947 Transferred to Royal Artillery.
Shoulder titles: 5 | IRISH | V | KINGS *(820)* in w.m.; T | 8 | IRISH | KING'S *(821)*.

9th 1861 80th Lancashire R.V.C. formed in Liverpool.
1880 Renumbered 19th.
1888 Redesignated 6th V.B. King's Regiment.
1908 Became 9th Bn (TF).
1920 Transferred to Royal Engineers.
Shoulder titles: 6 | V | KING'S in w.m.; T | 9 | KING'S *(822)*.

10th 1900 Formed as the 8th (Scottish) V.B. King's Regiment in Liverpool.
1908 Became 10th (Scottish) Bn (TF).
1937 Transferred to The Cameron Highlanders.
Shoulder titles: T | 10 | SCOTTISH | LIVERPOOL *(823)*; T | 10 | KING'S *(824)*. Most T.F. Bns wore T | KING'S *(825)* on their greatcoats.

Service Battalions

Four bns were raised by the Earl of Derby within the City of Liverpool during the 1st World War. They came to be known as the Liverpool Pals but their official titles were 17th (1st City), 18th (2nd City), 19th (3rd City) and 20th (4th City). All bns were raised in 1914 and disbanded by 1919.
Shoulder titles: CITY BATN. | 1 | THE KINGS *(826)* or with the relevant number *(827, 828, 829)*.

Cadets

The 1st Cadet Bn was recognized in 1910. HQ Castle St, Liverpool. The Territorial Force withdrew its recognition in 1912.
Shoulder title: 1 | C | KING'S.
The Liverpool Collegiate School Cadet Corps was recognized in 1915 and affiliated to 6th Bn (TF). Transferred to the O.T.C. in 1925.
Shoulder title: LIVERPOOL | C | COLLEGIATE *(830)*.
Cadets affiliated to 6th Bn (TF) wore C | 6 | LIVERPOOL.

The Royal Norfolk Regiment

Regular Battalions

1685 Raised.
1751 Numbered 9th Regiment of Foot.
1881 Became The Norfolk Regiment.
1935 Redesignated The Royal Norfolk Regiment.
1959 Amalgamated with The Suffolk Regiment as the 1st East Anglian Regiment (see chapter 6).

Shoulder titles: A semicircular NORFOLK, of which there were two versions, was the first title to be worn (*831, 832*). These were replaced in 1902 by *833*. Another version was worn by officers serving in India c1935 (*834*). ROYAL | NORFOLK (*835, 836*) were issued in 1937, the latter being an officers' pattern. Another title, R. NORFOLK, which is made from cast brass, was made in India in 1942 and worn until 1945.

Volunteer Battalions pre-1908

1st	see 4th Bn (TF).
2nd	see 5th Bn (TF).
4th	see 4th Bn (TF).

Volunteer Battalions 1918

The Norfolk Volunteer Regiment consisted of 7 battalions which formed the 1st to 4th Volunteer Bn of the Norfolk Regiment in 1918.

Shoulder titles: 1 | NORFOLK | VOLUNTEERS (*837*) and 2 | NORFOLK | VOLUNTEERS (*838*) are the only titles so far noted.

Territorial Battalions

4th   1859 Raised as 1st Norfolk (City of Norwich) R.V.C.
          1883 Redesignated 1st V.B. Norfolk Regiment.

          1859 4th Norfolk R.V.C. formed at Norwich.
          1883 Redesignated 4th V.B. Norfolk Regiment.

          1908 1st and 4th V.Bs amalgamated as 4th Bn (TF).

Shoulder titles: 1 | V | NORFOLK in w.m.; 4 | V | NORFOLK in w.m.; T | 4 | NORFOLK (*839, 840*).

5th   1860 1st Admin Bn of Norfolk R.V.s formed at East Dereham, the senior corps being the 5th which was formed in 1859.
          1872 Bn consolidated as 3rd Norfolk R.V.C.
          1883 Redesignated 3rd V.B. Norfolk Regiment.

          1877 1st Admin Bn of Norfolk R.V.s formed, the senior corps being the 2nd which was formed in 1859.
          1880 Bn consolidated as the 2nd Norfolk R.V.C. with HQ in Great Yarmouth.
          1883 Redesignated 2nd V.B. Norfolk Regiment.

          1908 2nd and 3rd V.Bs amalgamated to form 5th Bn (TF). HQ East Dereham.
          1947 Disbanded.

Shoulder titles: 2 | V | NORFOLK in w.m.; T | 5 | NORFOLK (*841, 842*).

6th   1908 Raised at Norwich as 6th (Cyclist) Bn (TF).
          1920 Transferred to Royal Engineers.

Shoulder titles: T | 6 | NORFOLK (*843*). A smaller version also exists.

Royal Lincolnshire Regiment

Regular Battalions

1685 Raised.
1751 Numbered 10th Regiment of Foot.
1881 Became The Lincolnshire Regiment.
1946 Became The Royal Lincolnshire Regiment.
1960 Amalgamated with The Northamptonshire Regiment to form 2nd East Anglian Regiment (see chapter 6).

Shoulder titles: The semicircular title, LINCOLN (*844*), was worn until 1902, when replaced by *845* or *846*. A smaller version (*847*) was worn by officers. After 1946 the titles changed to include the word Royal: ROYAL|LINCOLNSHIRE (*848*). An oval-shaped version of the title also exists but according to the Regiment was never worn.

Territorial Battalions

4th & 5th   1860 1st Admin Bn of Lincolnshire R.Vs formed in Lincoln, the senior corps being the 1st which was formed in 1859.
1880 Bn consolidated as 1st Lincolnshire R.V.C.
1883 Redesignated 1st V.B. Lincolnshire Regiment.

1860 2nd Admin Bn of Lincolnshire R.Vs formed at Grantham.
1880 Bn consolidated as 2nd Lincolnshire R.V.C.
1883 Redesignated 2nd V.B. Lincolnshire Regiment.

1900 3rd V.B. formed at Grimsby.

1908 1st, 2nd and 3rd V.Bs formed, the 4th and 5th Bns (TF) at Lincoln and Grimsby respectively.
1936 5th Bn transferred to Royal Engineers.

Shoulder titles: T|4|LINCOLN (*849*); T|5|LINCOLN (*850*).

The Devonshire Regiment

Regular Battalions

1685 Raised.
1751 Numbered 11th Regiment of Foot.
1881 Became The Devonshire Regiment.
1958 Amalgamated with The Dorset Regiment to form the Devonshire and Dorset Regiment (see chapter 6).

Shoulder titles: DEVON (*851, 852, 853, 854*). The last is an officers' pattern.

Volunteer Battalions

2nd   see 5th Bn (TF).
3rd   see 4th Bn (TF).

Territorial Battalions

4th   1852 Raised as The Exeter and South Devon Volunteers. HQ Exeter.

1859 Became 1st Devonshire (Exeter and South Devon) R.V.C.

1885 Redesignated 1st (Exeter and South Devon) V.B.

1860 1st Admin Bn of Devonshire R.Vs formed in Exeter.

1880 Bn consolidated as 3rd Devonshire R.V.C.

1885 Redesignated 3rd V.B. Devonshire Regiment.

1908 1st V.B. and 3rd V.B. amalgamated as 4th Bn (TF).

Shoulder titles: 3 | v | DEVON *(855)* in w.m.; T | 4 | DEVON *(856)*. A three-piece version of the 3rd V.B. title also exists.

5th   1860 2nd Admin Bn of Devonshire R.Vs formed.

1880 Bn consolidated as 2nd Devonshire R.V.C. with HQ at Plymouth.

1885 Redesignated 2nd (Prince of Wales's) V.B. Devonshire Regiment.

1860 4th Admin Bn of Devonshire R.Vs formed at Newton Abbot.

1880 Bn consolidated as 5th Devonshire R.V.C.

1885 Redesignated 5th (The Hay Tor) V.B. Devonshire Regiment.

1908 2nd and 5th V.Bs amalgamated as 5th (Prince of Wales's) Bn (TF). HQ Plymouth.

1941 Transferred to Royal Artillery.

Shoulder titles: 2 | v | DEVON *(857)* in w.m.; T | 5 | DEVON *(858, 859)*.

6th   1860 3rd Admin Bn of Devonshire R.Vs formed at Barnstable.

1880 Bn consolidated as 4th Devonshire R.V.C.

1885 Became 4th V.B. Devonshire Regiment.

1908 Became 6th Bn (TF).

1947 Transferred to Royal Artillery.

Shoulder title: T | 6 | DEVON *(860)*.

7th   1908 Formed as 7th (Cyclist) Bn (TF) from Cyclist sections of 1st and 5th V.Bs. HQ Exeter.

1920 Disbanded.

Shoulder title: T | 7 | DEVON *(861)*.

Cadets

The 1st Exeter Cadet Bn was recognized in September, 1916, and affiliated to the 4th Bn (TF).

Shoulder title: C | 1 | DEVON.

The Exeter Cathedral School Cadet Corps was affiliated to the Regiment. They were recognized in 1911 and were absorbed into the 1st Exeter C.B. in 1916.

Shoulder title: EXETER | CATH SCHOOL *(862)*.

Cadet Companies affiliated to the 5th and 6th Bns (TF) wore the titles C | 5 | DEVON *(863)* and C | 6 | DEVON respectively. Others wore CADETS | DEVON *(864)*.

The Suffolk Regiment
Regular Battalions
1685 Raised.

1751 Numbered 12th Regiment of Foot.

1881 Became The Suffolk Regiment.

1959 Amalgamated with the Royal Norfolk Regiment to form the 1st East Anglian Regiment (see chapter 6).

Shoulder titles: SUFFOLK (*865, 866*); the latter title is in cast brass and was made and worn overseas.

Volunteer Battalions
1st see 4th Bn (TF).

3rd 1862 1st Admin Bn of Cambridgeshire R.Vs formed at Cambridge, the senior corps being the 1st which was raised in 1860.

1880 Bn consolidated as 1st Cambridgeshire R.V.C.

1887 Redesignated 3rd (Cambridgeshire) V.B. Suffolk Regiment.

1908 Became Cambridgeshire Bn, The Suffolk Regiment.

1909 Became The Cambridgeshire Regiment.

Shoulder title: 3 | CAMBS | V | SUFFOLK (*867*) in w.m.

Territorial Battalions
4th 1860 2nd Admin Bn of Suffolk R.Vs formed at Ipswich, the senior corps being the 1st which was raised in 1859.

1880 Bn consolidated as 1st Suffolk R.V.C.

1887 Redesignated 1st V.B. Suffolk Regiment.

1908 Became 4th Bn (TF).

Shoulder titles: 1 | V | SUFFOLK and 1 | VB | SUFFOLK, both in w.m.; T | 4 | SUFFOLK (*868*).

5th 1860 1st Admin Bn of Suffolk R.Vs formed.

1880 Bn consolidated as 6th Suffolk R.V.C.

1887 Redesignated 2nd V.B. Suffolk Regiment with HQ in Bury St Edmunds.

1908 Became 5th Bn (TF).

1921 Absorbed into 4th Bn.

Shoulder title: T | 5 | SUFFOLK (*869*).

6th 1910 Raised as 6th (Cyclist) Bn at Ipswich.

1920 Transferred to Royal Artillery.

Shoulder titles: T | 6 | SUFFOLK (*870*); T | 6 | CYCLIST | SUFFOLK, made up privately for the men at a cost of 6d per pair.

Cambs and Suffolk Reserve Bn
1915 Raised as 3/4th Bn Suffolk Regiment.

1916 Renumbered 2/4th.

1916 Redesignated 4th (Reserve) Bn.

1917 Absorbed 1st (Reserve) Bn The Cambridgeshire Regiment and designated The Cambridgeshire and Suffolk Reserve Bn.

1919 Disbanded.

Shoulder title: CAMBS | SUFFOLK (*871*).

The Somerset Light Infantry (Prince Albert's)

Regular Battalions:
    1685 Raised.
    1751 Numbered 13th Regiment of Foot.
    1881 Became The Prince Albert's (Somerset Light Infantry).
    1959 Amalgamated with The Duke of Cornwall's Light Infantry to
    form The Somerset and Cornwall Light Infantry (see chapter 6).
Shoulder titles: The first title to be worn was SOMERSET which was worn with a separate bugle above (872). This was replaced by the end of the 1st World War with a one-piece version, bugle | SOMERSET, which were worn in pairs, (873 and 874). A slightly different version, in that the bugles had cords instead of ribbons, was worn on foreign service dress (875 and 876). White metal versions of 873 and 874 were issued in 1954.

Territorial Battalions
4th & 5th   1860 1st Admin Bn of Somersetshire R.Vs formed at Bath, the
    senior corps being the 1st which was raised in 1859.
    1880 Bn consolidated as 1st Somersetshire R.V.C.
    1881 Redesignated 1st V.B. Somersetshire L.I.

    1860 2nd Admin Bn of Somersetshire R.Vs formed at Taunton.
    1880 Bn consolidated as 2nd Somersetshire R.V.C.
    1881 Redesignated 2nd V.B. Somersetshire L.I.

    1860 3rd Admin Bn of Somersetshire R.Vs formed at Wells.
    1880 Bn consolidated as 3rd Somersetshire R.V.C.
    1881 Redesignated 3rd V.B. Somersetshire L.I.

    1908 1st, 2nd and 3rd V.Bs amalgamated and formed 4th and 5th
    Bns (TF), with HQs at Bath and Taunton respectively.
Shoulder titles: T | 4 | bugle and T | 5 | bugle were worn above a separate SOMERSET (877) and (878). Titles were also worn in three pieces, i.e. T | 4 over bugle over SOMERSET. The 4th Bn, who served in India throughout the 1st World War, had made in the local bazaars the title T | 4 | SOMERSET which is made from cast brass. All titles that included bugles were worn in pairs.

Cadets
    The Queen's College (Taunton) Cadet Bn was recognized in 1915
    and affiliated to the 5th Bn (TF).
Shoulder title: QCCB (879).

    Also affiliated to the 5th Bn was the Chard School Cadet Company
    which was recognized in 1922.
Shoulder title: CHARD SCHOOL | SOMERSET (880).

    The 1st Cadet Bn was also affiliated to the 5th Bn
Shoulder title: 1 | C | bugle | SOMERSET.

The West Yorkshire Regiment (The Prince of Wales's Own)

Regular Battalions

1685 Raised.

1751 Numbered 14th Regiment of Foot.

1881 Became The Prince of Wales's Own (West Yorkshire Regiment).

1958 Amalgamated with The East Yorkshire Regiment to form The Prince of Wales's Own Regiment of Yorkshire (see chapter 6).

Shoulder titles: W. YORK (881) was replaced by W. YORKSHIRE (882) in 1924. Another title, W. YORK.R., which is curved, was worn by officers.

Volunteer Battalions 1918

The 1st to 7th Volunteer Bns were formed from battalions of the West Riding Volunteer Regiment as follows: 3rd Bn became 1st V.B., 4th Bn became 2nd V.B., 5th Bn became 3rd V.B., 11th Bn became 5th V.B., 12th Bn became 6th V.B., 13th Bn became 7th V.B. and 21st Bn became 4th V.B.

Shoulder titles: 3│WRV; 5│WRV; 12│WRV; 21│WRV. No titles have so far been noted for the 4th, 11th and 13th Bns.

Territorial Battalions

5th

1860 1st Admin Bn of Yorkshire West Riding R.Vs formed at York, the senior corps being the 1st which was raised in 1859.

1880 Bn consolidated as 1st Yorkshire West Riding R.V.C.

1887 Redesignated 1st V.B. West Yorkshire Regiment.

1908 Became 5th Bn (TF).

Shoulder title: T│5│W. YORK (883).

6th

1859 5th and 6th Yorkshire West Riding R.V.C. formed.

1860 Amalgamated as the 3rd at Bradford.

1887 Redesignated 2nd V.B. West Yorkshire Regiment.

1908 Became 6th Bn (TF).

1937 Transferred to Royal Engineers.

Shoulder title: T│6│W. YORK (884).

7th & 8th

1859 11th Yorkshire West Riding R.V.C. raised in Leeds.

1860 Renumbered 7th.

1887 Redesignated 3rd V.B. West Yorkshire Regiment.

1908 Became 7th and 8th (Leeds Rifles) Bns (TF).

1936 8th transferred to Royal Artillery.

1938 7th transferred to Royal Tank Corps.

Shoulder titles: T│7│W. YORK│LEEDS RIFLES (885); T│8│W. YORK│LEEDS RIFLES (886).

Service Battalions

15th & 17th 1914 Raised as 15th (1st Leeds) and 17th (2nd Leeds) (Service) Bns.

1917 15th absorbed 17th.

1919 Disbanded.

Shoulder title: LEEDS | W. YORK (*887*).

16th 1914 Raised as 16th (1st Bradford) (S) Bn.

1918 Disbanded.

Shoulder title: 16 | W. YORK (*888*).

18th 1915 Raised as 18th (2nd Bradford) (S) Bn.

1918 Disbanded.

Shoulder title: 18 | W. YORK (*889*).

Cadets

The Ashville College Cadet Corps was recognized in 1916 and affiliated to the 5th Bn (TF); disbanded 1920.

Shoulder title: ASHVILLE | C | COLLEGE (*890*).

The East Yorkshire Regiment (The Duke of York's Own)

Regular Battalions

1685 Raised.

1751 Numbered 15th Regiment of Foot.

1881 Became The East Yorkshire Regiment.

1958 Amalgamated with The West Yorkshire Regiment to form The Prince of Wales's Own Regiment of Yorkshire (see chapter 6).

Shoulder titles: E YORK (*891, 892*) and E. YORK (*893*) with *894*, unvoided, and *895* for officers. These were replaced in 1921 by E. YORKSHIRE (*896*).

Volunteer Battalions pre-1908

1st see 4th Bn (TF).

Volunteer Battalions 1918

Shoulder title: V | E. YORK (*897*).

Territorial Battalions

4th 1859 1st Yorkshire East Riding R.V.C. raised in Hull.

1883 Redesignated 1st V.B. East Yorkshire Regiment.

1908 Became 4th Bn (TF).

Shoulder titles: 1 | V | E. YORK in w.m.; T | 4 | E. YORK (*898*).

5th 1908 Formed as 5th (Cyclist) Bn (TF) from the Cyclist Company of 1st V.B. HQ Hull.

1920 Transferred to Royal Corps of Signals.

Shoulder title: T | 5 | E. YORK (*899*).

Cadets

Shoulder title: CADETS | E. YORK (*900*).

The Bedfordshire and Hertfordshire Regiment

Regular Battalions
1688 Raised.
1751 Numbered 16th Regiment of Foot.
1881 Became The Bedfordshire Regiment.
1919 Redesignated The Bedfordshire and Hertfordshire Regiment.
1958 Amalgamated with The Essex Regiment to form the 3rd East Anglian Regiment (see chapter 6).
Shoulder titles: Two versions of the semicircular title BEDFORD (*901, 902*) were issued before 1902 when *903* appeared. This was replaced in 1921 by BEDFS & HERTS (*904*).

Volunteer Battalions pre-1908
3rd   see 5th Bn (TF)

Volunteer Battalions 1918
The 1st and 2nd Volunteer Bns were formed from the 1st and 2nd Bns of the Bedfordshire Volunteer Regiment.
Shoulder title: BEDFORD V.T.C on a solid tablet.

Territorial Battalions
5th   1860 1st Admin Bn of Bedfordshire R.Vs formed.
1880 Bn consolidated as 1st Bedfordshire R.V.C. HQ in Bedford.
1887 Redesignated 3rd V.B. Bedfordshire Regiment.
1908 Became 5th Bn (TF) after amalgamation with 4th (Huntingdonshire) V.B. which had been formed in 1900.
Shoulder titles: 3 | V | BEDFORD (*905*); T | 5 | BEDFORD (*906*).

The Royal Leicestershire Regiment

Regular Battalions
1688 Raised.
1751 Numbered 17th Regiment of Foot.
1881 Became The Leicestershire Regiment.
1946 Redesignated The Royal Leicestershire Regiment.
1964 Became 4th Bn, The Royal Anglian Regiment (see chapter 6).
Shoulder titles: The semicircular title LEICESTER (*907*) was replaced by *908* in 1902 and by LEICESTERSHIRE (*909*) in 1924. After becoming Royal in 1946 the Regiment adopted the title ROYAL | LEICESTER (*910*) for other ranks and R. LEICESTER (*911*) or R LEICESTERS (*912*) for officers. Officers of the 2nd Bn wore for a short time before 1908, 2 | LEIC (*913*).

Territorial Battalions
4th & 5th   1860 1st Admin Bn of Leicestershire R.Vs formed at Leicester, the senior corps being the 1st which was raised in 1859.

1880 Bn consolidated as 1st Leicestershire R.V.C.
1883 Redesignated 1st V.B. Leicestershire Regiment.
1908 Became 4th and 5th Bns (TF).
1936 4th Bn transferred to Royal Engineers.
Shoulder titles: T | 4 | LEICESTER (914); T | 5 | LEICESTER (915).

Cadets
Shoulder title: C | LEICESTER

The Royal Irish Regiment
Regular Battalions
1684 Raised.
1751 Numbered 18th Regiment of Foot.
1881 Became The Royal Irish Regiment.
1922 Disbanded.
Shoulder titles: R. IRISH (916) was the first shoulder title to be worn, being replaced by ROYAL IRISH (917) by 1902. RI (918, 919, 920, 921, 922) were worn by officers only until 1920.

The Green Howards (Alexandra, Princess of Wales's Own Yorkshire Regiment)
Regular Battalions
1688 Raised.
1751 Numbered 19th Regiment of Foot.
1881 Became The Princess of Wales's Own (Yorkshire) Regiment.
1920 Designated The Green Howards (Alexandra, Princess of Wales's Own Yorkshire Regiment).
Shoulder titles: YORK (923) was replaced by a larger version (924) in 1912 and by a curved GREEN HOWARDS in 1920. A two-tier GREEN | HOWARDS (925) replaced the latter in 1921, an anodised version following in the 1960s.

Volunteer Battalions
1st see 4th Bn (TF).
2nd see 5th Bn (TF).

Territorial Battalions
4th 1860 1st Admin Bn of Yorkshire North Riding R.Vs formed, the senior corps being the 2nd which was raised in 1859.
1880 Bn consolidated as 1st Yorkshire North Riding R.V.C.
1883 Redesignated 1st V.B. Yorkshire Regiment with HQ in Northallerton.
1908 Became 4th Bn (TF).
Shoulder titles: 1 | V | YORK in w.m.; T | 4 | YORK (926), changing to T4 | GREEN | HOWARDS in 1922.

5th   1860 2nd Admin Bn of Yorkshire North Riding R.Vs formed at Scarborough, the senior corps being the 1st which was formed in 1859.
1880 Bn consolidated as 2nd Yorkshire North Riding R.V.C.
1883 Redesignated 2nd V.B. Yorkshire Regiment.

1860 2nd Admin Bn of Yorkshire East Riding R.Vs formed.
1862 Renumbered 1st.
1880 Bn consolidated as 2nd Yorkshire East Riding R.V.C.
1883 Redesignated 2nd V.B. East Yorkshire Regiment.

1908 2nd V.B. Yorkshire Regiment and 2nd V.B. East Yorkshire Regiment amalgamated as 5th Bn (TF). HQ Scarborough.
1947 Transferred to Royal Artillery.
Shoulder titles: 2 | V | YORK in w.m.; T | 5 | YORK (927), changing to T5 | GREEN | HOWARDS (928) in 1922.

Cadets

The Scorton Grammar School Cadet Corps was formed in 1917 and affiliated to the 4th Bn (TF).
Shoulder title: SCORTON SCHOOL | CADETS | 4th YORKSHIRE REGT. which is on a solid tablet (929).

The Lancashire Fusiliers

Regular Battalions

1688 Raised.
1751 Numbered 20th Regiment of Foot.
1881 Became The Lancashire Fusiliers.
1968 Became 4th Bn, The Royal Regiment of Fusiliers (see chapter 6).

Shoulder titles: Other ranks' titles until 1916 were LF, worn with a separate grenade above (930). After 1916 the title changed to LgrenadeF, the ball of the grenade bearing the sphinx within a laurel wreath. The officers' bi-metal titles appeared in either brass and w.m. or silver and gilt. Some versions had the wreath meeting at the top while some left a gap. The plinth below the sphinx was either left blank or inscribed EGYPT, (931, 932 and 933). All titles were worn in pairs, the sphinx facing to the front. A smaller version was introduced in the 1950s (934), changing to gold and silver anodised in the 1960s. Another title LgrenadeF with plain ball (935) was worn on the K.D. jacket c1910.

Volunteer Battalions

1st   see 5th Bn (TF).
3rd   see 7th Bn (TF).

Territorial Battalions

5th   1859 8th Lancashire R.V.C. raised in Bury.

            1883 Redesignated 1st V.B. Lancashire Fusiliers.

            1908 Became 5th Bn (TF).

            1941 Transferred to Royal Armoured Corps.

Shoulder titles: 1 | V | grenade | LF in w.m. (*936*); T | 5 | grenade | LF. Titles were also worn in two pieces, i.e. T | 5 over grenade | LF (*937*).

6th   1860 24th Lancashire R.V.C. raised at Rochdale.

            1880 Renumbered 12th.

            1883 Redesignated 2nd V.B. Lancashire Fusiliers.

            1908 Became 6th Bn (TF).

            1941 Transferred to Royal Armoured Corps.

Shoulder titles: T | 6 | grenade | LF. A two piece version was also worn.

7th   1860 56th Lancashire R.V.C. raised in Salford.

            1880 Renumbered 17th.

            1881 Became a volunteer bn of The Manchester Regiment.

            1886 Transferred to The Lancashire Fusiliers as 3rd V.B.

            1908 Became 7th and 8th Bns (TF).

            1936 7th Bn transferred to Royal Engineers.

Shoulder titles: 3 | V | LF in w.m.; T | 7 | grenade | LF (*938*). A two-piece version was also worn.

8th   1908 Formed from 3rd V.B. HQ Salford.

            1947 Transferred to Royal Artillery.

Shoulder titles: T | 8 | grenade | LF (*939*). A two-piece version was also worn. T | LgrenadeF (*940*) has also been worn by Territorial Bns.

Service Battalions

Five battalions were raised in Salford during the 1st World War: the 15th (1st Salford), 16th (2nd Salford), 19th (3rd Salford), 20th (4th Salford) and the 21st (Salford) (Reserve). The last was transferred to The King's Liverpool Regiment in 1917.

Shoulder titles: LgrenadeF | SALFORD (*941*); 20th LANCS FUSLRS | grenade | SALFORD (*942*).

The Royal Scots Fusiliers

Regular Battalions

            1678 Raised.

            1751 Numbered 21st Regiment of Foot.

            1881 Became The Royal Scots Fusiliers.

            1959 Amalgamated with The Highland Light Infantry to form The Royal Highland Fusiliers (see chapter 6).

Shoulder titles: Dated photos in the Scottish United Services Museum show the titles SF (*943, 944*) being worn in the 1890s. By 1907 the title had changed to RSF (*945*), which was worn with a separate grenade above, senior NCOs wearing the bi-metal collar badge (*946*). Three other versions of the title have also been noted: *947*, which was worn on the greatcoat, *948*, made in cast brass and worn in India and *949*, which was also made and worn overseas. The latter title has been made from three separate pices.

Territorial Battalions
4th and 5th 1860 1st Admin Bn of Ayrshire R.Vs formed at Ayr.

1873 Divided into two bns, the 1st at Ayr and the 2nd at Kilmarnock.

1880 1st Bn consolidated as 2nd Ayrshire R.V.C; 2nd consolidated as 1st Ayrshire R.V.C.

1887 1st became 1st V.B. Royal Scots Fusiliers; 2nd became 2nd V.B. Royal Scots Fusiliers.

1908 1st V.B. became 4th Bn (TF); 2nd V.B. became 5th Bn (TF).

1921 Amalgamated as 4th/5th Bn.

Shoulder titles: T│4│grenade│RSF (*950*); T│5│grenade│RSF (*951*). Two-piece versions were also worn: T│4 and T│5 over grenade│RSF.

Ardeer Company
This unit was formed in 1913 from employees of the Nobel Explosives Company of Ardeer, the intention being to guard the factory in the event of war. However, soon after war was declared in 1914 the company was disbanded so that the men could follow their usual occupations inside the factory.

Shoulder title: ARDEER│COMPANY (*952*).

The Cheshire Regiment
Regular Battalions
1689 Raised.

1751 Numbered 22nd Regiment of Foot.

1881 Became The Cheshire Regiment.

Shoulder titles: The only shoulder title to be worn by the Regiment's regular battalions is CHESHIRE. Several variations exist, however. *953* was the first to be used, being gradually replaced, before 1902, by *954, 955* and *956* are officers' patterns, the latter appearing in gold anodised during the 1960s for all ranks.

Volunteer Battalions
1st   see 4th Bn (TF).
2nd   see 5th Bn (TF).

Territorial Battalions
4th   1860 1st Admin Bn of Cheshire R.Vs formed at Birkenhead, the senior corps being the 1st which was raised in 1859.

1880 Bn consolidated as 1st Cheshire R.V.C.

1887 Redesignated 1st V.B. Cheshire Regiment.

1908 Became 4th Bn (TF).

1921 Amalgamated with 5th (Earl of Chester's) Bn to form 4th/5th (Earl of Chester's) Bn.

Shoulder titles: 1│V│CHESHIRE in w.m. (*957*); T│4│CHESHIRE (*958*).

5th   1860 2nd Admin Bn of Cheshire R.Vs formed at Chester, the senior corps being the 6th which was raised in 1859.

1880 Bn consolidated as 2nd (The Earl of Chester's) R.V.C.

1887 Redesignated 2nd (Earl of Chester's) V.B. Cheshire Regiment.

1860 3rd Admin Bn of Cheshire R.Vs formed at Knutsford.

1880 Bn consolidated as 3rd Cheshire R.V.C.

1887 Redesignated 3rd V.B. Cheshire Regiment.

1908 2nd and 3rd V.Bs amalgamated as 5th (Earl of Chester's) Bn (TF). HQ Chester.

1921 Amalgamated with 4th Bn.

Shoulder titles: 2│V│CHESHIRE in w.m.; T│5│EC│CHESHIRE (959).

The title V│CHESHIRE in w.m. was also worn with the battalion number worn separate above.

6th   1860 4th Admin Bn of Cheshire R.Vs formed at Stockport.

1880 Bn consolidated as 4th Cheshire R.V.C.

1887 Redesignated 4th V.B. Cheshire Regiment.

1908 Became 6th Bn (TF).

1920 Transferred to Royal Artillery.

Shoulder title: T│6│CHESHIRE (960).

7th   1860 5th Admin Bn of Cheshire R.Vs formed at Congleton.

1880 Bn consolidated as 5th Cheshire R.V.C.

1887 Redesignated 5th V.B. Cheshire Regiment.

1908 Became 7th Bn (TF).

Shoulder title: T│7│CHESHIRE (961).

Service Company

The 1st Manx (Service) Company was formed in March, 1915, by the 7th (Isle of Man) V.B. The King's (Liverpool Regiment). They were attached to the 16th (Service) Bn until October, 1915, when they were transferred to the 3rd Bn Cheshire Regt. The Company joined the 2nd Bn in Salonika on 12 January, 1916, becoming 'A' Company.

Shoulder titles: The Arms of the Isle of Man within a circle (962) was worn above the regular pattern KING'S (808) and, later, CHESHIRE (954). One-piece specimens also exist.

Cadets

The cadets affiliated to the 4th Bn wore the title C│4│CHESHIRE (963).

The Royal Welch Fusiliers

Regular Battalions

1689 Raised.

1751 Numbered 23rd Regiment of Foot.

1881 Became The Royal Welsh Fusiliers (Welch after 1920).

Shoulder titles: The first title was WF (964), which was worn until 1898. After

1898 the titles changed to RWF (*965*), which was worn with a separate grenade above. Three variants have been noted: *966*, which was worn on the greatcoats, *967*, which is made from cast brass, and *968*. A much smaller version than any of those shown was worn by officers. One unidentified title is grenade | R.W.FUS (*969*) which, although made from cast brass, is of much better manufacture than usual.

Volunteer Battalions pre-1908
1st   see 4th Bn (TF).
2nd   see 5th Bn (TF).

Volunteer Battalions 1918
The 1st Carnarvonshire Volunteer Regiment formed the 3rd Volunteer Battalion of the Royal Welsh Fusiliers in 1918.
Shoulder title: 1 | CARNARVONSHIRE | V.T.C (*970*), the numeral in brass the remainder bronze.

Territorial Battalions
4th   1861 1st Admin Bn of Denbighshire R.Vs formed at Ruabon, the
                    senior corps being the 1st which was raised in 1860.
            1880 Bn consolidated as 1st Denbighshire R.V.C.
            1884 Redesignated 1st V.B. Royal Welsh Fusiliers. HQ Wrexham.
            1908 Became 4th (Denbighshire) Bn (TF).
Shoulder titles: 1 | V | grenade | RWF in w.m.; T | 4 | grenade | RWF (*971*). Also two-piece T | 4 over grenade | RWF.
5th   1860 1st Admin Bn of Flintshire R.V.s formed at Rhyl.
            1880 Bn consolidated as the 1st Flintshire and Carnarvonshire
                    R.V.C.
            1884 Redesignated 2nd V.B. Royal Welsh Fusiliers.
            1908 Became 5th (Flintshire) Bn (TF). HQ Hawarden.
            1938 Transferred to Royal Artillery.
Shoulder titles: 2 | V | grenade | RWF in w.m. (*972*); T | 5 | grenade | RWF (*973*); T | 5 | RWF. Also two-piece T | 5 over grenade | RWF.
6th   1897 3rd V.B. formed from part of 2nd V.B. HQ Carnarvon.
            1908 Became 6th (Carnarvonshire and Anglesey) Bn (TF).
            1947 Transferred to Royal Artillery.
Shoulder title: T | 6 | grenade | RWF (*974*). Also two-piece T | 6 over grenade | RWF.
7th   1897 Formed as 5th V.B. South Wales Borderers.
            1908 Became 7th (Montgomery) Bn Royal Welsh Fusiliers (TF).
                    HQ Newtown.
            1947 Transferred to Royal Artillery.
Shoulder titles: T | 7 | grenade | RWF (*975*); T | 7 | RWF. Also two-piece T | 7 over grenade | RWF.

Service Battalions
15th   1914 Raised with the sub-title (1st London Welsh).
            1918 Disbanded.
Shoulder title: grenade | RWF | 1st LONDON WELSH (*976*).

Cadets

The titles C|4|RWF (977) and C|5|RWF were worn by cadets affiliated to the 4th and 5th Bns (TF) respectively.

The South Wales Borderers

Regular Battalions

> 1689 Raised.
>
> 1751 Numbered 24th Regiment of Foot.
>
> 1881 Became The South Wales Borderers.
>
> 1969 Amalgamated with The Welch Regiment to form The Royal Regiment of Wales (see chapter 6).

Shoulder titles: The title SWB was the only pattern to be worn by the Regiment's regular battalions. There were, however, several variations. The first to be worn were 978, 979, 980, and 981 for other ranks, and 982 for officers. These were replaced in 1904 by 983 for other ranks and 984 for officers. Another pattern was 985, which was worn by officers during the 1930s.

Volunteer Battalions

1st   see Brecknockshire Bn.

Territorial Battalions

Brecknockshire Bn

> 1860 1st Admin Bn of Brecknockshire R.Vs formed at Brecon, the senior corps being the 1st which was raised in 1959.
>
> 1880 Bn consolidated as 1st Brecknockshire R.V.C.
>
> 1885 Redesignated 1st (Brecknockshire) V.B. South Wales Borderers.
>
> 1908 Became the Brecknockshire Bn, The South Wales Borderers. HQ Brecon.
>
> 1922 Amalgamated with 3rd Bn, The Monmouthshire Regiment to form 3rd (Brecknockshire and Monmouthshire) Bn, The Monmouthshire Regiment.

Shoulder titles: 1|V|SWB in w.m.; T|BRECKNOCK (986) which was also worn with the 'T' separate above. 2nd and 3rd Line Bns were formed during the 1st World War and on 29 October, 1914, the 1st/1st Bn sailed for India. While in India the battalion had made up the title T|1|BRECKNOCK (987) which is in cast brass.

The King's Own Scottish Borderers

Regular Battalions

> 1689 Raised.
>
> 1751 Numbered 25th Regiment of Foot.
>
> 1881 Became The King's Own Borderers
>
> 1887 Redesignated The King's Own Scottish Borderers.

Shoulder titles: KOB (988); KOSB (989). Several versions of the post-1887 title have been noted: 990, which was worn on the greatcoats, 991 which was worn by officers, 992 and the gold anodised pattern which was introduced in the 1960s (993). A curved version also exists (994), and K.O.S.B (995) which is of overseas manufacture.

Territorial Battalions

4th 1861 1st Roxburghshire and Selkirkshire Admin Bn formed, the senior corps being the 1st Roxburghshire which was formed in 1859.

1880 Bn consolidated as 1st Roxburghshire and Selkirkshire R.V.C.

1881 Became a volunteer bn of The Royal Scots Fusiliers.

1887 Transferred to The King's Own Scottish Borderers.

1863 1st Admin Bn of Berwickshire R.V.s formed at Duns, the senior corps being the 1st which was formed in 1859.

1880 Bn consolidated as 1st Berwickshire R.V.C.

1881 Became a volunteer bn of The Royal Scots.

1887 Transferred to The King's Own Scottish Borderers as 2nd (Berwickshire) V.B.

1908 1st Roxburgh and Selkirk R.V.C. and 2nd V.B. amalgamated as 4th (The Border) Bn (TF). HQ Melrose.

Shoulder title: T | 4 | KOSB *(996)*.

5th 1862 1st Admin Bn of Dumfrieshire R.Vs formed at Dumfries, the senior corps being the 1st which was formed in 1860.

1880 Bn consolidated as 1st Dumfrieshire R.V.C.

1881 Became a volunteer bn of The Royal Scots Fusiliers.

1887 Transferred to The King's Own Scottish Borderers as the 3rd (Dumfries) V.B.

1860 The Galloway Admin Bn formed.

1880 Bn consolidated as Galloway R.V.C.

1881 Became a V.B. of The Royal Scots Fusiliers.

1899 Transferred to The King's Own Scottish Borderers.

1908 3rd V.B. and the Galloway R.V.C. amalgamated as 5th (Dumfries and Galloway) Bn (TF) HQ Dumfries.

Shoulder title: T | 5 | KOSB *(997)*.

The Cameronians (Scottish Rifles)

Regular Battalions

1689 26th Regiment of Foot raised.

1794 90th Regiment of Foot raised.

1881 Linked as The Cameronians (Scottish Rifles).

1968 Disbanded.

Shoulder titles: Two sizes of the blackened brass title SR have been issued *(998, 999)*, the latter being worn on the greatcoat. These were replaced by CAMERONIANS *(1000)*, which is also blackened brass, in 1921

Volunteer Battalions

3rd Lanarkshire R.V.C. see 7th Bn (TF).

Territorial Battalions

5th 1859 1st Lanarkshire (Glasgow 1st Western) R.V.C. raised.

   1881 Became a volunteer bn of the Cameronians.

   1908 Became 5th Bn (TF).

   1921 Amalgamated with 8th Bn to form 5th/8th Bn.

   1940 Transferred to Royal Artillery.

Shoulder titles: T｜5｜SR (*1001*). The three-piece title T over 5/8 over CAMERONIANS was worn after 1921.

6th 1860 3rd Admin Bn of Lanarkshire R.Vs formed, the senior corps being the 16th which was raised in 1859.

   1861 Renumbered 1st.

   1873 Bn consolidated as 16th Lanarkshire R.V.C. HQ Hamilton.

   1880 Renumbered 2nd.

   1887 Redesignated 2nd V.B. Cameronians.

   1908 Became 6th Bn (TF).

Shoulder title: T｜6｜SR (*1002*).

7th 1859 3rd Lanarkshire (Glasgow 1st Southern) R.V.C. raised.

   1881 Became a volunteer bn of The Cameronians.

   1908 Became 7th Bn (TF).

Shoulder titles: 3｜V｜LANARK in w.m. (*1003*); T｜7｜SR (*1004*).

8th 1859 4th Lanarkshire (Glasgow 1st Northern) R.V.C. raised.

   1887 Redesignated 4th V.B. Cameronians.

   1908 Became 8th Bn (TF).

   1921 Amalgamated with 5th Bn.

Shoulder title: T｜8｜SR (*1005*).

Cadets

   The Glasgow High School Cadet Corps was affiliated to the old 1st Lanarkshire R.V.C. The School continued the affiliation when the 1st Lanarkshire R.V.C. The School continued the affiliation when the 1st Lanarks became the 5th Bn (TF) in 1908 but were later transferred to the O.T.C. in 1910.

Shoulder title: HIGH SCHOOL｜CC｜GLASGOW (*1006*).

   The 7th Cameronians (Scottish Rifles) Cadet Corps was formed c1931.

Shoulder title: 7｜C｜CAMERONIANS.

The Royal Inniskilling Fusiliers

Regular Battalions

   1689 27th Regiment of Foot raised.

   1854 108th Regiment of Foot raised.

   1881 Linked as The Royal Inniskilling Fusiliers.

   1968 Became 1st Bn, The Royal Irish Rangers (see chapter 6).

Shoulder titles: A sketch of a private of the 2nd Bn in the Tirah Campaign of 1897–98 in the *Regimental History* shows the badge being worn on the shoulder strap as a grenade bearing the Castle of Inniskilling, below the grenade a scroll inscribed ROYAL INNISKILLING FUSILIERS. The other ranks' title is in brass while the officers' is silver and gilt (*1007*). Other titles are INNG.F (*1008*) worn c1900,

R.INNIS (*1009*) worn c1908, RINNISKILLING (*1010*) worn c1914, INNISKILLINGS
(*1011*) worn c1927 and in w.m. by pipers, and INNISKILLING (*1012*) which was
the last pattern to be worn; all five titles were worn with a separate grenade
above. In addition to the above two other versions of the INNISKILLING title
were worn, both by officers (*1013, 1014*). The latter can be seen being worn
on a top coat in the Regimental Museum.

The Gloucestershire Regiment

Regular Battalions

      1694 28th Regiment of Foot raised.
      1756 61st Regiment of Foot raised.
      1881 Linked as The Gloucestershire Regiment.
Shoulder titles: The semicircular title GLOSTER was worn by other ranks until
1902 when replaced by *1015*. The pre-1902 officers' title was also semicircular
but worded GLOUCESTER. A smaller version of the GLOSTER title was worn by
officers after 1902 (*1016*). The 2nd Bn wore the title 2|GLOSTER (*1017*) until
1894. Another pattern worded simply GLOS exists but no information can be
found as to when it was worn.

Militia Battalions
4th   1760 Raised as North Bn of Gloucestershire Militia.
      1795 Redesignated Royal North Gloucestershire Militia.
      1881 Became 4th Bn, Gloucestershire Regiment.
      1908 Disbanded.
Shoulder title: The letters RNGM in script and intertwined. The title is in w.m.

Volunteer Battalions
1st see 4th Bn (TF).

Territorial Battalions
4th   1859 1st Gloucestershire (City of Bristol) R.V.C. raised.
      1883 Redesignated 1st (City of Bristol) V.B. Gloucestershire Regi-
            ment.
      1908 Became 4th (City of Bristol) Bn (TF).
      1940 Transferred to Royal Artillery.
Shoulder titles: 1|VB|GLOSTER in w.m.; T|4|GLOSTER (*1018*).
5th   1860 1st Admin Bn of Gloucestershire R.V.s formed in Gloucester,
            the senior corps being the 2nd which was raised in 1859.
      1880 Bn consolidated as 2nd Gloucestershire R.V.C.
      1883 Redesignated 2nd V.B. Gloucestershire Regiment.
      1908 Became 5th Bn (TF).
      1941 Transferred to Reconnaissance Corps.
Shoulder titles: T|5|GLOSTER (*1019*); T|5|GLOUCESTER.
6th   1900 3rd V.B. Gloucestershire Regiment formed at Bristol.
      1908 Became 6th Bn (TF).
      1938 Transferred to Royal Tank Regiment.
Shoulder title: T|6|GLOSTER (*1020*).

The Worcestershire Regiment

Regular Battalions

      1694 29th Regiment of Foot raised.

      1701 36th Regiment of Foot raised.

      1881 Linked as The Worcestershire Regiment.

      1970 Amalgamated with The Nottinghamshire and Derbyshire Regiment to form The Worcestershire and Sherwood Foresters Regiment (see chapter 6).

Shoulder titles: WORCESTER (*1021*) was the first shoulder title to be used, being semicircular until 1902. This was replaced in 1907 by WORCESTERSHIRE (*1022*), which appeared in gold anodised in the 1960s. Before 1908 two officers' patterns were worn, WORC (*1023*) and WORCS.

Territorial Battalions

7th   1860 1st Admin Bn of Worcestershire R.Vs formed, the senior corps being the 1st which was raised in 1859.

           1880 Bn consolidated as 1st Worcestershire R.V.C.

           1883 Redesignated 1st V.B. Worcestershire Regiment. HQ Kidderminster.

           1908 Became 7th Bn (TF).

Shoulder title: T | 7 | WORCESTERSHIRE (*1024*).

8th   1860 2nd Admin Bn of Worcestershire R.Vs formed at Worcester.

           1880 Bn consolidated as 2nd Worcestershire R.V.C.

           1883 Redesignated 2nd V.B. Worcestershire Regiment

           1908 Became 8th Bn (TF).

           1947 Transferred to Royal Artillery.

Shoulder title: T | 8 | WORCESTERSHIRE (*1025*).

Cadets

      The King Edward VI Grammar School Cadet Corps at Stourbridge was formed in 1915 and affiliated to the 7th Bn (TF). It became part of the Worcestershire Cadet Bn, later 1st Cadet Bn, The Worcestershire Regiment in 1916.

Shoulder title: A solid oval worded, K.E.VI.G.S. | CADET CORPS | STOURBRIDGE (*1026*).

The East Lancashire Regiment

Regular Battalions

      1702 30th Regiment of Foot raised.

      1755 59th Regiment of Foot raised.

      1881 Linked as The East Lancashire Regiment.

      1958 Amalgamated with The South Lancashire Regiment (Prince of Wales's Volunteers) to form The Lancashire Regiment (Prince of Wales's Volunteers) (see chapter 6).

Shoulder titles: ELANCASHIRE (*1027*) and E. LANCASHIRE (*1028*). Another version (*1029*) was worn by officers. Other patterns noted are E. LANC (*1030*), E. LANCS (*1031*) and E.LAN.R which is made from cast brass.

Volunteer Battalions

1st   see 4th Bn (TF).
2nd   see 5th Bn (TF).

Territorial Battalions

4th   1864 8th Admin Bn of Lancashire R.V.s formed at Blackburn, the
            senior corps being the 2nd which was raised in 1859.
            1880 Bn consolidated as 2nd Lancashire R.V.C.
            1889 Redesignated 1st V.B. East Lancashire Regiment.
            1908 Became 4th Bn (TF).
            1921 Amalgamated with 5th Bn to form 4th/5th Bn.
Shoulder titles: 1│v│ELANCASHIRE in w.m.; T│4│E. LANCASHIRE (*1032*).

5th   1860 3rd Admin Bn of Lancashire R.Vs formed in Burnley, the
            senior corps being the 4th which was raised in 1859.
            1880 Bn consolidated as 3rd Lancashire R.V.C.
            1889 Redesignated 2nd V.B. East Lancashire Regiment.
            1908 Became 5th Bn (TF).
            1921 Amalgamated with 4th Bn.
Shoulder titles: 2│v│ELANCASHIRE in three pieces (*1033*) w.m.; T│5│E.
LANCASHIRE which also exists with the lower tier solid (*1034*). Cast brass
versions were also made and worn in India during the 1st World War.

The East Surrey Regiment

Regular Battalion

            1702 31st Regiment of Foot raised.
            1756 70th Regiment of Foot raised.
            1881 Linked as The East Surrey Regiment.
            1959 Amalgamated with The Queen's Royal West Surrey Regi-
            ment to form The Queen's Royal Surrey Regiment (see chapter 6).
Shoulder titles: The semicircular title E. SURREY (*1035*) was worn until 1902
when replaced by *1036* and *1037*. Officers of the Regiment also wore the title E.
SURREY which appeared as *1038, 1039* and *1040*, the last being worn on the
foreign service tunic c1900. Another title, SURREYS (*1041*), was worn by the 2nd
Bn in India just prior to the 1st World War.

Volunteer Battalions

3rd   see 6th Bn (TF).
4th   1859 7th Surrey R.V.C. raised at Clapham Junction.
            1887 Redesignated 4th V.B. East Surrey Regiment.
            1908 Became 23rd (County of London) Bn The London Regiment.
Shoulder title: 4│v│E. SURREY in w.m. (*1042*).

Territorial Battalions

5th   1860 1st Admin Bn of Surrey R.Vs formed, the senior corps being
            the 2nd which was raised in 1859.
            1880 Bn consolidated as 3rd Surrey R.V.C.

1887 Redesignated 2nd V.B. East Surrey Regiment. HQ Wimbledon.

1908 Became 5th Bn (TF).

1938 Transferred to Royal Artillery.

Shoulder title: T | 5 | E. SURREY (*1043*).

6th   1860 2nd Admin Bn of Surrey R.Vs formed at Kingston-upon-Thames, the senior corps being the 6th which was raised in 1859.

1880 Bn consolidated as 5th Surrey R.V.C.

1887 Redesignated 3rd V.B. East Surrey Regiment.

1908 Became 6th Bn (TF).

Shoulder titles: 3 | v | E. SURREY in w.m.; T | 6 | E. SURREY (*1044*).

Cadets

The Beaumont College Cadet Corps of Old Windsor was affiliated to the 3rd V.B. They became part of the Junior Division O.T.C. in 1908.

Shoulder title: BEAUMONT | CC | COLLEGE (*1045*).

The Tiffin School Cadet Corps at Kingston-upon-Thames was recognized in 1915. They were affiliated to the 6th Bn (TF) and became a company of the 1st Cadet Bn in 1919.

Shoulder title: TIFFIN | C | SCHOOL (*1046*).

The Wimbledon College Cadet Corps also joined the 1st Cadet Bn in 1919. They were recognized in 1915 and affiliated to the 5th Bn (TF).

Shoulder title: WIMBLEDON | COLLEGE (*1047*).

Another unit to join the 1st Cadet Bn in 1919 was the Kingston Grammar School Cadet Corps which was recognized in 1915 and affiliated to the 6th Bn (TF).

Shoulder title: KINGSTON | C | GRAMMAR SCHOOL (*1048*).

The 1st Cadet Bn was formed in 1919 from various cadet corps within the Surrey area.

Shoulder titles: The general title to be worn by the Battalion was 1 | C | E. SURREY, but the Richmond Hill School Company had their own pattern, R.H.S. | C | 1 | E. SURREY (*1049*).

Other companies affiliated to the 6th Bn (TF) wore C | 6 | E. SURREY (*1050*).

The Duke of Cornwall's Light Infantry

Regular Battalions

1702 32nd Regiment of Foot raised.

1741 46th Regiment of Foot raised.

1881 Linked as The Duke of Cornwall's Light Infantry.

1959 Amalgamated with The Somersetshire Light Infantry to form The Somerset and Cornwall Light Infantry (see chapter 6).

Shoulder titles: The title worn until 1914 was CORNWALL (*1051*), which was worn with a separate bugle above. The lower part was being worn by other ranks on tropical dress c1903 and continued to be worn after 1914 on the greatcoat. The title introduced in 1914 was also a bugle over CORNWALL but this time in one piece (*1052, 1053*). These titles were worn in pairs with the mouthpiece facing front. The same title was introduced in w.m. c1954. According to photographs taken of officers in 1889 a similar title to the post-1914 pattern was being worn on the white mess tunic; the word CORNWALL, however, was non-voided (*1054*). This title is also shown in a c1893 photograph as being worn on the tropical jacket. Army Order 509 of 1920 states that the titles to be worn on the shoulder straps will change to a curved D.C.L.I (*1055*). This title was obviously manufactured but no evidence can be found to suggest that it was ever worn.

Territorial Battalions

4th   1860 1st Admin Bn of Cornwall R.Vs formed, the senior corps being the 1st which was raised in 1859.

1880 Bn consolidated as 1st Cornwall R.V.C.

1885 Redesignated 1st V.B. Duke of Cornwall's L.I. HQ Truro.

1908 Became 4th Bn (TF).

1921 Amalgamated with 5th Bn to form 4th/5th Bn.

Shoulder titles: The first title to be worn was in two pieces, T|4|bugle over CORNWALL (*1056*). These were worn in pairs. A one-piece version was adopted in 1914, the lower bugle|CORNWALL being the regular pattern of the period. After 1921 the titles changed to T|4/5|bugle|CORNWALL (*1057*) which were also worn in pairs. A change took place in 1930 when the numbers were discarded and the title appeared as T|bugle|CORNWALL, again in pairs (*1058, 1059*).

5th   1860 2nd Admin Bn of Cornwall R.Vs formed at Bodmin, the senior corps being the 4th which was raised in 1859.

1880 Bn consolidated as 2nd Cornwall R.V.C.

1885 Redesignated 2nd V.B. Duke of Cornwall's L.I.

1908 Became 5th Bn (TF).

1921 Amalgamated with 4th Bn (TF).

Shoulder title: T|5|bugle over CORNWALL (*1060*), two-piece and worn in pairs.

Cadets

The 1st Cadet Bn wore 1|C|CORNWALL (*1061*) between 1912 and 1931.

The Duke of Wellington's Regiment (West Riding)

Regular Battalions

1702 33rd Regiment of Foot raised.

1787 76th Regiment of Foot raised.

1881 Linked as The Duke of Wellington's (West Riding Regiment).

Shoulder titles: W. RIDING (*1062*) was worn up to 1915, with a smaller version, W RIDING (*1063*) for officers. This was replaced by DUKE|OF|WELLINGTON'S (*1064*) or DUKE|OF|WELLINGTON. A further change took place in 1931 when DW (*1065, 1066*) were issued, these being replaced by the anodised DWR (*1067*) in 1970. Other titles known are D of W (*1068*) and, D. of W's (*1069*) which were both worn in No. 1 dress c1920–31.

Volunteer Battalions pre-1908

1st   see 4th Bn (TF).

2nd   see 5th Bn (TF).

Volunteer Battalions 1918

Volunteer battalions were formed from the West Riding Volunteer Regiment in 1918 as follows: 2nd Bn became 1st V.B., 6th Bn became 5th V.B., 8th Bn became 3rd V.B., 9th Bn became 2nd V.B. and 20th Bn became 4th V.B.

Shoulder titles: 2 | WRV; 6 | WRV (*1070*); 8 | WRV; 9 | WRV; 20 | WRV.

Territorial Battalions

4th   1859 7th and 8th Yorkshire West Riding R.V.C. raised.
              1860 13th and 14th Corps raised and amalgamated with 7th and 8th to form 4th Yorkshire West Riding R.V.C. with HQ in Halifax.
              1883 Redesignated 1st V.B. Duke of Wellington's Regiment.
              1908 Became 4th Bn (TF).
              1938 Transferred to Royal Artillery.

Shoulder titles: 1 | V | W.RIDING in w.m.; T | 4 | W.RIDING (*1071*).

5th   1859 10th Yorkshire West Riding R.V.C. raised.
              1860 Renumbered 6th.
              1862 Formed 5th Admin Bn of Yorkshire West Riding R.Vs with the 32nd Corps.
              1880 Bn consolidated as 6th Yorkshire West Riding R.V.C. HQ Huddersfield.
              1883 Redesignated 2nd V.B. Duke of Wellington's Regiment.
              1908 Became 5th Bn (TF).
              1936 Transferred to Royal Engineers.

Shoulder titles: 2 | V | W.RIDING in w.m.; T | 5 | W.RIDING (*1072*) changing to 5 | D.OFW c1920 and T | 5 | DW (*1073*) c1931.

6th   1860 2nd Admin Bn of Yorkshire West Riding R.Vs formed.
              1880 Bn consolidated as 9th Yorkshire West Riding R.V.C.
              1883 Redesignated 3rd V.B. Duke of Wellington's Regiment.
              1908 Became 6th Bn (TF). HQ Skipton-in-Craven.
              1947 Transferred to Royal Artillery.

Shoulder title: T | 6 | W.RIDING (*1074*).

7th   1908 Formed from three companies of the 2nd V.B. at Milnsbridge.

Shoulder title: T | 7 | W.RIDING (*1075*) changing to T | 7 | DW in 1931.

The Border Regiment

Regular Battalions

              1702 34th Regiment of Foot raised.
              1755 55th Regiment of Foot raised.
              1881 Linked as The Border Regiment.
              1959 Amalgamated with The King's Own Royal Regiment (Lancaster) to form The King's Own Royal Border Regiment (see chapter 6).

Shoulder titles: The semicircular title BORDER (*1076*) was worn by the 1st Bn until 1902, when replaced by *1077, 1078* and *1079*, with a smaller version

(1080) for officers. The 2nd Bn wore a straight version, *(1081)* and *(1082)*. The two regular battalions were amalgamated in 1948, which year saw the curved title worn by other ranks while officers adopted the straight pattern. Another title, BORDER.REGT *(1083)*, also exists but so far no information can be found as to when it was worn.

Territorial Battalions
4th   1860 1st Admin Bn of Cumberland R.Vs formed.
1880 Bn consolidated as 1st Cumberland R.V.C.
1887 Redesignated 1st (Cumberland) V.B. Border Regiment at Carlisle.

1860 1st Admin Bn of Westmoreland R.Vs formed at Kendal.
1880 Bn consolidated as 1st Westmoreland R.V.C.
1887 Redesignated 2nd (Westmoreland) V.B. Border Regiment.

1908 1st and 2nd V.Bs amalgamated as 4th (Cumberland and Westmoreland) Bn (TF). HQ Kendal.
Shoulder title: T | 4 | BORDER *(1084)*.
5th   1900 3rd (Cumberland) V.B. raised at Workington.
1908 Became 5th (Cumberland) Bn (TF).
1941 Transferred to Royal Armoured Corps.
Shoulder title: T | 5 | BORDER *(1085)*.

Cadets
C | 4 | BORDER was worn by cadets affiliated to 4th Bn (TF).

The Royal Sussex Regiment
Regular Battalions
1701 35th Regiment of Foot raised.
1854 107th Regiment of Foot raised.
1881 Linked as The Royal Sussex Regiment.
1966 Became 3rd Bn, The Queen's Regiment (see chapter 6).
Shoulder titles: SUSSEX *(1086)* was the first title to be worn, changing, by 1902, to ROYAL SUSSEX *(1087)*. This was replaced by R.SUSSEX *(1088, 1089)* in 1920, the latter being an officers' pattern.

Volunteer Battalions pre-1908
1st   see 6th Bn (TF).
2nd   see 4th Bn (TF).

Volunteer Battalions 1918
The 1st to 9th Battalions of the Sussex Volunteer Regiment became the 1st to 6th Volunteer Bns of The Royal Sussex Regiment in 1918.
Shoulder title: The letters VTC intertwined over SUSSEX *(1090)*.

Territorial Battalions

4th   1860 1st and 2nd Admin Bns of Sussex R.Vs formed.

            1874 Bns amalgamated as 1st. HQ Worthing.

            1880 Bn consolidated as 2nd Sussex R.V.C.

            1887 Redesignated 2nd V.B. Royal Sussex Regiment.

            1908 Became 4th Bn (TF).

            1943 Amalgamated with 5th Bn to form 4th/5th Bn.

Shoulder titles: 2│v│ROYAL SUSSEX in w.m.; T│4│ROYAL SUSSEX *(1091)*.

5th   1861 1st Admin Bn of Cinque Ports R.Vs formed at Hastings. the senior corps being the 1st which was raised in 1859.

            1880 Bn consolidated as 1st Cinque Ports R.V.C.

            1881 Became a volunteer bn of The Royal Sussex Regiment.

            1908 Became 5th (Cinque Ports) Bn (TF).

            1943 Amalgamated with 5th Bn.

Shoulder title: T│5│ROYAL SUSSEX *(1092)*.

6th   1859 1st Sussex R.V.C. raised at Brighton.

            1887 Redesignated 1st Volunteer Bn The Royal Sussex Regiment.

            1908 The Bn was to be transferred to the Royal Field Artillery as 2nd Home Counties Brigade. but the officers flatly refused to comply, resulting in the Battalion being put upon the unattached list until 1912.

            1912 Became 6th (Cyclist) Bn (TF).

            1919 Disbanded.

Shoulder titles: 1│v│ROYAL SUSSEX in w.m.; T│6│ROYAL SUSSEX *(1093)*.

Cadets

CADETS│4│ROYAL SUSSEX *(1094)* and C│4│ROYAL SUSSEX were both worn by cadet companies affiliated to the 4th Bn (TF).

Cadets affiliated to the 5th Bn (TF) wore CADETS│5│ROYAL SUSSEX.

            The Mayfield College Cadet Corps was recognized in 1921 and affiliated to the 5th Bn (TF).

Shoulder title: MAYFIELD│C.C│COLLEGE *(1095)*.

The Royal Hampshire Regiment

Regular Battalions

            1702 37th Regiment of Foot raised.

            1756 67th Regiment of Foot raised.

            1881 Linked as The Hampshire Regiment.

            1946 Redesignated The Royal Hampshire Regiment.

Shoulder titles: A semicircular title, HAMPSHIRE *(1096)*, was worn until 1902 when replaced by HANTS *(1097)*. This was worn until the mid-1920s when HAMPSHIRE *(1098, 1099)* was once again introduced. The first title to be worn after 1946 was ROYAL│HAMSPHIRE but these were soon withdrawn and another title R. HAMPSHIRE issued. Two versions exist, *1100* for other ranks and *1101* for officers.

Volunteer Battalions pre-1908
1st to 5th   see 4th to 8th Bns (TF).

Volunteer Battalions 1918
The Portsmouth Volunteer Training Corps formed part of the 1st
V.B. in 1918.
Shoulder title: V.T.C | PORTSMOUTH.

Territorial Battalions
4th   1860 1st Admin Bn of Hampshire R.Vs formed at Winchester, the
senior corps being the 1st which was raised in 1859.

1880 Bn consolidated as 1st Hampshire R.V.C.

1885 Redesignated 1st V.B. Hampshire Regiment.

1908 Became 4th Bn (TF).

Shoulder titles: IVB | HANTS in w.m.; T | 4 | HANTS *(1102)*; 4 | HANTS* *(1103)*.

5th   1860 4th Admin Bn of Hamsphire R.Vs formed, the senior corps
being the 2nd which was raised in 1859.

1880 Bn consolidated as 2nd Hampshire R.V.C.

1885 Redesignated 2nd V.B. Hampshire Regiment.

1908 Became 5th Bn (TF). HQ Southampton.

1921 Amalgamated with 7th Bn to form 5th/7th Bn.

1948 Transferred to Parachute Regiment.

Shoulder titles: 2 | VB | HANTS in w.m.; T | 5 | HANTS *(1104)*; 5 | HANTS* *(1105)*. A
three-piece title T over 5/7 over HANTS was issued to the 5th/7th Bn in 1930.

6th   1860 2nd Admin Bn of Hampshire R.Vs formed at Portsmouth.

1880 Bn consolidated as 3rd Hampshire R.V.C.

1885 Redesignated 3rd V.B. Hampshire Regiment.

1893 Redesignated 3rd (Duke of Connaught's Own) V.B.

1908 Became 6th (Duke of Connaught's Own) Bn (TF).

1938 Transferred to Royal Artillery.

Shoulder titles: 3 | VB | HANTS in w.m.; T | 6 | HANTS *(1106)*; 6 | HANTS* *(1107* and
1108), the latter made in India from cast brass in 1916.

7th   1860 19th Hampshire R.V.C. raised at Bournemouth.

1880 Renumbered 4th

1885 Redesignated 4th V.B. Hampshire Regiment.

1908 Became 7th Bn (TF).

1921 Amalgamated with 5th Bn

Shoulder titles: 4 | V | HANTS in w.m.; V | 4 | HANTS *(1109)*, which was worn on full-
dress tunics in blackened brass; T | 7 | HANTS *(1110)*.

8th   1860 1st Admin Bn of Isle of Wight R.Vs formed at Newport.

1880 Bn consolidated as the 1st Isle of Wight R.V.C.

1885 Redesignated 5th (Isle of Wight, Princess Beatrice's) V.B.
Hampshire Regiment.

1908 Became 8th (Isle of Wight Rifles, Princess Beatrice's) Bn
(TF).

---

*No satisfactory answer has been found regarding territorial shoulder titles that were made without
the 'T'. Those marked above have not had the 'T' removed or broken off. This type of title has been
noted in photos being worn on tunics both with a separate 'T' and without and on greatcoats without
the 'T'.

1937 Transferred to Royal Artillery.
Shoulder titles: 5│V│HANTS (*1111*) in blackened brass; T│8│HANTS (*1112*).
9th   1911 Formed as 9th (Cyclist) Bn (TF). HQ Southampton.
            1920 Disbanded.
Shoulder title: T│9│HANTS (*1113*).

Cadets
Cadets of the pre-1908 period wore the blackened brass title C│V│HANTS (*1114*).
1st Cadet Bn
            Recognized in 1912; redesignated 4th Bn, Hampshire Regiment
            Cadet Bn in 1918.
Shoulder title: 1│C│HANTS (*1115*).
2nd Cadet Bn
            Recognized in 1914; redesignated 6th Bn, Hamsphire Regiment
            Cadet Bn in 1918.
Shoulder title: C│2│HANTS (*1116*).
3rd (Isle of Wight) Cadet Bn
            Recognized in 1914; became the 8th Bn, Hampshire Regiment
            Cadet Bn in 1918.
Shoulder title: 3│C│HANTS.
4th Bn, Hampshire Regiment Cadet Bn
            Formed in 1918 by the amalgamation of the 1st Cadet Bn, the
            Peter Symonds School Cadet Corps and the Aldershot County
            School Cadet Corps.
Shoulder titles: C│4│HANTS (*1117*), changing to C│4│HAMPSHIRE (*1118*) after
1921.
5th Bn, Hampshire Regiment Cadet Bn
            Formed in 1918 by the amalgamation of the King Edward VI
            School, Southampton, Cadet Corps and the Taunton's School
            Cadet Corps. The Battalion was amalgamated in 1922 with the
            Cadet Bn of the 7th Bn, Hampshire Regiment to form the 5th/7th
            Bn, Hampshire Regiment Cadet Bn.
Shoulder title: C│5│HANTS.
6th Bn, Hampshire Regiment Cadet Bn
            Formed in 1918 from the 2nd Cadet Bn.
Shoulder title: C│6│HANTS (*1119*).
7th Bn, Hampshire Regiment Cadet Bn
            Formed in 1918. Amalgamated with the 5th Bn, Hampshire Regi-
            ment Cadet Bn in 1922.
Shoulder title: C│7│HANTS.
8th (Isle of Wight) Bn, Hampshire Regiment Cadet Bn
            Formed in 1918 from the 3rd Cadet Bn.
Shoulder title: C│8│HANTS.
            The Peter Symonds School Cadet Corps was recognized in 1913. It
            was amalgamated with the 1st Cadet Bn and the Aldershot School
            Cadet Corps in 1918 to form the 4th Bn, Hampshire Regiment
            Cadet Bn.
Shoulder title: P.S.S.C.C (*1120*).

The South Staffordshire Regiment

Regular Battalions

1702 38th Regiment of Foot raised.

1793 80th Regiment of Foot raised.

1881 Linked as The South Staffordshire Regiment.

1959 Amalgamated with The North Staffordshire Regiment to form The Staffordshire Regiment (The Prince of Wales's) (see chapter 6).

Shoulder titles: The semicircular title s. STAFFORD *(1121)* was worn until 1902 when replaced by SSTAFFORD *(1122)*. Officers of the Regiment wore *1123*. One of the companies of the 1st Battalion wore the title 4MI while serving with the 4th Mounted Infantry during the Boer War.

Volunteer Battalions pre-1908

1st & 2nd   see 5th Bn (TF).

3rd   see 6th Bn (TF).

Volunteer Battalions 1918

Shoulder title: V | SSTAFFORD; WVRC with a Staffordshire Knot above was worn by the Wolverhampton Companies.

Territorial Battalions

5th   1860 5th Admin Bn of Staffordshire R.Vs formed at Walsall, the senior corps being the 4th which was raised in 1859.

1880 Bn consolidated as 3rd Staffordshire R.V.C.

1883 Redesignated 2nd V.B. South Staffordshire Regiment.

1860 3rd Admin Bn of Staffordshire R.Vs formed at Handsworth, the senior corps being the 1st which was raised in 1859.

1880 Bn consolidated as 1st Staffordshire R.V.C.

1883 Redesignated 1st V.B. South Staffordshire Regiment.

1908 2nd V.B. plus one company of the 1st amalgamated as 5th Bn (TF).

Shoulder titles: 1 | V | SSTAFFORD and 2 | V | SSTAFFORD both in w.m.; T | 5 | SSTAFFORD *(1124)*.

6th   1860 4th Admin Bn of Staffordshire R.Vs formed at Wolverhampton, the senior corps being the 5th which was formed in 1859.

1880 Bn consolidated as 4th Staffordshire R.V.C.

1883 Redesignated 3rd V.B. South Staffordshire Regiment.

1908 Became 6th Bn (TF).

1947 Transferred to Royal Artillery.

Shoulder titles: 3 | V | SSTAFFORD in w.m.; T | 6 | SSTAFFORD *(1125)*.

Cadets

The Queen Mary's School Walsall Cadet Corps was affiliated to the 2nd V.B. It became part of the Junior Division O.T.C. in 1908.

Shoulder title: QMSCC *(1126)*.

The Dorset Regiment

Regular Battalions

1702 39th Regiment of Foot raised.

1755 54th Regiment of Foot raised.

1881 Linked as The Dorsetshire Regiment.

1958 Amalgamated with the Devonshire Regiment to form The Devon and Dorset Regiment (see chapter 6).

Shoulder titles: Three versions of the title DORSET have so far been noted: *1127, 1128* and *1129*, the last being an officers' pattern. Another title, castle/DORSET (*1130*), was worn but no information can be found as to when.

Volunteer Battalions

1st see 4th Bn (TF).

Territorial Battalions

4th   1860 1st Admin Bn of Dorsetshire R.Vs formed at Dorchester, the senior corps being the 1st which was formed in 1859.

1880 Bn consolidated as 1st Dorsetshire R.V.C.

1887 Redesignated 1st V.B. Dorsetshire Regiment.

1908 Became 4th Bn (TF).

Shoulder titles: 1 | v | DORSET in w.m.; T | 4 | DORSET (*1131*).

Cadets

c/DORSET (*1132*).

The South Lancashire Regiment (The Prince of Wales's Volunteers)

Regular Battalions

1717 40th Regiment of Foot raised.

1793 82nd Regiment of Foot raised.

1881 Linked as The Prince of Wales's Volunteers (South Lancashire Regiment).

1958 Amalgamated with The East Lancashire Regiment to form The Lancashire Regiment (Prince of Wales's Volunteers) (see chapter 6).

Shoulder titles: The title S. LANCS (*1133, 1134*), was worn until 1902 when S. LANCASHIRE was introduced. Again two versions were issued (*1135, 1136*). P.W.V (*1137, 1138, 1139, 1140*) were introduced in 1922 and worn until amalgamation in 1958. The officers of the Regiment wore the straight title S. LAN (*1141*) before 1902.

Volunteer Battalions

1st   see 4th Bn (TF).

2nd   see 5th Bn (TF).

Territorial Battalions

4th   1859 9th and 49th Lancashire R.V.C. raised.
             1865 Grouped as 9th Admin Bn of Lancashire R.Vs at Warrington.
             1880 Bn consolidated as 9th Lancashire R.V.C.
             1886 Redesignated 1st V.B. South Lancashire Regiment.
             1908 Became 4th Bn (TF).
Shoulder titles: 1│V│S LANCASHIRE in w.m. *(1142)*; T│4│S. LANCASHIRE *(1143)*, which also exists with no gap between the 'S' and 'L' as in the regular pattern *(1136)*.

5th   1860 47th Lancashire R.V.C. raised at St Helens.
             1880 Renumbered 21st.
             1886 Redesignated 2nd V.B. South Lancashire Regiment.
             1908 Became 5th Bn (TF).
             1940 Transferred to Royal Artillery.
Shoulder titles: 2│V│S LANCASHIRE in w.m.; T│5│S. LANCASHIRE *(1144)*. T│S. LANCASHIRE *(1145)* was worn by both bns on the greatcoats.

The Welch Regiment

Regular Battalions

             1719 41st Regiment of Foot raised.
             1756 69th Regiment of Foot raised.
             1881 Linked as The Welsh Regiment.
             1920 Redesignated The Welch Regiment.
             1969 Amalgamated with The South Wales Borderers to form The Royal Regiment of Wales (see chapter 6).
Shoulder titles: Four versions of the title WELSH have so far been noted. *1146* and *1147* are officers' patterns, *1148* and *1149* for other ranks. The spelling of Welsh changed to Welch in 1920, the shoulder titles changing shortly after. WELCH *(1150, 1151)* are the officers' versions; *1152* is for other ranks. An anodised version *(1153)* appeared in the 1960s.

Volunteer Battalions

3rd   see 5th Bn (TF).

Territorial Battalions

4th   1861 1st Admin Bn of Pembrokeshire R.Vs formed at Haverfordwest, the senior corps being the 1st which was raised in 1859.
             1880 Bn consolidated as 1st Pembrokeshire R.V.C.
             1887 Redesignated 1st (Pembrokeshire) V.B. Welsh Regiment.
             1908 Became 4th Bn (TF).
Shoulder titles: T│4│WELSH *(1154)*, changing to T│4│WELCH in 1921.

5th   1860 3rd Admin Bn of Glamorganshire R.Vs formed, the senior corps being the 2nd which was raised in 1859.
             1880 Bn consolidated as 2nd Glamorganshire R.V.C.
             1887 Redesignated 3rd (Glamorgan) V.B. Welsh Regiment. HQ Pontypridd.
             1908 Became 5th Bn (TF).
Shoulder titles: 3│V│WELSH in w.m. *(1155)*; T│5│WELSH *(1156)*, changing to T│5│WELCH in 1921.

6th   1859 3rd Glamorganshire R.V.C. raised in Swansea.
     1881 Became a volunteer bn of the Welsh Regiment.
     1908 Became 6th (Glamorgan) Bn (TF).
     1921 Amalgamated with the 7th (Cyclist) Bn.
     1940 Transferred to Royal Artillery.
Shoulder titles: T | 6 | WELSH *(1157)*, changing to T | 6 | WELCH in 1921.
7th   1908 Formed as 7th (Cyclist) Bn. HQ Cardiff.
     1921 Amalgamated with the 6th Bn (TF).
Shoulder title: T | 7 | WELSH *(1158)*.

The Black Watch (Royal Highland Regiment)

Regular Battalions
     1725 42nd Regiment of Foot raised.
     1780 73rd Regiment of Foot raised.
     1881 Linked as The Black Watch (Royal Highlanders).
Shoulder titles: The first title to be worn was RH *(1159)*. A larger version *(1160)* was worn on the greatcoat. These were replaced in 1921 by BLACK WATCH *(1161)* and, in 1927, by BW *(1162, 1163)*. A smaller version is now worn in gold anodised.

Volunteer Battalions
2nd   see 5th Bn (TF).
3rd   see 5th Bn (TF).
4th   see 6th Bn (TF).

Territorial Battalions
4th   1859 1st Forfarshire (City of Dundee) R.V.C. raised.
     1887 Redesignated 1st (Dundee) V.B. Black Watch.
     1908 Became 4th (City of Dundee) Bn (TF).
     1921 Amalgamated with 5th Bn to form 4th/5th (Dundee and Angus) Bn.
     1939 Redesignated 4th Bn.
Shoulder titles: T | 4 | RH *(1164)*; T | 4/5 | BW.
5th   1861 1st Admin Bn of Forfarshire R.Vs formed, the senior corps being the 3rd which was formed in 1859.

          2nd Admin Bn of Forfarshire R.Vs formed, the senior corps being the 2nd which was formed in 1859.

     1874 Bns amalgamated as 1st Admin Bn.
     1880 Bn consolidated as 2nd Forfarshire R.V.C.
     1887 Redesignated 2nd (Angus) V.B. Black Watch. HQ Arbroath.

     1860 10th Forfarshire R.V.C. raised in Dundee.
     1861 14th Forfarshire R.V.C. raised in Dundee.
     1868 Amalgamated as the 10th.
     1880 Renumbered 3rd.
     1887 Redesignated 3rd (Dundee Highland) V.B. Black Watch.
     1908 2nd and 3rd V.Bs amalgamated as 5th (Angus and Dundee)

Bn (TF). HQ Arbroath.

1921 Amalgamated with 4th Bn.

Shoulder titles: 2│v│RH (*1165*) and 3│v│RH, both in w.m.: T│5│RH (*1166*).

6th   1860 1st Admin Bn of Perthshire R.Vs formed at Perth, the senior corps being the 1st which was raised in 1859.

1880 Bn consolidated as 1st Perthshire R.V.C.

1887 Redesignated 4th (Perthshire) V.B. Black Watch.

1908 Became 6th (Perthshire) Bn (TF).

1921 Amalgamated with 7th Bn as 6th/7th Bn.

1939 Redesignated 6th Bn.

Shoulder titles: 4│v│RH (*1167*) in w.m.: T│6│RH (*1168*), which also exists with the smaller RH; T│6/7│BLACK WATCH (*1169*).

7th   1860 1st Admin Bn of Fifeshire R.Vs formed at St Andrews.

1880 Bn consolidated as 1st Fifeshire R.V.C.

1887 Redesignated 6th (Fifeshire) V.B. Black Watch.

1908 Became 7th (Fife) Bn (TF).

1921 Amalgamated with 6th Bn.

Shoulder title: T│7│RH (*1170*).

Cadets

The 1st County of Fife Cadet Corps was recognized in 1915 and disbanded in 1920. It was affiliated to the 7th Bn (TF).

Shoulder title: 1│c│COUNTY OF FIFE (*1171*).

The Oxfordshire and Buckinghamshire Light Infantry

Regular Battalions

1741 43rd Regiment of Foot raised.

1755 52nd Regiment of Foot raised.

1881 Linked as The Oxfordshire Light Infantry.

1908 Redesignated The Oxfordshire and Buckinghamshire Light Infantry.

1958 Redesignated 1st Green Jackets.

1966 Became 1st Bn, Royal Green Jackets (see chapter 6).

Shoulder titles: The full dress tunics of the 1887-1902 period had on the shoulder straps the embroidered title of a French Horn over OXFORD. An almost exact replica of this title in metal was the first to be worn on the khaki service dress (*1172, 1173*). By 1900 a smaller bugle│OXFORD (*1174, 1175*) had been introduced for other ranks, the officers having the same title but without the bugles. Two-piece titles, OXFORD worn with a separate bugle (*1176*), were introduced for other ranks by 1907 and were retained by the 2nd Bn until 1914, the 1st changing to OXF & BUCKS (*1177*) in 1908. One-piece titles were reintroduced during the 1st World War: bugle│OXF & BUCKS (*1178* and *1179*). These were worn in brass until 1954 when w.m. titles were ordered to be worn. Although w.m. titles were manufactured, the order stated that 'existing stocks of gilding metal titles will be dipped to approximate the new pattern'. This would account for the odd, chromed specimen that turns up. The old two-piece titles (*1177*) were retained for men joining the Regiment. A photo in the Regimental Museum shows them being worn by recruits passing through the depot at Cowley Barracks in 1939.

The last title to be worn was issued in 1958 on joining the Green Jackets Brigade: 43RD & 52ND (*1180*) in blackened brass.

Volunteer Battalions pre-1908

1st   1859 Raised as 1st Oxfordshire (Oxford University) R.V.C.

1887 Redesignated 1st (Oxford University) V.B. Oxfordshire L.I.

1908 Became Oxford University O.T.C.

Shoulder title: O.U.V.B which is straight and measures 15mm wide by 55mm long.

Volunteer Battalions 1918

The Oxfordshire Volunteer Regiment became the 1st and 2nd Volunteer Bns Oxfordshire L.I. in 1918.

Shoulder title: O.V.T.C (*1181*).

Territorial Battalions

4th   1860 2nd Admin Bn of Oxfordshire R.Vs formed at Oxford.

1861 Renumbered 1st.

1873 Bn consolidated as 2nd Oxfordshire R.V.C.

1887 Redesignated 2nd V.B. Oxfordshire L.I.

1908 Became 4th Bn (TF).

Shoulder titles: A distinctive shoulder title was worn by the 4th Bn: bugle/OXF & BUCKS with the addition of T4 within the strings of the bugle (*1182, 1183*). The more usual title, T | 4 | OXF & BUCKS (*1184*), was manufactured but probably never worn. Titles were reintroduced to the battalion in 1958 and the pattern chosen was *1178, 1179*, but with a black finish.

Bucks Bn   1860 1st Admin Bn of Buckinghamshire R.Vs formed at Great Marlow, the senior corps being the 1st which was raised in 1859.

1875 Bn consolidated as 1st Buckinghamshire R.V.C.

1881 Became a volunteer bn of The Oxfordshire L.I.

1908 Became the Buckinghamshire Bn, The Oxfordshire L.I.

1947 Transferred to Royal Artillery.

Shoulder titles: Two patterns have been worn, the first, according to photographs, was T | BUCKS (*1185*) which was listed in the 1920 *P.V.C.N*. The second, T | BUCKINGHAMSHIRE (*1186*), was also worn with the T separate.

The Essex Regiment

Regular Battalions

1741 44th Regiment of Foot raised.

1755 56th Regiment of Foot raised.

1881 Linked as The Essex Regiment.

1958 Amalgamated with The Bedfordshire and Hertfordshire Regiment to form the 3rd East Anglian Regiment (see chapter 6).

Shoulder titles: ESSEX (*1187, 1188*).

Volunteer Battalions pre-1908

4th   see 7th Bn (TF)

Volunteer Battalions 1918
Shoulder title: v | ESSEX.

Territorial Battalions
4th   1861 3rd Admin Bn of Essex R.Vs formed, the senior corps being the 1st which was raised in 1859.

        1880 Bn consolidated as 1st Essex R.V.C.

        1883 Redesignated 1st V.B. Essex Regiment. HQ Brentwood.

        1908 Became 4th Bn (TF).

Shoulder title: T | 4 | ESSEX (*1189*).

5th   1860 1st Admin Bn of Essex R.Vs formed, the senior corps being the 4th which was raised in 1859.

        1880 Bn consolidated as 2nd Essex R.V.C.

        1883 Redesignated 2nd V.B. Essex Regiment. HQ Colchester.

        1908 Became 5th Bn (TF).

        1947 Transferred to Royal Artillery.

Shoulder title: T | 5 | ESSEX (*1190*).

6th   1859 5th Essex R.V.C. raised.

        1880 Renumbered 3rd.

        1883 Redesignated 3rd V.B. Essex Regiment. HQ West Ham.

        1908 Became 6th Bn (TF).

        1940 Transferred to Royal Artillery.

Shoulder title: T | 6 | ESSEX (*1191*).

7th   1860 9th Essex R.V.C. raised.

        1880 Renumbered 4th.

        1883 Redesignated 4th V.B. Essex Regiment.

        1908 Became 7th Bn (TF). HQ Leyton.

        1935 Transferred to Royal Artillery.

Shoulder titles: 4 | v | ESSEX in w.m. (*1192*); T | 7 | ESSEX (*1193*).

8th   1908 Formed as Essex and Suffolk Cyclist Bn.

        1911 Redesignated 8th (Cyclist) Bn, Essex Regiment. HQ Colchester.

        1920 Transferred to Royal Engineers.

Shoulder title: T | 8 | ESSEX (*1194*).

16th   1915 Formed as the 66th Provisional Bn (TF).

        1917 (January) Transferred to The Essex Regiment as 16th Bn (TF).

        1917 (December) Disbanded.

Shoulder title: T | 16 | ESSEX (*1195*).

Cadets
      The Southend Technical School Cadet Corps was recognized in 1910 and affiliated to the 6th Bn (TF). It was redesignated The Southend High School Cadet Corps in 1913.

Shoulder title: S.T.S/CADET CORPS (*1196*).

Twelve Cadet battalions were raised by 1922. Shoulder titles so far noted are C | 1 | ESSEX; C | 2 | ESSEX; C | 3 | ESSEX; C | 4 | ESSEX; C | 10 | ESSEX.

The Sherwood Foresters (Nottinghamshire and Derbyshire Regiment)

Regular Battalions

1741 45th Regiment of Foot raised.

1823 95th Regiment of Foot raised.

1881 Linked as The Sherwood Foresters (Derbyshire Regiment).

1902 Redesignated The Sherwood Foresters (Nottinghamshire and Derbyshire Regiment).

1970 Amalgamated with The Worcestershire Regiment to form The Worcestershire and Sherwood Foresters Regiment (see chapter 6).

Shoulder titles: DERBY (*1197, 1198*), the latter worn by officers. The 2nd Bn, before 1902, had their own title 2│DERBY (*1199*). The first title to be used after 1902 was NOTTS│AND│DERBY (*1200*), with a smaller version for officers (*1201*). These were replaced in 1920 with FORESTERS (*1202*), the officers once again having a smaller version (*1203*). A straight version (*1204*) can be seen worn on the K.D. jacket in photos taken in the 1930s.

Militia Battalions

3rd   1885 2nd Derbyshire Militia or Chatsworth Rifles raised.

1881 Became 3rd Bn Sherwood Foresters.

1953 Disbanded.

Shoulder title: SHERWOOD│FORESTERS (*1205*) in w.m.

4th   1775 Nottinghamshire Militia raised.

1881 Became 4th Bn Sherwood Foresters.

1953 Disbanded.

Shoulder title: SHERWOOD│4│FORESTERS (*1206*).

Volunteer Battalions

1st   see 5th Bn (TF).

Territorial Battalions

5th   1860 1st Admin Bn of Derbyshire R.Vs formed at Derby, the senior corps being the 1st which was raised in 1859.

1880 Bn consolidated as 1st Derbyshire R.V.C.

1887 Redesignated 1st V.B. Sherwood Foresters.

1908 Became 5th Bn (TF).

Shoulder titles: 1│V│NOTTS│AND│DERBY in w.m.; T│5│NOTTS│AND│DERBY (*1207*).

6th   1861 3rd Admin Bn of Derbyshire R.Vs formed at Bakewell, the senior corps being the 3rd which was formed in 1860.

1880 Bn consolidated as 2nd Derbyshire R.V.C.

1887 Redesignated 2nd V.B. Sherwood Foresters.

1908 Became 6th Bn (TF). HQ Chesterfield.

1936 Transferred to Royal Engineers.

Shoulder title: T│6│NOTTS│AND│DERBY (*1208*).

7th   1859 1st Nottinghamshire (Robin Hood) R.V.C. raised in
                 Nottingham.
                 1881 Became a volunteer Bn of the Sherwood Foresters.
                 1908 Became 7th (Robin Hood) Bn (TF).
                 1936 Transferred to Royal Engineers.
Shoulder title: T | 7 | NOTTS & DERBY (*1209*).

8th   1862 1st Admin Bn of Nottinghamshire R.Vs formed at East Ret-
                 ford, the senior corps being the 2nd which was raised in 1860.
                 1880 Bn consolidated as 2nd Nottinghamshire R.V.C.
                 1887 Redesignated 4th (Nottinghamshire) V.B. Sherwood
                 Foresters.
                 1908 Became 8th Bn (TF). HQ Newark.
Shoulder title: T | 8 | NOTTS & DERBY (*1210*).

Cadets

                 The 1st Cadet Bn was recognized in 1914 and affiliated to the 7th
                 Bn (TF).
Shoulder title: 1 | CB | 7TH NOTTS & DERBY (*1211*).
Companies affiliated to the 6th Bn (TF) wore the title C | 6 | NOTTS & DERBY
(*1212*).
C | FORESTERS (*1213*) was worn by cadets affiliated to the Regiment after 1920.

The Loyal Regiment (North Lancashire)

Regular Battalions

                 1741 47th Regiment of Foot raised.
                 1793 81st Regiment of Foot raised.
                 1881 Linked as The Loyal North Lancashire Regiment.
                 1970 Amalgamated with The Lancashire Regiment to form The
                 Queen's Lancashire Regiment (see chapter 6).
Shoulder titles: The following patterns have been recorded: L. N. LANCS (*1214*);
N. LANCS (*1215*); NLANC (*1216*); N.LANC (*1217*), all of which have not been positively identified. NLANCASHIRE (*1218*) was being worn by 1907 and was replaced
in 1920 by LOYALS (*1219, 1220*). A straight version LOYALS. (*1221*), which is in
cast brass, was worn overseas.

Territorial Battalions

4th   1861 6th Admin Bn of Lancashire R.Vs formed at Preston, the
                 senior corps being the 11th which was raised in 1859.
                 1880 Bn consolidated as 11th Lancashire R.V.C.
                 1883 Redesignated 1st V.B. Loyal North Lancashire Regiment.
                 1908 Became 4th Bn (TF).
                 1940 Transferred to Royal Artillery.
Shoulder titles: T | 4 | NLANCASHIRE (*1222*); T | 4 | N. LANCASHIRE (*1223*), changing
to T | 4 | LOYALS after 1920.

5th   1860 27th Lancashire R.V.C. raised at Bolton.
                 1880 Renumbered 14th.
                 1883 Redesignated 2nd V.B. Loyal North Lancashire Regiment.

1908 Became 5th Bn (TF).

1941 Transferred to Reconnaissance Corps.

Shoulder titles: T|5|NLANCASHIRE (*1224*); T|5|N. LANCASHIRE, changing to T|5|LOYALS (*1225*) after 1920.

T|N. LANCASHIRE (*1226*) was worn by both battalions on the greatcoats.

Cadets

C|4|N. LANCASHIRE worn by cadet companies affiliated to the 4th Bn (TF).

The Northamptonshire Regiment

Regular Battalions

1741 48th Regiment of Foot raised.

1755 58th Regiment of Foot raised.

1881 Linked as The Northamptonshire Regiment.

1960 Amalgamated with The Royal Lincolnshire Regiment to form the 2nd East Anglian Regiment (see chapter 6).

Shoulder titles: NORTHAMPTON, of which no less than six versions have been noted: *1228*, which was worn before 1902; *1229*, which is unusual in that it has three lugs; *1230*; *1231*, which is an officers' pattern; *1232*, which is the other ranks' normal issue and *1233*, which is in cast brass. The title changed to NORTHAMPTONSHIRE in 1921, *1234* being for officers, *1235* for other ranks.

Militia Battalions

3rd and 4th 1759 Rutland Militia raised.

1860 Amalgamated with Northampton Militia (raised 1763) to form Northampton and Rutland Militia.

1874 Divided into two bns.

1881 Became 3rd and 4th Bns, The Northamptonshire Regiment.

1899 Amalgamated as 4th Bn.

1953 Disbanded.

Shoulder titles: NORTHAMPTONSHIRE (*1236, 1237*) the latter is in cast brass. One of the badges of the Northampton and Rutland Militia was a horseshoe, the titles quite clearly resembling one.

Territorial Battalions

4th 1860 1st Admin Bn of Northamptonshire R.Vs formed in Northampton, the senior corps being the 1st which was raised in 1859.

1880 Bn consolidated as 1st Northamptonshire R.V.C.

1887 Redesignated 1st V.B. Northamptonshire Regiment.

1908 Became 4th Bn (TF).

1937 Transferred to Royal Engineers.

Shoulder title: T|4|NORTHAMPTON (*1238*).

Cadets

The Kettering Grammar School Cadet Corps was recognized in 1916 and affiliated to the 4th Bn (TF).

Shoulder title: KETTERING | C | GRAMMAR SCHOOL (*1239*).
 The Magdalen College School Cadets were also affiliated to the 4th
 Bn, being recognized in 1915.
Shoulder title: M.C.S | C | BRACKLEY (*1240*).

The Royal Berkshire Regiment (Princess Charlotte of Wales's)

Regular Battalions
 1744   49th Regiment of Foot raised.
 1755   66th Regiment of Foot raised.
 1881   Linked as Princess Charlotte of Wales's Berkshire Regiment.
 1885   Royal title granted.
 1959   Amalgamated with The Wiltshire Regiment to form The
 Duke of Edinburgh's Royal Regiment (see chapter 6).
Shoulder titles: The first title to be worn by the Regiment was R. BERKS (*1241*)
which was replaced by ROYAL BERKS (*1242, 1243*) c1907. Army Order 509 of
1920 directs that ROYAL BERKS will be replaced by R. BERKSHIRE (*1244*) which
was worn until the mid-1930s when ROYAL BERKS was once again issued.

Volunteer Battalions
1st   see 4th Bn (TF).

Territorial Battalions
4th   1860 1st Admin Bn of Berkshire R.Vs raised at Reading, the senior
 corps being the 1st which was raised in 1859.
 1874   Bn consolidated as the 1st Berkshire R.V.C.
 1882   Redesignated 1st V.B. Berkshire Regiment.
 1908   Became 4th Bn (TF).
Shoulder titles: 1 | V | ROYAL BERKS in w.m.; T | 4 | ROYAL BERKS (*1245*).

Cadets
 The senior company of the cadets affiliated to the 4th Bn (TF) was
 formed in 1914 at Maidenhead. The 2nd and 3rd Companies were
 raised in Windsor.
Shoulder title: C | 4 | ROYAL BERKS.

The Queen's Own Royal West Kent Regiment

Regular Battalions
 1755   50th Regiment of Foot raised.
 1824   97th Regiment of Foot raised.
 1881   Linked as The Queen's Own (Royal West Kent) Regiment.
 1961   Amalgamated with The Buffs (Royal East Kent Regiment) to
 form The Queen's Own Buffs, Royal Kent Regiment (see
 chapter 6).
Shoulder titles: Three sizes of the title R. W. KENT have been noted: *1246, 1247*
and *1248*, the last being an officers' pattern, while the larger can be seen being
worn in photos taken in the 1920s. A cast brass title, R.W.K (*1249*), was worn by
officers in India before the 1st World War. Another title, W. KENT (*1250*), also

exists but no information can be found as to when it was worn. It is possible that it was a variant of the West Kent Yeomanry.

Volunteer Battalions pre-1908

1st   see 4th Bn (TF).

2nd   1860 1st Admin Bn of Kent R.Vs formed at Blackheath, the senior corps being the 3rd which was raised in 1859.
1880 Bn consolidated as the 3rd Kent R.V.C.
1883 Redesignated 2nd V.B. Royal West Kent Regiment.
1908 Amalgamated with 3rd V.B. to form the 20th (County of London) Bn, The London Regiment.
Shoulder title: 2│V│R.W.KENT in w.m.

Volunteer Battalions 1918

The West Kent Volunteer Fencibles formed the 1st to 4th Volunteer Bns of the Royal West Kent Regiment in 1918.
Shoulder title: WKVF *(1251)* worn with the battalion number separate above.

Territorial Battalions

4th & 5th 1860 2nd Admin Bn of Kent R.Vs formed at Tonbridge, the senior corps being the 11th which was raised in 1859.
1887 Bn consolidated as 1st Kent R.V.C.
1883 Redesignated 1st V.B. Queen's Own Royal West Kent Regiment.
1908 Became 4th and 5th Bns (TF). The 4th Bn was at Tonbridge while the 5th was at Bromley.
1947 Amalgamated as the 4th/5th Bn.
Shoulder titles: 1│V│R.W.KENT in w.m.; T│4│R.W.KENT *(1252)*; T│5│R.W.KENT *(1253)*.

Service Battalions

10th   1915 Raised with the sub-title (Kent County).
1919 Disbanded.
Shoulder title: R.W.KENT│KENT.COUNTY *(1254)*.

Cadets

The Dartford Grammar School, which already had an O.T.C. unit, formed a cadet company. The company, which was formed in 1931, was affiliated to the 5th Bn (TF).
Shoulder title: DARTFORD│CADETS *(1255)*.

The 1st Cadet Bn was recognized in 1913.
Shoulder title: 1│C│R.W.KENT *(1256)*.

The King's Own Yorkshire Light Infantry

Regular Battalions

1755 51st Regiment of Foot raised.

1839 105th Regiment of Foot raised.

1881 Linked as The King's Own Light Infantry (South Yorkshire Regiment).

1887 Redesignated The King's Own (Yorkshire Light Infantry).

1968 Became 2nd Bn, The Light Infantry.

Shoulder titles: The first title to be worn by the regiment was K.O.L.I., which was curved and measured 53mm by 15mm. This was replaced after 1887 by YORKSHIRE (*1257*) which was worn with a separate bugle above. A further change took place in 1921 when the title K.O.Y.L.I was introduced and worn with the bi-metal collar badge above (*1258*). The title was worn in w.m. after 1954. Another title, which was the letters KOYLI mounted on a bar, was made and worn in India by the 2nd Bn c1930 (*1259*).

Volunteer Battalions pre-1908

1st   see 4th and 5th Bns (TF)

Volunteer Battalions 1918

The 1st, 2nd and 3rd Volunteer Bns of the 1918 period were formed from battalions of the West Riding Volunteer Regiment as follows: 7th Bn became 2nd V.B., 10th Bn became 1st V.B. and 19th Bn became 3rd V.B.

Shoulder titles: 7│WRV and 19│WRV. No title has so far been noted for the 10th Bn.

Territorial Battalions

4th & 5th   1860 3rd Admin Bn of Yorkshire West Riding R.V.s formed at Wakefield.

1880 Bn consolidated as 5th Yorkshire West Riding R.V.C.

1883 Redesignated 1st V.B. King's Own Light Infantry.

1908 Became 4th and 5th Bns (TF), the 4th at Wakefield and the 5th at Doncaster.

1940 5th Bn transferred to Royal Artillery.

Shoulder titles: The 1st V.B. wore a three-piece title, 1/V over a French Horn over YORKSHIRE, all in w.m., the bugle being the cap/collar badge (*1258*). Titles for the 4th and 5th Bns were issued in two or three pieces: T│4 over bugle over YORKSHIRE (*1260*); T│4│bugle over YORKSHIRE (*1261*); T│5 over bugle over YORKSHIRE (*1262*). The 5th Bn also wore the title T│5│K.O.Y.L.I after 1921.

The King's Shropshire Light Infantry

Regular Battalions

1755 53rd Regiment of Foot raised.
1794 85th Regiment of Foot raised.
1881 Linked as The King's Light Infantry (Shropshire Regiment).
1968 Became 3rd Bn, The Light Infantry (see chapter 6).

Shoulder titles: The first title to be worn was SLI (*1263*) which was replaced, before 1902, by a smaller version (*1264*). The title introduced in 1902 was SHROPSHIRE (*1265*) which was worn with a bugle above by 1907. Officers wore the same title but in bronze and without the bugle. The title KSLI (*1266*) was taken into use by the 1st Bn while serving in India between the 1st and 2nd World Wars, the officers having a smaller version (*1267*). In 1920 the officers' title changed to the letters K.S.L.I. mounted on a curved w.m. plate. A larger version of KSLI which measured $1\frac{1}{4}$in by $\frac{1}{4}$in, was worn on the greatcoats. The SHROPSHIRE title was discontinued in 1921 and replaced by K.S.L.I (*1268*) which was worn in brass by other ranks while the officers had the title in bronze. Another version was in gilt (*1269*), worn on K.D. by officers. The bugle was once again worn above by other ranks. A cast w.m. version was issued to the 2nd Bn while serving in Egypt in 1946 (*1270*). White metal titles replaced brass in the early 1950s, the separate bugle once again being worn by other ranks. Silver titles were worn by officers. A small w.m. pattern (*1271*) was worn without the bugle by other ranks on K.D.

Volunteer Battalions 1918

SHROPSHIRE V.T.C on a solid tablet was worn by the Shropshire Volunteer Regiment until 1918 when they became 1st and 2nd Volunteer Bns of the King's Shropshire L.I. with the title V | SHROPSHIRE.

Territorial Battalions

4th
1860 1st Admin Bn of Shropshire R.Vs formed at Shrewsbury, the senior corps being raised in 1859.
1880 Bn consolidated as 1st Shropshire R.V.C.
1887 Redesignated 1st V.B. King's Shropshire L.I.

1860 2nd Admin Bn of Shropshire R.Vs formed at Shrewsbury, the senior corps being the 2nd which was raised in 1859.
1880 Bn consolidated as 2nd Shropshire R.V.C.
1887 Redesignated 2nd V.B. King's Shropshire L.I.

1908 1st and 2nd V.Bs amalgamated as 4th Bn (TF).

Shoulder titles: The battalion's titles have been issued as follows: T | 4 over bugle over SHROPSHIRE (*1272*); T | 4 | bugle | SHROPSHIRE (*1273*) and T | 4 | bugle over SHROPSHIRE (*1274*), the last, which is cast brass, was made and worn while the battalion was serving in India during the 1st World War.

Cadets

The 3rd Company of the 1st Cadet Bn was formed in 1915 and wore the title 3 | C | SHROPSHIRE, changing to 3 | C | KSLI after 1921.

The 6th Company was also formed in 1915 but was disbanded in 1922.
The title worn for the last year of its existence was 6 │ C │ KSLI (*1275*).

The Middlesex Regiment (Duke of Cambridge's Own)

Regular Battalions

1755 57th Regiment of Foot raised.
1787 77th Regiment of Foot raised
1881 Linked as The Duke of Cambridge's Own (Middlesex Regiment).
1966 Became 4th Bn, The Queen's Regiment (see chapter 6).

Shoulder titles: MIDDLESEX (*1276, 1277, 1278, 1279*), the semicircular versions being worn before 1902. Another title, MIDDLESEX.REGT (*1280*), was worn for a short time in K.D. during the 1950s. Straight titles with the name of the Regiment misspelt as MIDDLESSEX were made in Cawnpore, India, for the 3rd Bn just prior to the 1st World War.

Volunteer Battalions 1918

V │ MIDDLESEX (*1281*) was worn by the Volunteer Battalions of the 1st World War.

Territorial Battalions

7th   1860 2nd Admin Bn of Middlesex R.Vs formed, the senior corps being the 3rd which was raised in 1859.
1880 Bn consolidated as 3rd Middlesex R.V.C. with HQ in Hornsey.
1898 Redesignated 1st V.B. Middlesex Regiment.
1908 Became 7th Bn (TF).

Shoulder titles: T │ 7 │ MIDDLESEX (*1282*). The w.m. version was also worn in three separate pieces.

8th   1861 7th Admin Bn of Middlesex R.Vs formed, the senior corps being the 16th which was raised in 1860.
1880 Bn consolidated as 8th Middlesex R.V.C.
1887 Redesignated 2nd V.B. Middlesex Regiment.
1908 Became 8th Bn (TF). HQ Hounslow.
1947 Transferred to Parachute Regiment.

Shoulder titles: T │ 8 │ MIDDLESEX (*1283*). The w.m. version was also worn in three separate pieces.

9th   1859 9th Middlesex R.V.C. raised.
1880 Renumbered 5th.
1881 Became a volunteer bn of the Royal Fusiliers.
1883 Transferred to The King's Royal Rifle Corps.
1908 Became 9th Bn Middlesex Regiment (TF). HQ St John's Wood.
1940 Transferred to Royal Artillery.

Shoulder titles: T │ 9 │ MIDDLESEX (*1284*). The w.m. version was also worn in three pieces.

10th   1908 Formed at Ravenscourt Park.
                1920 Disbanded.
Shoulder titles: T | 10 | MIDDLESEX (*1285*). A cast brass version was made and
worn in India during the 1st World War. The w.m. pattern was also worn in
three pieces.

Service Battalions
20th   1915 Raised with the sub-title (Shoreditch).
                1919 Disbanded.
Shoulder title: 20 | MIDDLESEX.

Cadets
                The 1st, 2nd, 3rd and 4th Cadet Bns were all formed in 1916.
Their titles were C | 1 | MIDDLESEX (*1286*), C | 2 | MIDDLESEX (*1287*), C | 3 |
MIDDLESEX and C | 4 | MIDDLESEX. 1 | C | MIDDLESEX (*1288*) was worn by the
Tottenham Grammar School Company of the 1st Bn.

                Other cadet units were the Christ's College Cadet Company of
                Finchley which was formed in 1912, affiliated to the 7th Bn (TF)
                and absorbed into the 1st Cadet Bn in 1916. The John Lyon School
                Cadet Company of Harrow was formed in 1915, affiliated to the
                9th Bn (TF) and absorbed into the 3rd Cadet Bn in 1916.
Shoulder titles: CHRIST'S COLLEGE | FINCHLEY (*1289*) and LOWER SCHOOL |
HARROW | OF JOHN LYON (*1290*).

The King's Royal Rifle Corps

Regular Battalions
                1755 60th Regiment of Foot raised.
                1881 Became The King's Royal Rifle Corps.
                1958 Became 2nd Green Jackets.
                1966 Became 2nd Bn, The Royal Green Jackets (see chapter 6).
Shoulder titles: Until 1958 only one pattern of shoulder title had been worn by
the Regiment. There were, however, several variations: KRR (*1291, 1292, 1293,
1294, 1295, 1296*) KRRC (*1297*) was introduced when the Regiment joined the
Green Jackets Brigade in 1958. All titles were in blackened brass.

Volunteer Battalions
25th Middlesex R.V.C.
                see 15th Bn, The London Regiment.

Territorial Battalions
                Two of the Regiment's territorial bns were The Queen Victoria's
                Rifles (7th Bn) and The Queen's Westminsters (11th Bn). They
                were amalgamated in 1961 as The Queen's Royal Rifles.
Shoulder title: QRR (*1298*) in blackened brass.

Cadets

The 1st Cadet Bn of the Regiment was formed in 1894 and bears the distinction of being the only cadet unit to be awarded a battle honour, 'South Africa 1900–02'. The battalion formed a special contingent which served with the City Imperial Volunteers.

Shoulder title: 1 | C | KRR (*1299*).

Many of the cadet companies of the 1st World War period affiliated to the Regiment were formed from members of the Church Lads Brigade.

Two of the titles worn were CLB (*1300*) and 17 | LONDON | C.L.B. (*1301*).

The Wiltshire Regiment (The Duke of Edinburgh's)

Regular Battalions

1756　62nd Regiment of Foot raised.

1824　99th Regiment of Foot raised.

1881　Linked as The Duke of Edinburgh's (Wiltshire Regiment).

1959　Amalgamated with The Royal Berkshire Regiment to form The Duke of Edinburgh's Royal Regiment (see chapter 6).

Shoulder titles: A straight version of WILTS (*1302*) was the first title to be worn, the curved pattern (*1303*) being introduced by 1902.

Territorial Battalions

4th　　1860　1st Admin Bn of Wiltshire R.V.s formed at Salisbury, the senior corps being the 1st which was raised in 1859.

1880　Bn consolidated as 1st Wiltshire R.V.C.

1881　Became a volunteer bn of The Wiltshire Regiment.

1860　2nd Admin Bn of Wiltshire R.Vs formed at Chippenham, the senior corps being the 3rd which was raised in 1859.

1880　Bn consolidated as 2nd Wiltshire R.V.C.

1887　Redesignated 2nd V.B. Wiltshire Regiment.

1908　1st Wiltshire R.V.C. and 2nd V.B. amalgamated as 4th Bn (TF). HQ Trowbridge.

Shoulder title: T | 4 | WILTS (*1304*).

The Manchester Regiment

Regular Battalions

1757　63rd Regiment of Foot raised.

1824　96th Regiment of Foot raised.

1881　Linked as The Manchester Regiment.

1958　Amalgamated with The King's Regiment (Liverpool) to form The King's Regiment (see chapter 6).

Shoulder titles: The semicircular title MANCHESTER (*1305*) was the first shoulder title to be worn, changing to *1306* by 1902. Another semicircular shaped title, but this time with much narrower letters, was worn by officers after the 2nd World War. Another version of the MANCHESTER title (*1307*) was also worn.

Volunteer Battalions
4th   see 7th Bn (TF).
5th   see 8th Bn (TF).
6th   see 10th Bn (TF).

Territorial Battalions
5th   1860 4th Admin Bn of Lancashire R.Vs formed at Wigan.
           1880 Bn consolidated as 4th Lancashire R.V.C.
           1888 Redesignated 1st V.B. Manchester Regiment.
           1908 Became 5th Bn (TF).
           1941 Transferred to Royal Armoured Corps.
Shoulder title: T | 5 | MANCHESTER *(1308)*.

6th   1859 Raised as 6th Lancashire (1st Manchester) R.V.C.
           1888 Redesignated 2nd V.B. Manchester Regiment.
           1908 Became 6th Bn (TF).
           1921 Amalgamated with 7th Bn to form 6th/7th Bn.
           1936 Transferred to Royal Artillery.
Shoulder titles: T | 6 | MANCHESTER *(1309)*. After 1921 the three-piece title T over
6/7 over MANCHESTER *(1310)* was worn.

7th   1860 40th Lancashire (3rd Manchester) R.V.C. raised.
           1880 Renumbered 16th.
           1888 Redesignated 4th V.B. Manchester Regiment.
           1908 Became 7th Bn (TF).
           1921 Amalgamated with 6th Bn
Shoulder titles: 4 | V | MANCHESTER and T | 7 | MANCHESTER *(1311)*.

8th   1860 33rd Lancashire (2nd Manchester) R.V.C. raised.
           1880 Renumbered 20th.
           1888 Redesignated 5th (Ardwick) V.B. Manchester Regiment.
           1908 Became 8th (Ardwick) Bn (TF).
Shoulder titles: 5 | V | MANCHESTER and T | 8 | MANCHESTER *(1312)*.

9th   1860 23rd and 31st Lancashire R.V.C. raised.
           1863 Grouped as 7th Admin Bn of Lancashire R.Vs.
           1880 Bn consolidated as 7th Lancashire R.V.C.
           1882 The Oldham Companies of the battalion, who were the old
31st Corps, were withdrawn and designated 22nd Lancashire
R.V.C.
           1888 Redesignated 3rd V.B. Manchester Regiment at Ashton-
under-Lyne.
           1908 Became 9th Bn (TF).
Shoulder title: T | 9 | MANCHESTER *(1313)*.

10th   1882 Oldham Companies of the 7th Lancashire R.V.C. withdrawn
to form the 22nd Lancashire R.V.C. (see 9th Bn above).
           1888 Redesignated 6th V.B. Manchester Regiment.
           1908 Became 10th Bn (TF).
           1938 Transferred to Royal Tank Regiment.

Shoulder titles: 6│VB│MANCHESTER in w.m.; T│10│MANCHESTER *(1314).*
Titles were issued to all Territorial bns between 1908 and 1921, either with the lower tier voided or non-voided.

Service Battalions

16th to   The 16th to 23rd or 1st to 8th City Bns were all formed in 1914 and
23rd   disbanded by 1919.
Shoulder titles: CITY│1│MANCHESTER *(1315)* or with the relevant number: *(1316* to *1322).* All titles were made of brass with a bronze finish.
24th   The 24th (Oldham) Bn was formed in 1914 and disbanded in 1919.
Shoulder title: OLDHAM│24│MANCHESTER *(1323)* which was brass with a bronze finish.

Cadets

The 1st Cadet Bn was formed in 1884 in Manchester.
Shoulder title: 1│C│MANCHESTER *(1324).* Cadets affiliated to the Bn wore the title C│5│MANCHESTER *(1325).*

The Hulme Grammar School Cadet Corps was also affiliated to the Regiment (6th Bn). It was recognized in 1915.
Shoulder title: H.G.S│CADET CORPS *(1326).*

The North Staffordshire Regiment (The Prince of Wales's)

Regular Battalions

1756 64th Regiment of Foot raised.
1824 98th Regiment of Foot raised.
1881 Linked as The Prince of Wales's (North Staffordshire Regiment).
1959 Amalgamated with The South Staffordshire Regiment to form The Staffordshire Regiment (see chapter 6).

Shoulder titles: Semicircular titles were worn before 1902, N. STAFFORD *(1327, 1328),* the latter being an officers' pattern. After 1902 *1329* was issued to other ranks while officers had *1330.* Another title exists, N. STAFFS *(1331),* but no information can be found as to when it was worn.

Volunteer Battalions pre-1908

1st see 5th Bn (TF).
2nd see 6th Bn (TF).

Volunteer Battalions 1918

Shoulder title: V│NSTAFFORD.

Territorial Battalions

5th   1860 1st Admin Bn of Staffordshire R.Vs formed at Stoke-on-Trent, the senior corps being the 2nd which was raised in 1859.
1880 Bn consolidated as 2nd Staffordshire R.V.C.
1883 Redesignated 1st V.B. North Staffordshire Regiment.
1908 Became 5th Bn (TF). HQ Hanley.

1936 Transferred to Royal Engineers.
1961 Reconverted to infantry and amalgamated with 6th Bn as
5th/6th Bn.
Shoulder titles: 1 | v | NSTAFFORD in w.m.; T | 5 | N. STAFFORD (*1332*)). T | 5/6 | N.
STAFFORD was introduced after 1961.

6th　　　1860 2nd Admin Bn of Staffordshire R.Vs formed at Lichfield.
1880 Bn consolidated as 5th Staffordshire R.V.C.
1883 Redesignated 2nd V.B. North Staffordshire Regiment.
1908 Became 6th Bn (TF). HQ Burton-on-Trent.
1961 Amalgamated with 5th Bn.
Shoulder titles: 2 | v | NSTAFFORD (*1333*) in w.m.; T | 6 | N. STAFFORD (*1334*).

The York and Lancaster Regiment

Regular Battalions

1756 65th Regiment of Foot raised.
1793 84th Regiment of Foot raised.
1881 Linked as The York and Lancaster Regiment.
1968 Disbanded.
Shoulder titles: Y&L (*1335*). Another title exists, YORK & LANCS (*1336*), but no
information can be found as to when it was worn.

Volunteer Battalions pre-1908

1st see 4th Bn (TF).

Volunteer Battalions 1918

The 1st, 16th, 17th and 18th Bns of The West Riding Volunteer
Regiment formed the 1st to 4th Volunteer Bns of The York and
Lancaster Regiment in 1918.
Shoulder titles: 1 | WRV (*1337*); 16 | WRV (*1338*); 17 | WRV; 18 | WRV.

Territorial Battalions

4th　　　1859 2nd, 3rd and 4th Yorkshire West Riding R.V.C. formed.
1860 Amalgamated as 2nd Yorkshire West Riding (Hallamshire)
R.V.C. at Sheffield.
1883 Redesignated 1st (Hallamshire) V.B. York and Lancaster
Regiment.
1908 Became 4th (Hallamshire) Bn (TF).
1924 Redesignated The Hallamshire Bn.
Shoulder titles: 1 | v | Y&L in w.m. (*1339*); T | 4 | Y&L (*1340*). A w.m. Tudor Rose
was worn above the title Y&L (*1335*) after 1924.

5th　　　1860 4th Admin Bn of Yorkshire West Riding R.V.C. formed.
1880 Bn consolidated as 8th Yorkshire West Riding R.V.C.
1883 Redesignated 2nd V.B. York and Lancaster Regiment.
1908 Became 5th Bn (TF). HQ Rotherham.
1936 Transferred to Royal Artillery.
Shoulder title: T | 5 | Y&L (*1341*).

Service Battalions
The 12th (Sheffield) Bn was raised in 1914 and disbanded in 1918.
Shoulder title: Y&L│SHEFFIELD *(1342)*.

The Durham Light Infantry

Regular Battalions
1756 68th Regiment of Foot raised.
1826 106th Regiment of Foot raised.
1881 Linked as The Durham Light Infantry.
1968 Became 4th Bn, The Light Infantry (see chapter 6).

Shoulder titles: A one-piece bugle│DURHAM *(1343, 1344)* was worn on the K.D. jackets c1885. A variant exists where ribbons replace the strings of the bugles, and the titles, which were made in India, are in cast brass *(1345, 1346)*. After 1907 two-piece titles were worn: DURHAM with a separate bugle above *(1347)*. One-piece titles, but this time slightly larger, were reintroduced during the 1st World War, *(1348, 1349)*, only to be replaced in 1920 by D.L.I *(1350)* which was worn with the separate bugle above. In 1952 the Regiment once again adopted the one-piece bugle│DURHAM titles *(1348, 1349)*, but this time in w.m., changing to chrome in 1958 and silver anodised in 1966.

Militia Battalions
3rd & 4th   1745 The Militia of County Durham raised.
1853 Divided into three regiments, 1st or South Durham, 2nd or North Durham and an artillery unit.
1881 2nd Regt became 4th Bn, Durham Light Infantry.
1908 Redesignated 3rd Bn.
1953 Disbanded.

1881 3rd Regt became 3rd Bn, Durham Light Infantry
1908 Redesignated 4th Bn.
1953 Disbanded.

Shoulder titles: bugle│DURHAM with a 3 within the ribbons of the bugle *(1351)*. The bugle is gilt and the numeral silver — worn by officers. Other ranks of both bns wore a w.m. version of *1343* and *1344* on the K.D. jackets during the Boer War.

Volunteer Battalions pre-1908
1st to 5th   see 5th to 9th Bns (TF).

Volunteer Battalions 1918
The Durham Volunteer Regiment consisted of 11 battalions which formed the 1st to 11th Volunteer Bns of The Durham Light Infantry in 1918.
Shoulder titles: Titles so far noted are 3│V.T.C│DURHAM; 1│V│DURHAM; 3│V.B│DURHAM; V│DURHAM.

Territorial Battalions

5th   1862 4th Admin Bn of Durham R.Vs formed at Stockton-on-Tees, the senior corps being the 1st which was raised in 1859.
1880 Bn consolidated as 1st Durham R.V.C.
1887 Redesignated 1st V.B. Durham Light Infantry.
1908 Became 5th Bn (TF).
1940 Transferred to Royal Artillery.

Shoulder titles: 1│v│bugle over DURHAM in w.m.; T│5│bugle over DURHAM (*1352*); T│5│bugle over D.L.I introduced c1934.

6th   1860 2nd Admin Bn of Durham R.Vs formed at Bishop Auckland.
1880 Bn consolidated as 2nd Durham R.V.C.
1887 Redesignated 2nd V.B. Durham Light Infantry.
1908 Became 6th Bn (TF).

Shoulder titles: 2│v│bugle over DURHAM in blackened brass. T│6│bugle over DURHAM. T│6│bugle over D.L.I was introduced c1934.

7th   1860 3rd Durham R.V.C. raised at Sunderland.
1887 Redesignated 3rd (Sunderland) V.B. Durham Light Infantry.
1908 Became 7th Bn (TF).
1936 Transferred to Royal Engineers.

Shoulder titles: 3│v│bugle over DURHAM in w.m.; T│7│bugle over DURHAM. T│7│bugle over D.L.I was introduced c1934.

8th   1860 1st Admin Bn of Durham R.Vs formed at Chester-le-Street.
1880 Bn consolidated as 4th Durham R.V.C.
1887 Redesignated 4th V.B. Durham Light Infantry.
1908 Became 8th Bn (TF). HQ Gilesgate.

Shoulder titles: 4│v│bugle over DURHAM in blackened brass; T│8│bugle over DURHAM. T│8│bugle over D.L.I was introduced c1934.

9th   1861 3rd Admin Bn of Durham R.Vs formed at Gateshead, the senior corps being the 6th which was formed in 1860.
1880 Bn consolidated as 5th Durham R.V.C.
1887 Redesignated 5th V.B. Durham Light Infantry.
1908 Became 9th Bn (TF).
1947 Transferred to Parachute Regiment.

Shoulder titles: 5│v│bugle over DURHAM in w.m.; T│9│bugle over DURHAM. T│9│bugle over D.L.I was introduced c1934.

Cadets

C│DURHAM worn by cadet units until 1926 when replaced by C│bugle│D.L.I.

All titles that include a bugle were worn in pairs with the mouthpiece to the front.

The Highland Light Infantry (City of Glasgow Regiment)

Regular Battalions

    1777 71st Regiment of Foot raised.

    1787 74th Regiment of Foot raised.

    1881 Linked as The Highland Light Infantry.

    1959 Amalgamated with The Royal Scots Fusiliers to form The Royal Highland Fusiliers (see chapter 6).

Shoulder titles: HLI alone was worn on the khaki drill tunics from 1884, other ranks adding the bugle in 1908. Patterns so far noted are *1353, 1354* and *1355*, the last being an officers' title, H.L.I *(1356)*, which is made from cast brass, was also worn. A new title was issued c1930, bugle/HIGHLAND *(1357, 1358)*. These were worn for a few years, only being replaced in 1936 with the old HLI and bugle pattern *(1353)*. Titles changed to w.m. in 1954, the officers having silver. A one-piece pattern with a slightly different bugle was also worn *(1359)*, the title is in w.m. A curved version of HLI has also been noted.

Militia Battalions

3rd   1796 Raised as the Lanark Militia.

    1881 Became 3rd Bn, Highland Light Infantry.

    1953 Disbanded.

Shoulder title: 3 | HLI.

Territorial Battalions

5th   1859 19th Lanarkshire R.V.C. raised in Glasgow.

    1880 Renumbered 5th.

    1887 Redesignated 1st V.B. Highland Light Infantry.

    1908 Became 5th (City of Glasgow) Bn (TF).

    1947 Amalgamated with 6th, 10th and 11th Bns to form 5th/6th Bn.

Shoulder title: T | 5 | bugle | HLI *(1360)*.

6th   1860 6th Bn of Lanarkshire R.Vs formed in Glasgow, the senior corps being the 25th which was raised in 1859.

    1861 Bn consolidated as 25th Lanarkshire R.V.C.

    1880 Renumbered 6th.

    1887 Redesignated 2nd V.B. Highland Light Infantry.

    1908 Became 6th (City of Glasgow) Bn (TF).

    1947 Amalgamated with 5th Bn.

Shoulder title: T | 6 | bugle | HLI *(1361)*.

7th   1860 4th Bn of Lanarkshire R.Vs formed in Glasgow.

    1861 Redesignated 2nd Admin Bn.

    1865 Bn consolidated as 31st Lanarkshire R.V.C.

    1880 Renumbered 8th.

    1887 Redesignated 3rd (Blythswood) V.B. Highland Light Infantry.

    1908 Became 7th (Blythswood) Bn (TF).

    1938 Transferred to Royal Artillery.

Shoulder title: T | 7 | bugle | HLI *(1362)*.

8th   1860   8th Bn of Lanarkshire R.Vs formed.

           1861   Redesignated 3rd Admin Bn at Lanark.

           1880   Bn consolidated as 9th Lanarkshire R.V.C.

           1881   Became a volunteer bn of The Highland Light Infantry.

           1908   Became 8th (Lanark) Bn (TF).

           1914   Disbanded.

Shoulder title: T | 8 | bugle | HLI.

9th   1868   105th Lanarkshire (Glasgow Highland) R.V.C. raised.

           1880   Renumbered 10th.

           1887   Redesignated 5th (Glasgow Highland) V.B. Highland Light Infantry.

           1908   Became 9th (Glasgow Highland) Bn (TF).

           1939   Redesignated 1st Bn, The Glasgow Highlanders.

Shoulder title: T | 9 | bugle | HLI *(1363)*.

           All titles were worn in pairs with the mouthpiece to the front.

           Another title, TB | HLI, also exists but it is not known what battalion wore it.

Cadets

           The Fairfield Cadet Corps was recognized in 1918 and affiliated to the 6th Bn.

Shoulder title: FAIRFIELD | HLI | CADET CORPS.

           The Allan Glen's School Glasgow Cadet Corps was also recognized in 1918, being affiliated to the 5th Bn.

Shoulder title: ALLAN GLEN'S | C.C | SCHOOL *(1364)*.

Seaforth Highlanders (Ross-shire Buffs, The Duke of Albany's)

Regular Battalions

           1778   72nd Regiment of Foot raised.

           1793   78th Regiment of Foot raised.

           1881   Linked as Seaforth Highlanders.

           1961   Amalgamated with The Cameron Highlanders to form The Queen's Own Highlanders (see chapter 6).

Shoulder titles: SEAFORTH *(1365, 1366)*, the latter being an officers' pattern. Another title *(1367)*, which is solid, also exists but no information can be found as to when it was worn.

Territorial Battalions

4th   1861   1st Admin Bn of Ross-shire R.Vs formed at Dingwall, the senior corps being the 1st which was formed in 1860.

           1880   Bn consolidated as 1st Ross-shire R.V.C.

           1887   Redesignated 1st (Ross Highland) V.B. Seaforth Highlanders.

           1908   Became 4th (Ross Highland) Bn (TF).

           1921   Amalgamated with 5th Bn to form 4th/5th Bn.

Shoulder title: T | 4 | SEAFORTH *(1368)*.

5th   1864 1st Admin Bn of Sutherland R.Vs formed at Golspie, the senior corps being the 1st which was raised in 1859.
1880 Bn consolidated as 1st Sutherland R.V.C.
1881 Became a volunteer bn of the Seaforth Highlanders.
1908 Became 5th (The Sutherland and Caithness Highland) Bn (TF).
1921 Amalgamated with 4th Bn.
Shoulder title: T | 5 | SEAFORTH (*1369*).

6th   1860 1st Admin Bn of Elgin R.Vs formed.
1880 Bn consolidated as 1st Elgin R.V.C.
1887 Redesignated 3rd (Morayshire) V.B. Seaforth Highlanders.
1908 Became 6th (Morayshire) Bn (TF).
Shoulder titles: T | 6 | SEAFORTH (*1370*).

The Gordon Highlanders

Regular Battalions
1787 75th Regiment of Foot raised.
1794 92nd Regiment of Foot raised.
1881 Linked as The Gordon Highlanders.
Shoulder titles: Two semicircular versions of the title GORDON were worn before 1902 (*1371, 1372*), the latter being the officers' pattern. These were replaced by *1373* for other ranks and *1374* or *1375* for officers. A change took place in 1922 when the title became GORDONS (*1376*). Both other ranks' (*1377*) and officers' (*1378*) versions were made and worn overseas. An anodised version of *1376* was issued in the 1960s.

Volunteer Battalions pre-1908
5th   see 7th Bn (TF).

Volunteer Battalions 1918
Volunteer battalions of the 1st World War period wore the two-piece title V over GORDON (*1379*).

Territorial Battalions
4th   1859 6th to 9th and 11th to 13th Aberdeenshire R.V.C. raised.
1860 Amalgamated as 1st. HQ Aberdeen.
1884 Redesignated 1st V.B. The Gordon Highlanders.
1908 Became 4th (Aberdeen) Bn (TF).
1941 Transferred to Royal Artillery.
Shoulder title: T | 4 | GORDON (*1380*).

5th   1860 2nd Admin Bn of Aberdeenshire R.Vs formed.
1880 Bn consolidated as 2nd Aberdeenshire R.V.C.
1884 Redesignated 2nd V.B. The Gordon Highlanders.

1862 3rd Admin Bn of Aberdeenshire R.Vs formed, the senior corps being the 5th which was raised in 1860.

1880 Bn consolidated as 3rd Aberdeenshire R.V.C.
1884 Redesignated 3rd (The Buchan) V.B. The Gordon Highlanders.
1908 2nd and 3rd V.Bs amalgamated as 5th (Buchan and Formartin) Bn (TF). HQ Peterhead.
1921 Amalgamated with 7th Bn to form 5th/7th Bn.
1942 Transferred to Royal Armoured Corps.
Shoulder title: T | 5 | GORDON (*1381*).

6th 1860 1st Admin Bn of Aberdeenshire R.Vs formed.
1880 Bn consolidated as 4th Aberdeenshire R.V.C. HQ Aberdeen.
1884 Redesignated 4th V.B. The Gordon Highlanders.

1860 1st Admin Bn of Banffshire R.Vs formed.
1880 Bn consolidated as 1st Banffshire R.V.C.
1884 Redesignated 6th V.B. The Gordon Highlanders. HQ Keith.

1908 4th and 6th V.Bs amalgamated as 6th (Banff and Donside) Bn (TF). HQ at Keith.
Shoulder title: T | 6 | GORDON (*1382*).

7th 1860 1st Admin Bn of Kincardineshire R.Vs formed.
1880 Bn consolidated as 1st Kincardineshire R.V.C.
1884 Redesignated 5th (Deeside Highland) V.B. The Gordon Highlanders. HQ at Banchory.
1908 Became 7th (Deeside Highland) Bn (TF).
1921 Amalgamated with 5th Bn.
Shoulder titles: 5 | V | GORDON (*1383*) in blackened brass; T | 7 | GORDON (*1384*).

The Shetland Companies
1900 Formed as the 7th V.B. The Gordon Highlanders at Lerwick.
1908 Became the Shetland Companies.
1920 Disbanded.
Shoulder title: T | S | GORDON (*1385*).

London Scottish
The 14th Bn, The London Regiment (London Scottish) was transferred to the Gordon Highlanders in 1937.
Shoulder title: From correspondence in Regimental Magazines published in 1941 and 1942 it would appear that the oval title LONDON SCOTTISH with the word GORDON in the centre was manufactured. What is not clear, however, is whether the titles were ever issued or if they were, in fact, cloth and not brass.

The Queen's Own Cameron Highlanders
Regular Battalions
1793 79th Regiment of Foot raised.
1881 Became The Queen's Own Cameron Highlanders.
1961 Amalgamated with the Seaforth Highlanders to form The Queen's Own Highlanders (see chapter 6).

Shoulder titles: The semicircular title CAMERON *(1386)* was the first pattern to be worn. This changed to *1387* in 1902 for other ranks and *1388* for officers. These continued to be used until 1922 when a new title CAMERONS *(1389)* was introduced.

Territorial Battalions

4th   1860 1st Admin Bn of Inverness-shire R.Vs formed at Inverness, the senior corps being the 1st which was raised in 1859.

1880 Bn consolidated as the 1st Inverness-shire R.V.C.

1887 Redesignated 1st (Inverness Highland) V.B. Cameron Highlanders.

1908 Became 4th Bn (TF).

Shoulder title: T | 4 | CAMERON *(1390)*.

Liverpool Scottish

The 10th Bn, The King's Liverpool Regiment (Liverpool Scottish) were transferred to the Regiment in 1937.

Shoulder title: LIVERPOOL | T | CAMERONS | SCOTTISH *(1391)*.

The Royal Ulster Rifles

Regular Battalions

1793 83rd Regiment of Foot raised.

1793 86th Regiment of Foot raised.

1881 Linked as The Royal Irish Rifles.

1920 Redesignated The Royal Ulster Rifles.

1968 Became 2nd Bn The Royal Irish Rangers (see chapter 6).

Shoulder titles: Three versions of the pre-1920 RIR title have been noted, two straight and one curved: *1392, 1393* and *1394*. After 1920 the title changed to RUR *(1395, 1396)*, the former being worn in both silver and chrome by pipers, the latter by officers.

Service Battalions

13th   1914 Raised as 13th (1st County Down) Bn.

1919 Disbanded.

Shoulder title: DOWN, which is curved.

14th   1914 Raised as 14th (Young Citizens) Bn.

1918 Disbanded.

Shoulder title: YCV; see also the Ulster Volunteer Force, chapter 14.

The Royal Irish Fusiliers (Princess Victoria's)

Regular Battalions

1793 87th Regiment of Foot raised.

1793 89th Regiment of Foot raised.

1881 Linked as Princess Victoria's (Royal Irish Fusiliers).

1968 Became 3rd Bn The Royal Irish Rangers (see chapter 6).

Shoulder titles: Shoulder titles, or 'Quails', as they are known in the Regiment, were worn as follows: IF *(1397)* until c1890; replaced by RIF *(1398)* which was worn with a separate grenade above and in w.m. by pipers. Just before the 1st World War the pattern changed to I grenade F (*1399*) which had an eagle on the ball of the grenade. The eagle commemorates the capture by the 87th of the Standard of the French 8th Regiment at the battle of Barrosa in 1811.

After the war the titles changed to bi-metal, the eagle being in w.m. These titles were worn in pairs and in silver and gilt by officers. A variation exists where the eagle appears as a much slimmer bird (*1400*). In 1938 the word ROYAL on a scroll was added to the title: (*1401, 1402*). Another title that was worn by the Regiment was IRISH.FUS (*1403*), but no information can be found as to when it was used.

The Connaught Rangers

Regular Battalions
> 1793 88th Regiment of Foot raised.
> 1823 94th Regiment of Foot raised.
> 1881 Linked as The Connaught Rangers.
> 1922 Disbanded.

Shoulder titles: The first title worn was CONNAUGHT (*1404*), changing by 1914 to CONN.RANGERS (*1405*). The letters CR (*1406*) were worn on greatcoats. Another title, which is unusual in that both tiers curve downwards, was CONNAUGHT│RANGERS.

The Argyll and Sutherland Highlanders (Princess Louise's)

Regular Battalions
> 1794 91st Regiment of Foot raised.
> 1800 93rd Regiment of Foot raised.
> 1881 Linked as The Princess Louise's (Argyll and Sutherland Highlanders).

Shoulders titles: Only one title has been worn by the Regiment: A&SH. There are, however, several size variations. The general other ranks issue was *1407*, which was worn on the jackets, and *1408*, which was worn on the greatcoats. Officers had a slightly smaller pattern (*1409*), which is also worn in w.m. by pipers. Other variants are *1410*, which is in cast brass, *1411* and *1412*, which is the gold anodised version now worn.

Territorial Battalions
5th   1860 1st Admin Bn of Renfrewshire R.Vs formed at Greenock, the senior corps being the 1st which was raised in 1859.
> 1880 Bn consolidated as 1st Renfrewshire R.V.C.
> 1887 Redesignated 1st (Renfrewshire) V.B. Argyll and Sutherland Highlanders.
> 1908 Became 5th (Renfrewshire) Bn (TF).
> 1921 Amalgamated with 6th Bn as 5th/6th Bn.
> 1939 Redesignated 6th Bn.
> 1941 Transferred to Royal Artillery.

Shoulder title: T│5│A&SH (*1413*).

6th   1860 2nd Admin Bn of Renfrewshire R.Vs formed at Paisley, the

senior corps being the 3rd which was raised in 1859.
1880 Bn consolidated as 2nd Renfreshire R.V.C.
1887 Redesignated 2nd (Renfreshire) V.B. Argyll and Sutherland Highlanders.

1860 3rd Admin Bn of Renfrewshire R.Vs formed at Barrhead, the senior corps being the 7th which was raised in 1859.
1880 Bn consolidated as 3rd Renfrewshire R.V.C.
1887 Redesignated 3rd (Renfrewshire) V.B. Argyll and Sutherland Highlanders.

1908 2nd and 3rd V.Bs amalgamated as 6th (Renfrewshire) Bn (TF). HQ Paisley.
1921 Amalgamated with 5th Bn.
Shoulder title: T | 6 | A&SH (*1414*).

7th   1860 1st Admin Bn of Stirlingshire R.Vs formed at Stirling, the senior corps being the 1st which was raised in 1859.
1880 Bn consolidated as 1st Stirlingshire R.V.C.
1887 Redesignated 4th (Stirlingshire) V.B. Argyll and Sutherland Highlanders.

1867 1st Admin Bn of Clackmannanshire R.Vs formed at Alloa, the senior corps being the 1st which was raised in 1860.
1873 1st Kinross R.V.C. added.
1880 Bn consolidated as 1st Clackmannanshire and Kinross R.V.C.
1887 Redesignated 7th (Clackmannanshire and Kinross) V.B. Argyll and Sutherland Highlanders.

1908 4th and 7th V.Bs amalgamated as 7th Bn (TF). HQ Stirling.
Shoulder title: T | 7 | A&SH (*1415*).

8th   1861 1st Admin Bn of Argyllshire R.Vs formed at Oban, the senior corps being the 2nd which was raised in 1860.
1880 Bn consolidated as 1st Argyllshire R.V.C.
1887 Redesignated 5th V.B. Argyll and Sutherland Highlanders.
1908 Became 8th Bn (TF). HQ Dunoon.
Shoulder title: T | 8 | A&SH (*1416*)

9th   1860 1st Admin Bn of Dumbartonshire R.Vs formed at Balloch.
1880 Bn consolidated as the 1st Dumbartonshire R.V.C.
1881 Became a volunteer bn of the Argyll and Sutherland Highlanders.
1908 Became 9th (Dumbartonshire) Bn (TF). HQ Helensburgh.
1938 Transferred to Royal Artillery.
Shoulder titles: T | 9 | A&SH | DUMBARTON, which was also worn with the lower part separate.

Cadets

Cadets affiliated to the 8th Bn (TF) wore the title 8 | A&SH | CC.

The Prince of Wales's Leinster Regiment (Royal Canadians)

Regular Battalions

1858 100th Regiment of Foot raised.

1853 109th Regiment of Foot raised.

1881 Linked as The Prince of Wales's Leinster Regiment (Royal Canadians).

1922 Disbanded.

Shoulder titles: Five patterns of the title LEINSTER have been noted: *1417*, which was worn before 1902, *1418* and *1419*. Officers' versions were *1420* and *1421*. By 1914 a second title, LEINSTER.R.C (*1422*), was being worn. This pattern also appeared with the letters non-voided.

The Royal Munster Fusiliers

Regular Battalions

1756 101st Regiment of Foot raised.

1839 104th Regiment of Foot raised.

1881 Linked as The Royal Munster Fusiliers.

1922 Disbanded.

Shoulder titles: MF with a separate grenade above (*1423*) was worn until 1903 when replaced by RMF, again with the loose grenade (*1424*). A larger version measuring $1\frac{1}{4}$in wide was worn on the greatcoats. Officers wore M grenade F (*1425*), the ball of the grenade bearing the figure of a tiger in silver; a smaller version was also worn. By the end of the 1st World War a one-piece title was worn by other ranks, the title being the same as that for officers but in all brass. An other ranks' half-size pattern also exists (*1426*). Both versions of the officers' title were worn in pairs with the tiger facing to the front. Other ranks' patterns, however, have only been noted with the tiger facing one way.

The Royal Dublin Fusiliers

Regular Battalions

1746 102nd Regiment of Foot raised.

1661 103rd Regiment of Foot raised.

1881 Linked as The Royal Dublin Fusiliers.

1922 Disbanded.

Shoulder titles: DF, which was worn with a separate grenade above (*1427*) was replaced in 1903 by RDF, which also had the separate grenade (*1428*). A larger version, which was $1\frac{1}{4}$in long, was worn on greatcoats. Three versions of the officers' one-piece title, D grenade F, have been noted, all bearing the figures of an elephant below a tiger on the ball of the grenade (*1429, 1430*). The third type is larger and has the grenade dropping below the lower bar of the title. On all three titles the animals are in either w.m. or silver and are worn facing to the front. Other ranks were also issued with one-piece titles, the first being worn in India c1897 (*1431*), and the second on K.D. jackets c1910 (*1432*).

The Rifle Brigade (Prince Consort's Own)

Regular Battalions

1800 Raised as The Rifle Corps.
1803 Numbered 95th Regiment of Foot.
1816 Redesignated The Rifle Brigade.
1958 Became 3rd Green Jackets.
1966 Became 3rd Bn, The Royal Green Jackets (see chapter 6).

Shoulder titles: Six versions of the title RB have been noted: *1433* and *1434*, which are officers' patterns, and *1435, 1436, 1437* and *1438* for other ranks. Photographs show the officers' pattern, (*1434*) and the other ranks', (*1435, 1436, 1437*), being worn overseas before the 1st World War.

Volunteer Battalions

19th Middlesex R.V.C.
see 9th Bn, The London Regiment.

24th Middlesex R.V.C.
see 8th Bn, The London Regiment.

Parachute Regiment

Formed 1942
Shoulder title: PARACHUTE | REGIMENT (*1439*), introduced in 1950.

6
Infantry Regiments formed since 1958

The Queen's Royal Surrey Regiment
Formed 14 October, 1959, from the amalgamation of The Queen's Royal West Surrey and East Surrey Regiments.
Shoulder title: QUEEN'S | SURREYS (*1440*).
> The Regiment was amalgamated in 1966 with The Queen's Own Buffs, The Royal Sussex and Middlesex Regiments to form The Queen's Regiment.

The Queen's Own Buffs
Formed 1 March, 1961, from the amalgamation of The Buffs (Royal East Kent) and Royal West Kent Regiments.
Shoulder title: QUEEN'S OWN | BUFFS (*1441*).
> Amalgamated in 1966 with The Queen's Royal Surrey, The Royal Sussex and The Middlesex Regiments to form The Queen's Regiment.

The Queen's Regiment
Formed 31 December, 1966, from the amalgamation of The Queen's Royal Surrey, The Queen's Own Buffs, The Royal Sussex and The Middlesex Regiments.
Shoulder title: QUEEN's in gold anodised (*1442*).

The King's Own Royal Border Regiment
Formed 1 October, 1959, from the amalgamation of The King's Own Lancaster and Border Regiments.
Shoulder title: KING'S OWN | BORDER (*1443*) issued in both brass and gold anodised.

The Royal Regiment of Fusiliers
Formed on 23 April, 1968, from the amalgamation of The Royal Northumberland Fusiliers, The Royal Warwickshire Fusiliers, The Royal Fusiliers and The Lancashire Fusiliers.
Shoulder title: RRF in gold anodised (*1444*).

The King's Regiment
Formed 1 September, 1958, from the amalgamation of The King's Liverpool and Manchester Regiments.
Shoulder title: KING'S in gold anodised (*1445*).

1st, 2nd and 3rd East Anglian Regiments

The three regiments were formed as follows:

1st formed in 1959 by the amalgamation of The Royal Norfolk and Suffolk Regiments.

2nd formed in 1960 from the amalgamation of The Royal Lincoln and Northamptonshire Regiments.

3rd formed 1958 from the amalgamation of The Bedfordshire and Hertfordshire and Essex Regiments.

Shoulder title: EAST ANGLIA (*1446*).

The three regiments were amalgamated in 1964 with The Royal Leicestershire Regiment to form The Royal Anglian Regiment.

The Royal Anglian Regiment

Formed 1 September, 1964, from the amalgamation of the 1st, 2nd and 3rd East Anglian Regiments and The Royal Leicestershire Regiment.

Shoulder title: ROYAL | ANGLIAN in gold anodised (*1447*).

The Devon and Dorset Regiment

Formed on 17 May, 1958, from the amalgamation of The Devonshire and Dorset Regiments.

Shoulder title: DEVON | & | DORSET (*1448*) issued in both brass and gold anodised.

The Somerset and Cornwall Light Infantry

Formed on 6 October, 1959, from the amalgamation of The Somerset Light Infantry and The Duke of Cornwall's Light Infantry.

Shoulder titles: bugle | SOMERSET & CORNWALL in w.m. and worn in pairs (*1449, 1450*). These were replaced c1966 by S.C.L.I (*1451*) which is in silver anodised.

The Regiment amalgamated with The King's Own Yorkshire Light Infantry, The King's Shropshire Light Infantry and The Durham Light Infantry in 1968 to form The Light Infantry.

The Light Infantry

Formed on 10 July, 1968, from the amalgamation of The Somerset and Cornwall Light Infantry, The King's Own Yorkshire Light Infantry, The King's Shropshire Light Infantry and the Durham Light Infantry.

Shoulder titles: bugle | LIGHT INFANTRY (*1452, 1453*). Other ranks wear the title in silver anodised while the officers have the same pattern but in bronze. Titles are worn in pairs with the mouthpieces facing front.

The Prince of Wales's Own Regiment of Yorkshire

Formed on 25 April, 1958, from the amalgamation of The West and East Yorkshire Regiments.

Shoulder titles: PRINCE OF | WALES'S OWN (*1454*), changing to PWO (*1455*) in gold anodised in the late 1960s.

The Royal Highland Fusiliers

Formed on 20 January, 1959, from the amalgamation of The Royal Scots Fusiliers and The Highland Light Infantry.

Shoulder title: RHF (*1456*).

The Royal Regiment of Wales

Formed on 11 June, 1969, from the amalgamation of The South Wales Borders and The Welch Regiment.

Shoulder title: RRW in gold anodised (*1457*).

The Royal Irish Rangers

Formed on 1 July, 1968, from the amalgamation of The Royal Inniskilling Fusiliers, The Royal Ulster Rifles and The Royal Irish Fusiliers.

Shoulder title: IRISH | RANGERS (*1458*) in gold anodised.

The Worcestershire and Sherwood Foresters

Formed on 28 February, 1970, from the amalgamation of The Worcestershire and Notts and Derby Regiments.

Shoulder title: WORCESTERS | & | FORESTERS (*1459*).

The Lancashire Regiment, Prince of Wales's Volunteers

Formed on 1 July, 1958, from the amalgamation of The East and South Lancashire Regiments.

Shoulder titles: LANCASHIRE | (PWV) (*1460*), which has been issued in both brass and gold anodised.

The Regiment amalgamated with The Loyal North Lancashire Regiment in 1970 to form The Queen's Lancashire Regiment.

The Staffordshire Regiment

Formed on 31 January, 1959, from the amalgamation of The North and South Staffordshire Regiments.

Shoulder titles: The first title to be issued to the Regiment was STAFFORD (*1461*) which was worn by all ranks. In the late 1960s other ranks were issued with a new title STAFFORDS (*1462*) in gold anodised. Officers retained the original issue.

The Queen's Lancashire Regiment

Formed on 25 March, 1970, from the amalgamation of The Lancashire Regiment (PWV) and The Loyal North Lancashire Regiment.

Shoulder title: LANCASHIRES (*1463*) in gold anodised.

The Duke of Edinburgh's Royal Regiment

Formed on 9 June, 1959, from the amalgamation of The Royal Berkshire and Wiltshire Regiments.

Shoulder titles: DUKE OF EDINBURGH'S | ROYAL REGT (*1464*) in gilding metal for officers and WO1s. A solid anodised version is worn by other ranks (*1465*). The raised letters are in gold while the background is in silver.

The Queen's Own Highlanders
Formed on 7 February, 1961, from the amalgamation of the Seaforth and Cameron Highlanders.

Shoulder title: QO | HIGHLANDERS (*1466*).

The Royal Green Jackets
Formed on 1 January, 1966, from the amalgamation of The Oxfordshire and Buckinghamshire Light Infantry, The King's Royal Rifle Corps and The Rifle Brigade.

Shoulder title: bugle | RGJ (*1467*).

Territorial Army and Volunteer Reserve

Lancastrian Volunteers

1967 Formed from territorials of The Lancashire Regiment (Prince of Wales's Volunteers), The King's Own Border Regiment, The Manchester Regiment, The King's Liverpool Regiment and The Loyal North Lancashire Regiment.

1971 Increased to 2 bns.

1975 Both bns were broken up and formed Volunteer Bns of The King's Regiment, The King's Own Royal Border Regiment and The Queen's Lancashire Regiment.

Shoulder title: ILV (*1468*). None recorded for the 2nd Bn.

Wessex Volunteers

1967 Formed from territorials of The Devonshire Regiment, The Gloucestershire Regiment, The Royal Hampshire Regiment, The Dorset Regiment and The Wiltshire Regiment.

A 2nd Bn was later formed, the 1st being designated 1st Wessex Regiment (Rifle Volunteers).

Shoulder title: WESSEX (*1469*) which is a solid tablet, the letters are brass while the background has been blackened.

7
Territorial Regiments

The Honourable Artillery Company
1537 Chartered by Henry VIII as the Fraternity or Guild of St George.
1670 First known as Artillery.
1860 Term 'Honourable' confirmed.
1871 Divided into two branches, Artillery and Infantry.
1899 Artillery divided into 'A' and 'B' Batteries.
1922 Artillery batteries brigaded with the City of London Yeomanry as 11th (H.A.C. and C.L.Y.) Brigade R.H.A.
1938 Formed 11th (H.A.C.) Regiment R.H.A.
1939 12th (H.A.C.) Regiment R.H.A. formed, including 'C' and 'D' Batteries.
R.H.A. Regiments increased to three batteries, 'E' Battery to 11th and 'F' to 12th.
1945 11th absorbed 12th.
1947 Redesignated 235 R.H.A. Regiment, H.A.C. (A,B and C Batteries).

Shoulder titles: A | H.A.C (*1470, 1471*); B | H.A.C (*1472*); E | HAC (*1473*); H.A.C (*1474*); HAC (*1475, 1476*). Officers' patterns are *1477* and *1478* which is silver. The smaller title (*1476*) was introduced to the Artillery Section in 1952. A gold anodised title (*1479*) was introduced in the 1960s.

Cadets
The 1st Cadet Bn was recognized in 1916.
Shoulder title: 1 | CB | HAC.
The Imperial Yeomanry Cadets (City of London Squadron) was recognized in 1911 and affiliated to the H.A.C. in 1921.
Shoulder title: 1 | Y | CADETS | CITY OF LONDON (*1480*).

The Monmouthshire Regiment

1st Bn
1860 1st Admin Bn of Monmouthshire R.Vs formed at Newport.
1880 Bn consolidated as 1st Monmouthshire R.V.C.
1885 Redesignated 2nd V.B. South Wales Borderers.
1908 Became 1st Bn, Monmouthshire Regiment.
1940 Transferred to Royal Artillery.

2nd Bn
1859 2nd Monmouthshire R.V.C. formed at Pontypool.
1885 Redesignated 3rd V.B. South Wales Borderers.
1908 Became 2nd Bn, Monmouthshire Regiment.

3rd Bn   1860 2nd Admin Bn Monmouthshire R.Vs formed at Abergavenny.
1880 Bn consolidated as 3rd Monmouthshire R.V.C.
1885 Redesignated 4th V.B. South Wales Borderers.
1908 Became 3rd Bn, Monmouthshire Regiment.
1947 Transferred to Royal Artillery.

Shoulder titles: T | 1 | MONMOUTHSHIRE *(1481)*; T | 2 | MONMOUTHSHIRE *(1482)*; T | 3 | MONMOUTHSHIRE *(1483)*. T | MONMOUTHSHIRE *(1484)* was introduced for all battalions after 1920. The 'T' was also worn separate.

Cambridgeshire Regiment

1860 1st Admin Bn of Cambridgeshire R.Vs formed at Cambridge.
1880 Bn consolidated as 1st Cambridgeshire R.V.C.
1887 Redesignated 3rd (Cambridgeshire) V.B. Suffolk Regiment.
1908 Became The Cambridgeshire Bn, The Suffolk Regiment.
1909 Redesignated 1st Bn, The Cambridgeshire Regiment.
1947 Transferred to Royal Artillery.

Shoulder titles: 3 | CAMBS | V | SUFFOLK in w.m. *(867)*; CAMBRIDGESHIRE *(1485)*. T | CAMBRIDGE *(1486)* was introduced after 1920.

The London Regiment

The London Regiment existed between 1908 and 1937 and consisted of 26 bns numbered 1 to 28. The numbers 26 and 27 were intended for the H.A.C. and the Inns of Court Regiment who were not satisfied with their high numbers and chose to ignore them. The 1st to 8th Bns were formed within the City while the 9th to 28th were spread around the County of London. A further six bns were raised during the 1st World War and numbered 29 to 34. They were all disbanded by 1919 and wore no shoulder titles.

The change in the lower tier of the London Regiment shoulder titles from CITY OF LONDON or COUNTY OF LONDON to, simply, LONDON took place during the 1st World War.

1st   1859 19th Middlesex R.V.C. raised.
1880 Renumbered 10th.
1883 Redesignated 1st V.B. Royal Fusiliers.
1908 Became 1st (City of London) Bn, The London Regiment (Royal Fusiliers).
1937 Became 8th Bn, Royal Fusiliers.

Shoulder titles: T | 1 | grenade | RF | CITY OF LONDON *(1487, 1488* and the two-piece *1489)*.

2nd   1860 46th Middlesex R.V.C. raised.
1880 Renumbered 23rd.
1883 Redesignated 2nd V.B. Royal Fusiliers.
1908 Became 2nd (City of London) Bn, The London Regiment (Royal Fusiliers).

1937 Became 9th Bn. Royal Fusiliers.

Shoulder titles: T | 2 | grenade | RF | CITY OF LONDON (*1490*). A two-piece version also exists.

3rd   1859 20th Middlesex R.V.C. raised.

           1880 Renumbered 11th.

           1881 Became a volunteer bn of The Middlesex Regiment.

           1890 Transferred to Royal Fusiliers as 3rd V.B.

           1908 Became 3rd (City of London) Bn. The London Regiment (Royal Fusiliers).

           1937 Became 10th Bn. Royal Fusiliers.

Shoulder titles: T | 3 | grenade | RF | CITY OF LONDON (*1491* and the two-piece *1492*).

4th   1860 2nd Tower Hamlets R.V.C. raised.

           1867 Amalgamated with 4th Tower Hamlets R.V.C. as 1st or Tower Hamlets Rifle Volunteer Brigade.

           1881 Became a volunteer bn of The Rifle Brigade.

           1904 Transferred to Royal Fusiliers as 4th V.B.

           1908 Became 4th (City of London) Bn. The London Regiment (Royal Fusiliers).

           1935 Transferred to Royal Artillery.

Shoulder titles: 4 | V | grenade | RF and 4 | VB | RF both in w.m.; the latter is illustrated in a Gaunt's catalogue of 1904; T | 4 | grenade | RF | CITY OF LONDON (*1493*). A one-piece version also exists.

5th   1859 1st London R.V.C. raised.

           1881 Became a volunteer bn of The King's Royal Rifle Corps.

           1908 Became 5th (City of London) Bn. The London Regiment (London Rifle Brigade).

           1937 Became The London Rifle Brigade. The Rifle Brigade.

Shoulder titles: T | 5 | CITY OF LONDON (*1494*); T | 5 | LONDON (*1495*). LRB (*1496*) was worn by officers.

Cadets

           The Cooper's Company School Cadet Corps was recognized in 1911 and affiliated to the 5th Bn. It was absorbed into the 2nd City of London Cadet Battalion in 1916.

Shoulder title: COOPER'S COMPANY | CADET CORPS | SCHOOL.

6th   1860 2nd London R.V.C. raised.

           1881 Became a volunteer bn of The King's Royal Rifle Corps.

           1908 Became 6th (City of London) Bn. The London Regiment (City of London Rifles).

           1935 Transferred to Royal Engineers.

Shoulder titles: T | 6 | CITY OF LONDON (*1497, 1498*). CLR (*1499*) was worn by officers.

7th   1861 3rd London R.V.C. raised.

           1881 Became a volunteer bn of The King's Royal Rifle Corps.

           1908 Became 7th (City of London) Bn. The London Regiment.

           1921 Amalgamated with 8th Bn to form 7th (City of London) Bn. The London Regiment (Post Office Rifles).

      1935   Transferred to Royal Engineers.
Shoulder titles: T | 7 | CITY OF LONDON (*1500, 1501*).
Cadets
      The 7th Bn, Cadet Corps was recognized in 1915 and became part
of the 1st Cadet Bn, Royal Fusiliers in 1922.
Shoulder title: CADETS | 7 | CITY OF LONDON

8th   1868   49th Middlesex R.V.C. raised.
      1880   Renumbered 24th.
      1881   Became a volunteer bn of The Rifle Brigade.
      1908   Became 8th (City of London) Bn, The London Regiment
(Post Office Rifles).
      1921   Amalgamated with 7th Bn.
Shoulder titles: Two patterns exist for the 24th Middlesex Rifles, a curved
24MXRV and 24 | MXVRC (*1502*). Rifle Volunteers were designated Rifle Volunteer
Corps until 1891 when they were styled Volunteer Rifle Corps. From this it
would seem that the curved title was worn prior to *1502*. T | 8 | CITY OF LONDON
(*1503, 1504*); T | 8 | LONDON.

9th   1803   Raised as the Duke of Cumberland's Sharpshooters.
      1835   Redesignated Royal Victoria Rifle Club.
      1853   Redesignated Victoria Rifles.
      1859   Became 1st Middlesex (Victoria) R.V.C.
      1881   Became a volunteer bn of The King's Royal Rifle Corps.

      1860   11th Middlesex (St George's) R.V.C. raised.
      1880   Renumbered 6th.
      1881   Became a volunteer bn of The King's Royal Rifle Corps.

      1892   1st and 6th amalgamated as the 1st Middlesex (Victoria and
St George's Rifles) R.V.C.

      1860   37th Middlesex (St Giles and St George's, Bloomsbury)
R.V.C.
      1880   Renumbered 19th.
      1881   Became a volunteer bn of The Rifle Brigade.

      1908   1st and 19th amalgamated as 9th (County of London) Bn,
The London Regiment (Queen Victoria's).
      1937   Became The Queen Victoria's Rifles, The King's Royal Rifle
Corps.
Shoulder titles: 19 | VR | MIDDLESEX (*1505*); T | 9 | COUNTY OF LONDON (*1506*);
T | 9 | LONDON (*1507*); 1 | 9 | LONDON (*1508*) which was worn between 1915 and
1918, when the bn was designated 1/1st; QVR (*1509, 1510*) and Q.V.R (*1511*)
which were all officers' patterns.

10th   1860   36th Middlesex R.V.C. raised.
      1880   Renumbered 18th.
      1881   Became a volunteer bn of The Rifle Brigade.
      1908   Became 10th (County of London) Bn, The London Regiment
(Paddington Rifles).
      1912   Disbanded.

1912 Reformed with subtitle (Hackney).

1937 Became 5th (Hackney) Bn, Royal Berkshire Regiment.

Shoulder titles: T│10│COUNTY OF LONDON *(1512)*; T│10│LONDON *(1513)*. 10LDN *(1514)* is hand-cut and so far remains unidentified.

11th   1860 39th Middlesex R.V.C. raised.

1880 Renumbered 21st.

1881 Became a volunteer bn of The King's Royal Rifle Corps.

1908 Became 11th (County of London) Bn, The London Regiment (Finsbury Rifles).

1935 Transferred to Royal Artillery.

Shoulder titles: T│11│COUNTY OF LONDON *(1515)*; T│11│LONDON *(1516)*.

12th   1860 40th Middlesex R.V.C. raised.

1880 Renumbered 22nd.

1881 Became a volunteer bn of The King's Royal Rifle Corps.

1908 Became 12th (County of London) Bn, The London Regiment (The Rangers).

1937 Became The Rangers, The King's Royal Rifle Corps.

Shoulder titles: T│12│COUNTY OF LONDON *(1517)*; T│12│LONDON *(1518)*.

Cadets

The Polytechnic School Cadet Corps was recognized in 1914.

Shoulder title: POLYTECHNIC│SCHOOL│CADET CORPS *(1519)*.

13th   1859 4th Middlesex R.V.C. raised.

1860 Grouped with 7th Middlesex R.V.C. as 1st Admin Bn of Middlesex R.Vs.

1861 Bn consolidated as 4th Middlesex R.V.C.

1881 Became a volunteer bn of The King's Royal Rifle Corps.

1908 Became 13th (County of London) Bn, The London Regiment (Kensington). Subtitle soon changed to (Princess Louise's Kensington).

1937 Became Princess Louise's Kensington Regiment, The Middlesex Regiment.

Shoulder titles: T│13│COUNTY OF LONDON *(1520)*; T│13│LONDON *(1521)*; KENSINGTON *(1522)* in w.m. worn by bandsmen. Another title, PRINCESS│KENSINGTON│LOUISE'S *(1523)*, also exists but so far remains unidentified.

Cadets

The Latymer Upper School Hammersmith Cadet Corps was recognized in 1916.

Shoulder title: LUSCC *(1524)*.

Other cadet companies affiliated to the battalion wore C│13│LONDON *(1525)*.

14th   1859 15th Middlesex R.V.C. raised.

1880 Renumbered 7th.

1881 Became a volunteer bn of The Rifle Brigade.

1908 Became 14th (County of London) Bn, The London Regiment (London Scottish).

1937 Became The London Scottish, The Gordon Highlanders.

Shoulder titles: L.S.R.V in w.m.; T | 14 | COUNTY OF LONDON (*1526*); T | 14 | LONDON (*1527*). LONDON | SCOTTISH (*1528*)) was introduced in 1915.

Cadets

The London Scottish Cadet Corps was recognized in 1917. Recognition was withdrawn by the War Office in 1922.

Shoulder title: LSCC (*1529*).

15th   1860 21st Middlesex R.V.C. raised.

1880 Renumbered 12th.

1881 Became a volunteer bn of The King's Royal Rifle Corps.

1875 50th Middlesex R.V.C. raised.

1880 Renumbered 25th.

1881 Became a volunteer bn of The King's Royal Rifle Corps.

1892 12th and 25th amalgamated as the 12th.

1908 Became 15th (County of London) Bn, The London Regiment (Civil Service Rifles).

1921 Amalgamated with 16th Bn.

Shoulder titles: 25 | VR | MIDDLESEX (*1530*); T | 15 | COUNTY OF LONDON (*1531*); T | 15 | LONDON (*1532*).

Cadets

The Civil Service Cadet Corps was affiliated to the old 12th Middlesex R.V.C. They were still affiliated in 1908 when the 12th became the 15th (County of London) Bn, The London Regiment. By 1913 the Corps had been redesignated 2nd (Civil Service) Cadet Bn, The London Regiment connections with the 15th were maintained until disbandment in 1920.

Shoulder titles: Two patterns have been recorded: 2C.S.C.B. (*1533*) which is in blackened brass and CIVIL SERVICE | 2C.B | LONDON REGT. (*1534*) which is in w.m.

16th   1860 22nd Middlesex R.V.C. raised.

1880 Renumbered 13th.

1881 Became a volunteer bn of The King's Royal Rifle Corps.

1908 Became 16th (County of London) Bn, The London Regiment (Queen's Westminster Rifles).

1921 Amalgamated with 15th Bn as 16th (County of London) Bn, The London Regiment (Queen's Westminster and Civil Service Rifles).

1937 Became The Queen's Westminsters, The King's Royal Rifle Corps.

Shoulder titles: T | 16 | COUNTY OF LONDON (*1535*); T | 16 | LONDON (*1536*).

17th   1860 1st Admin Bn of Tower Hamlets R.Vs formed.
                1880 Bn consolidated as 2nd Tower Hamlets R.V.C.
                1881 Became a volunteer bn of The Rifle Brigade.

                1860 26th Middlesex R.V.C. raised.
                1880 Renumbered 15th.
                1881 Became a volunteer bn of The Rifle Brigade.

                1908 2nd Tower Hamlets and 15th Middlesex amalgamated as
                17th (County of London) Bn, The London Regiment (Poplar and
                Stepney Rifles).
                1937 Became The Tower Hamlets Rifles, The Rifle Brigade.

Shoulder titles: T|17|COUNTY OF LONDON (*1537*); T|17|LONDON (*1538*). THR
(*1539*) was worn by officers in blackened brass.

18th   1860 28th Middlesex R.V.C. raised.
                1880 Renumbered 16th.
                1881 Became a volunteer bn of The Rifle Brigade.
                1908 Became 18th (County of London) Bn, The London Regiment
                (London Irish Rifles).
                1937 Became The London Irish Rifles, The Royal Ulster Rifles.

Shoulder titles: T|18|COUNTY OF LONDON (*1540*); T|18|LONDON (*1541*). The
unofficial title T|18|shamrock|LONDON was worn for a short time.

19th   1860 29th Middlesex R.V.C. raised.
                1880 Renumbered 17th.
                1881 Became a volunteer bn of The Middlesex Regiment.
                1908 Became 19th (County of London) Bn, The London Regiment
                (St Pancras).
                1935 Transferred to Royal Engineers.

Shoulder titles: T|19|COUNTY OF LONDON (*1542*); T|19|LONDON (*1543*).

Cadets
                The St Pancras Cadet Corps was recognized in 1917 and affiliated
                to the 8th Bn, County of London Volunteer Regiment. It was
                transferred to the 19th in 1918 and redesignated 19th Bn, London
                Regiment Cadet Corps in 1921.

Shoulder title: C|19|LONDON.

20th   1859 4th Kent R.V.C. raised.
                1860 26th Kent R.V.C. raised.
                1880 Amalgamated as 4th.
                1883 Redesignated 3rd V.B. Queen's Royal West Kent Regiment.

                1860 1st Admin Bn of Kent R.Vs formed, the senior corps being
                the 3rd which was raised in 1859.
                1880 Bn consolidated as 3rd Kent R.V.C.
                1883 Redesignated 2nd V.B. Queen's Royal West Kent Regiment.

                1908 2nd and 3rd V.Bs amalgamated as 20th (County of London)
                Bn, The London Regiment (Blackheath and Woolwich).

1935 Transferred to Royal Engineers.
Shoulder titles: 2│v│R.W.KENT in w.m.: T│20│COUNTY OF LONDON (1544);
T│20│LONDON (1545).

Cadets

The Lewisham Cadet Battalion was recognized in 1913 and
affiliated to the Royal Field Artillery. Transferred to the 20th in
1918.
Shoulder title: C│20│LONDON (1546).

21st   1859 1st Surrey R.V.C. raised.
           1881 Became a volunteer bn of The East Surrey Regiment.
           1908 Became 21st (County of London) Bn. The London Regiment
           (First Surrey Rifles).
           1935 Transferred to Royal Engineers.
Shoulder titles: T│21│COUNTY OF LONDON (1547); T│21│LONDON (1548).

Cadets
Cadet Companies affiliated to the 21st wore C│21│LONDON (1549). The Askes
Hatcham School Cadet Corps was recognized in 1914.
Shoulder title: ASKES HATCHAM│CC│SCHOOL.

22nd   1860 10th Surrey R.V.C. raised.
           1861 23rd Surrey R.V.C. raised.
           1868 Grouped as 4th Admin Bn of Surrey R.Vs.
           1880 Bn consolidated as 6th Surrey R.V.C.
           1883 Redesignated 3rd V.B. Queen's (Royal West Surrey Regi-
           ment).
           1908 Became 22nd (County of London) Bn. The London Regi-
           ment (Queen's).
           1937 Became 6th Bn. Queen's Royal Regiment (West Surrey).
Shoulder titles: T│22│COUNTY OF LONDON (1550); T│22│LONDON (1551).

23rd   1859 7th Surrey R.V.C. raised.
           1887 Redesignated 4th V.B. East Surrey Regiment.
           1908 Became 23rd (County of London) Bn. The London Regi-
           ment.
           1927 Subtitle (The East Surrey Regiment) added.
           1937 Became 7th Bn. The East Surrey Regiment.
Shoulder titles: 4│v│E. SURREY in w.m. (1042); T│23│COUNTY OF LONDON;
T│23│LONDON (1552 and 1553, which is hand-cut).

Cadets

The St Thomas's (Wandsworth) Cadet Corps was recognized in
1914. It became part of the 1st Cadet Battalion of the 4th City of
London Regiment in 1920.
Shoulder title: ST. THOMAS'S│CADETS│WANDSWORTH (1554).
The 23rd Cadet Battalion was recognized in 1921.
Shoulder title: C│T│23│LONDON (1555).

24th   1860 19th Surrey R.V.C. raised.

1880 Renumbered 8th.

1883 Redesignated 4th V.B. The Queen's (Royal West Surrey Regiment).

1908 Became 24th (County of London) Bn, The London Regiment (The Queen's).

1937 Became 7th Bn, The Queen's (Royal West Surrey Regiment).

Shoulder titles: T | 24 | COUNTY OF LONDON (*1556*); T | 24 | LONDON (*1557*).

Cadets

C | 24 | LONDON (*1558*) was worn by cadet companies affiliated to the bn.

25th   1888 26th Middlesex R.V.C. raised.

1908 Became 25th (County of London) (Cyclist) Bn, The London Regiment.

1920 Transferred to Royal Signals.

Shoulder titles: T | 25 | COUNTY OF LONDON (*1559*); T | 25 | LONDON (*1560*).

28th   1860 38th Middlesex R.V.C. raised.

1880 Renumbered 20th.

1881 Became a volunteer bn of The Rifle Brigade.

1908 Became 28th (County of London) Bn, The London Regiment (Artists Rifles).

1937 Became The Artists Rifles, The Rifle Brigade.

Shoulder titles: T | 28 | COUNTY OF LONDON (*1561*); T | 28 | LONDON (*1562*); A four-piece version of the latter has also been noted.

T | CITY OF LONDON (*1563, 1564*) and T | LONDON (*1565*) are listed in the 1920 *Priced Vocabulary of Clothing and Necessaries* for wear by City and County Bns respectively. These titles are often seen in photographs being worn on the jackets. They are more frequently seen, however, being worn on the greatcoat. Subsequent issues show the titles as once again including the bn number.

Inns of Court

1859 23rd Middlesex (Inns of Court) R.V.C. raised.

1880 Renumbered 14th.

1908 Transferred to the T.F. as 27th Bn, London Regiment but order ignored. Became The Inns of Court Officer Training Corps producing officers for the Special Reserve and the Territorial Force.

1932 Redesignated The Inns of Court Regiment.

1961 Amalgamated with The City of London Yeomanry as The Inns of Court and City Yeomanry.

1967 Became 'A' Coy, The London Yeomanry and Territorials.

Shoulder titles: T | OTC | INNS OF COURT (*1566, 1567*); INNS OF COURT (*1568*) was worn after 1932; IC&CY (*1569*).

Hertfordshire Regiment

1861 2nd Admin Bn of Hertfordshire R.Vs formed, the senior corps being the 1st which was raised in 1859.
1880 Bn consolidated as 1st Hertfordshire R.V.C.
1887 Redesignated 1st (Hertfordshire) V.B. Bedfordshire Regiment.

1860 1st Admin Bn of Hertfordshire R.Vs formed.
1880 Bn consolidated as 2nd Hertfordshire R.V.C.
1887 Redesignated 2nd (Hertfordshire) V.B. Bedfordshire Regiment.

1908 1st and 2nd V.Bs amalgamated as Hertfordshire Bn, The Bedfordshire Regiment. HQ Hertford.
1909 Redesignated 1st Bn, The Hertfordshire Regiment.
Shoulder titles: T | HERTS (*1570, 1571*). The ·T· was also worn separate.

Cadets

The 6th Hertfordshire Cadets (Watford Grammar School) were raised in 1915 and disbanded in 1924.
Shoulder title: HERTS | 6 | CADETS (*1572*).

Herefordshire Light Infantry

1860 1st Admin Bn of Herefordshire and Radnorshire R.Vs formed at Hereford.
1880 Bn consolidated as 1st Herefordshire R.V.C.
1881 Became a volunteer bn of The King's Shropshire Light Infantry.
1908 Redesignated Herefordshire Bn, The King's Shropshire Light Infantry.
1909 Redesignated 1st Bn, The Herefordshire Regiment.
1947 Redesignated The Herefordshire Light Infantry.
Shoulder titles: The Regiment has had four shoulder titles: T | HEREFORD which was worn in two pieces (*1573*); 1 | HEREFORD (*1574*) which was also worn in two pieces; HEREFORDS (*1575*) and T | HEREFORDSHIRE (*1576*) which was also worn with the ·T· separate. The titles were worn as follows: *1573*—1908-1914; *1574*—1914-1915; *1575*—1915-1920; *1576*—1920-

8
Cyclists

It was not until 1888 that a battalion completely dedicated to a cyclist role was formed, the 26th Middlesex Rifle Volunteer Corps. There were, however, several cyclist companies formed within the Rifle Volunteer Corps during the Easter manoeuvres of 1885.

By 1908, when the Territorial Force was created, the military cyclist had proved himself and the reorganizations saw the formation of several battalions of cyclists. Most of these were linked to Infantry of the Line Regiments; these will be dealt with under their respective regiments. Others, although in most cases joining infantry regiments, were later to become independent; these are listed here.

Northern Cyclist Battalion

1908 Formed as 8th (Cyclist) Bn. Northumberland Fusiliers (TF).
1910 Redesignated Northern Cyclist Bn at Newcastle-on-Tyne.
1920 Transferred to Royal Garrison Artillery.

Shoulder titles: T | CYCLIST | NORTHERN (1577) and T | NORTHERN (1578). The latter is first listed in the *Priced Vocabulary of Clothing and Necessaries* for 1920.

Kent Cyclist Battalion

1908 Formed as 6th (Cyclist) Bn. The Queen's Royal West Kent Regiment.
1910 Redesignated Kent Cyclist Bn. HQ Tonbridge.
1920 Transferred to Royal Garrison Artillery.

Shoulder titles: T | KENT | CYCLISTS (1579). By 1916 2nd and 3rd line bns had been formed and it was in February of that year that the 1/1st Bn sailed for India. The title worn for this period was 1 | KENT (1580) which is in cast brass. A third title T | KENT was also worn.

Highland Cyclist Battalion

1861 2nd Admin Bn of Perthshire R.V.s formed, the senior corps being the 3rd which was raised in 1860.
1880 Bn consolidated as 2nd Perthshire R.V.C.
1887 Redesignated 5th (Perthshire Highland) V.B. The Black Watch.
1908 Became 8th (Cyclist) Bn. The Black Watch (TF).
1909 Redesignated Highland Cyclist Bn. HQ Birnam.
1920 Transferred to Royal Signals.

Shoulder titles: Three titles have so far been noted: T | HIGHLAND | CYCLISTS (1581) was the first to be issued, with T | HC (1582) and T | HCB (1583) following.

Huntingdonshire Cyclist Battalion

1914 Raised. HQ Huntingdon.
1920 Redesignated 5th Bn. Northamptonshire Regiment.

Shoulder title: T | HUNTS (1584).

Essex and Suffolk Cyclist Battalion

1908 Formed. HQ Colchester.
1911 Redesignated 8th (Cyclist) Bn, The Essex Regiment.

Shoulder title: T | CYCLISTS | ESSEX & SUFFOLK (1585).

City of London Cyclists
1916 Formed as 1/1st London Divisional Cyclist Company.
Disbanded after a few months.

Shoulder title: T | CYCLIST | CITY OF LONDON (*1586*).

Army Cyclist Corps
1914 Formed.
1919 Disbanded.

Shoulder titles: The title worn was CYCLIST (*1587*) with T | CYCLISTS (*1588*) and T | CYCLIST (*1589*) being worn by Divisional Cyclist Companies of the Territorial Force.

9
Reserve Regiments 1900

The South African War of 1899–1902 saw the formation of several Reserve Regiments of Cavalry and Infantry, the intention being to relieve regular forces at home for overseas service.

Army Order 79 of 1900 gives details of badges, clothing etc. for infantry regiments. Following is part of item 6 of that order. The left hand column lists the regiments that were formed, while the column on the right gives the titles to be worn, (men only), on the shoulder straps. All items are in brass except the bugle of the Rifles, which is in bronze, and the w.m. thistle of the Scots.

Royal Guards Reserve Regt	A Royal Crown surmounting GUARDS over R.R.
Royal Home Counties Reserve Regt	H.C. over R.R.
Royal Northern Reserve Regt	NORTHERN over R.R.
Royal Rifles Reserve Regt	A bugle over R.R.
Royal Southern Reserve Regt	SOUTHERN over R.R.
Royal Lancashire Reserve Regt	LANCS over R.R.
Royal Scottish Reserve Regt	A thistle over R.R.
Royal Eastern Reserve Regt	EASTERN overR.R.
Royal Irish Reserve Regt	A Shamrock over R.R.
Royal Irish Fusiliers Reserve Regt	A Shamrock over F.R.R.

Similar details were published in Army Order 127 of 1900 for the Cavalry. An extract from part 2 of that order follows:

'On the field cap: In gilt letters, H.M.R.R. surmounted by a crown; below the letters a scroll inscribed, "Dragoon Guards" or "Dragoons". On the collar and shoulder chain: As for the field cap badge, with the crown omitted.' The same badges are listed for the Hussars but with the word 'Hussars' on the scroll. *1590, 1591* and *1592* are the other ranks' patterns. Officers' titles had a slight variation on the scrolls and were of better quality. 'Lancers: On the field cap, collar and shoulder chain: In gilt metal a pair of crossed lances, on the lances a crown above the letters, R.R., below the letters a scroll inscribed, "Lancers".' What is not mentioned, however, is that each lance bears a pennant of which the lower half is w.m. (*1593*).

Royal Garrison Regiment

Formed by Royal Warrant dated 20 February, 1900, as the Royal Reserve Battalions, redesignated in 1901. The Regiment officially consisted of eight battalions and was disbanded in 1908, but in fact only five battalions existed and there was no personnel after March, 1906.

Shoulder title: RGR (*1594*).

10
Royal Marines

Royal Marine Artillery

The straight title R.M.A (*1595*) was worn until 1923. Another version exists with the letters joined at the top and minus the full stops. Curved titles also exist but these were worn by the Royal Military Academy. Officers also wore RMA but the title was only 35mm × 10mm.

Royal Marine Light Infantry

Two sizes of the RMLI title were worn until 1923, *1596* for officers and *1597* for other ranks.

Royal Marines

After the amalgamation of the Royal Marine Artillery and the Royal Marine Light Infantry in 1923, the title RM was adopted. Two sizes have been issued (*1598, 1599*). The larger title was worn by other ranks until 1964 in both brass and gold anodised. The smaller pattern, previous to 1964, was only worn by officers, in brass on the blue uniform and tropical dress, and in bronze on khaki service dress. After 1964 all ranks adopted the smaller title which was worn in gold anodised on the blue and tropical uniforms and in bronze in lovat and in shirt sleeve order.

Royal Marine Police

Formed in 1923. RMP (*1600*) for other ranks (*1601*) for officers, both in w.m. The Royal Marine Police were merged into the Admiralty Constabulary in 1949 and are now part of the Ministry of Defence Police.

Royal Marine Engineers

Formed in 1917 with the title RME (*1602*). Disbanded in 1919.

Royal Marine Labour Corps

Formed on 2 February, 1917, from two companies of the Army Service Corps. The title worn until disbandment in 1919 was RMLC (*1603*). Officers wore the same title but measuring only 38mm × 10mm.

Royal Marine Bands

RMB (*1604*).

Volunteers

The Volunteers of the Royal Marines were formed in 1948 and known as The Royal Marine Forces Volunteer Reserve until 1964 when they were redesignated The Royal Marine Reserve. Titles worn were RMFVR (*1605*) and RMR (*1606*), both appearing in brass, bronze and gold anodised.

Cadets

The Marine section of the Sea Cadet Corps wear the title MARINE | SCC | CADETS (*1607*) which has been issued in both brass and gold anodised.

11
Royal Naval Division

The 1st and 2nd Royal Naval Brigades were formed as follows:

1st Brigade

1st (Drake) Bn, 2nd (Hawke) Bn, 3rd (Benbow) Bn and 4th (Collingwood) Bn.

2nd Brigade

5th (Nelson) Bn, 6th (Howe) Bn, 7th (Hood) Bn and 8th (Anson) Bn.

Originally khaki sailor caps were worn with the name of the battalion embroidered on the tally bands. It was not until May, 1916, that service dress caps were issued together with a metal badge. It will be of interest to note that the Benbow and Collingwood Battalions were disbanded in June, 1915, due to severe losses incurred at Gallipoli, and were never issued with metal cap badges, their shoulder titles being the only form of metal insignia to be worn.

Shoulder titles: DRAKE *(1608)*; HAWKE *(1609)*; BENBOW *(1610)*; COLLING-WOOD *(1611)*; NELSON *(1612)*; HOWE *(1613)*; HOOD *(1614)*; ANSON *(1615)*.

The Royal Naval Division also had a Machine Gun Battalion who wore the curved title R.N.D *(1616)*. This title also formed part of the cap badge. A straight version also exists *(1617)*.

The Divisional Engineers wore the title ENGINEERS | R.N.D. The word ENGINEERS was a solid tablet while the lower part was the curved R.N.D of the Machine Gun Battalion.

12
Schools and Training Establishments

Army Apprentices School

The above has, since being formed at Chepstow in the early 1920s, been known as The Boys Technical School, The Army Technical School (Boys) and The Army Apprentices College, as it is now known.

Shoulder titles: BTS (*1618*); ATS (*1619*); ARMY | APPRENTICES | SCHOOL (*1620*).

Army Cadet Force

Cadets were first recognized by the War Office in 1863 and by 1892 were attached to Volunteer Corps. The reforms of 1908 saw the various cadet units formed within the Public Schools System transferred to the Officer Training Corps. The remainder went to form the Territorial Cadet Force. The T.C.F. was redesignated the Army Cadet Force in 1942.

Shoulder title: ACF (*1621*), which also appears in gold anodised.

Army Technical School (Boys)

See Army Apprentices School.

Boys Technical School

See Army Apprentices School.

Combined Cadet Force

The Junior Division of the Officer Training Corps was redesignated the Junior Training Corps in 1940, then the Combined Cadet Force in 1948.

Shoulder title: CCF (*1622*).

Infantry Boys Battalion

See Junior Leaders Regiment.

Junior Leaders Regiments

Formed in 1954 as the Infantry Boys Battalion, being redesignated Junior Leaders Regiments in 1956.

Shoulder titles: INFANTRY | BOYS | BATTALION (*1623*); JL (*1624*).

153

Officer Cadet Battalions

Although 22 battalions existed during the 1st World War only two metal shoulder titles have so far been noted. Officer Cadet Battalions were formed in 1916 and were separate from the O.T.C. and other training units.

Shoulder titles: 4 | OCB and 6 | OCB (*1625*) both in two pieces. Both units were formed at Oxford University.

The Officer Training Corps

The Officer Training Corps, which was created in 1908, was divided into two divisions, the Senior, consisting of university units, and the Junior, which was formed from public schools.

Contingents of the O.T.C. came directly under the administration of the War Office and had no affiliations to regular or other regiments.

The Senior Division was known as the University Training Corps (TA) between 1948 and 1955, the Junior Division became the Junior Training Corps in 1940.

The Inns of Court Officer Training Corps, which is not dealt with here, was not part of either the Senior or Junior Divisions. This unit was part of the Territorial Force and administered by the County of London Association. It's object was to provide trained officers for the Territorial Force and Special Reserve.

|U: University; C: College; S: School|

Senior Division

Aberdeen U	ABERDEEN	O.T.C	UNIVERSITY (*1626*)
Belfast U redesignated Queen's in 1931	BELFAST	O.T.C	UNIVERSITY (*1627*)
	QUEEN'S UNIVERSITY	O.T.C	BELFAST CONTINGENT The top and bottom tiers are non-voided. (*1628*)
Birmingham U	BIRMINGHAM	O.T.C	UNIVERSITY (*1629*)
Bristol U	BRISTOL	OTC	UNIVERSITY (*1630*)
Cambridge U	CAMBRIDGE	O.T.C	UNIVERSITY (*1631*)
Cork U	UNIVERSITY COLLEGE	O.T.C	CORK (*1632*)
Dublin U	DUBLIN	O.T.C	UNIVERSITY (*1633*)
	DUBLIN	OTC	UNIVERSITY (*1634*)
Durham U	DURHAM	O.T.C	UNIVERSITY (*1635*)
Edinburgh U	EDINBURGH	OTC	UNIVERSITY (*1636*)
Exeter U	UNIV.COLL.	O.T.C	EXETER
Glasgow U	GLASGOW	O.T.C	UNIVERSITY (*1637*)
Leeds U	LEEDS	O.T.C	UNIVERSITY (*1638*)
Liverpool	LIVERPOOL	O.T.C	UNIVERSITY
London U	UNIVERSITY	O.T.C	OF LONDON (*1639*)
	U.L.O.T.C (*1640*)

The first title was also issued in three
separate pieces.

Manchester U	MANCHESTER|O.T.C|UNIVERSITY (*1641*)
Nottingham U	UNIVERSITY. COLL|O.T.C|NOTTINGHAM (*1642*)
Oxford U	OXFORD|O.T.C|UNIVERSITY (*1643*)
Reading U	READING|O.T.C|UNIVERSITY (*1644*) READING|O.T.C|UNIV.COLL (*1645*)
Royal Agricultural Coll	R.A.C|CIRENCESTER|O.T.C
Royal College of Surgeons in Ireland	SURGEONS|O.T.C|IRELAND (*1646*) COLLEGE OF|OTC|SURGEONS (*1647*)
Royal (Dick) Veterinary College, Edinburgh	VETERINARY|OTC|EDINBURGH (*1648*)
Royal Veterinary College of Ireland	VETERINARY|O.T.C|IRELAND
St Andrew's U	ST.ANDREWS|O.T.C|UNIVERSITY (*1649*)
Sheffield U	SHEFFIELD|O.T.C|UNIVERSITY (*1650*)
Southampton U	SOUTHAMPTON|O.T.C|UNIVERSITY
University of Wales	UNIVERSITY|OTC|OF WALES (*1651*) and (*1652*)

Junior Division

Abingdon S. Formed as Roysse's S. Redesignated in 1925	ABINGDON|OTC (*1653*)
Aldenham S	ALDENHAM|OTC|SCHOOL (*1654*)
Alleyn's S	OTC|ALLEYN'S (*1655*)
All Hallows S	ALL HALLOWS|O.T.C|SCHOOL (*1656*)
Ampleforth C	AMPLEFORTH|OTC|COLLEGE (*1657*)
Archbishop Abbot's S	none recorded
Ardlingly C	ARDLINGLY|O.T.C|COLLEGE (*1658*)
Ardrossan Academy	none recorded
Army S	ARMY|O.T.C|SCHOOL
Barnard Castle S. Formed as North Eastern County S. Redesignated in 1924	BARNARD|O.T.C|CASTLE (*1659*)
Bath C	BATH|O.T.C|COLLEGE (*1660*)
Beaumont C	BEAUMONT|O.T.C|COLLEGE (*1661*)
Bedford Grammar S. Formed as above but redesignated Bedford S in 1918	BEDFORD|O.T.C|GRAMMAR SCHOOL (*1662*) and BEDFORD|O.T.C|SCHOOL (*1663*)
Bedford Modern S	BEDFORD|O.T.C|MODERN SCHOOL (*1664*)
Berkhamsted S	BERKHAMSTED|O.T.C|SCHOOL (*1665*)
Birkenhead S	BIRKENHEAD|O.T.C|SCHOOL
Bishop's Stortford S	none recorded.
Bishop Vesey's Grammar S	BISHOP VESEY'S|O.T.C|GRAMMAR SCHOOL (*1666*)

Bloxham S	BLOXHAM│O.T.C│SCHOOL *(1667)*
Blundell's S	OTC│BLUNDELLS *(1668)*
Bournemouth S	BOURNEMOUTH│O.T.C│SCHOOL
Bradfield C	OTC│BRADFIELD *(1669)*
Bradford Grammar S	BRADFORD│O.T.C│SCHOOL
	OTC│BRADFORD
Brentwood S	BRENTWOOD│O.T.C│SCHOOL
Bridlington Grammar S	BRIDLINGTON│O.T.C│SCHOOL *(1670)*
Brighton C	BRIGHTON│OTC│COLLEGE *(1671)*
Brighton Grammar S	BRIGHTON│O.T.C│GRAMMAR SCHOOL *(1672)*
Bristol Grammar S	OTC│BRISTOL *(1673)*
Bromsgrove S	BROMSGROVE│O.T.C│SCHOOL *(1674)*
Buckland S. Formed as West	WEST│O.T.C│BUCKLAND *(1675)*
Buckland S. Redesignated in 1913	BUCKLAND│O.T.C│SCHOOL
Bury Grammar S	BURY│O.T.C│SCHOOL
Cambridge and County S	CAMB. & COUNTY│O.T.C│SCHOOL
Campbell C	CAMPBELL│O.T.C│COLLEGE *(1676)*
Canford S	CANFORD│OTC│SCHOOL *(1677)*
Charterhouse S	OTC│CHARTERHOUSE *(1678)*
Chatham House C	none recorded.
Cheltenham C	CHELT│OTC│COLL *(1679)* replaced by CHELTENHAM│OTC│COLLEGE *(1680)*
Chigwell S	CHIGWELL│O.T.C│SCHOOL *(1681)*
Christ C, Brecon	CHRIST COLLEGE│O.T.C│BRECON
Christ's Hospital	CHRISTS│OTC│HOSPITAL *(1682)* and *(1683)*
Churcher's C	CHURCHER'S│OTC│COLLEGE *(1684)*
City of London S	CITY OF LONDON│O.T.C│SCHOOL *(1685)*
Clifton C	O.T.C│CLIFTON *(1686)* worn by infantry coys. RE│O.T.C│CLIFTON *(1687)* worn by engineer coys.
Coatham S	COATHAM│O.T.C│SCHOOL
Cork Grammar S	none recorded.
Cranbrook S	CRANBROOK│O.T.C│SCHOOL *(1689)*
Cranleigh S	CRANLEIGH│O.T.C│SCHOOL *(1688)*
Daniel Stewart's C	STEWART'S│O.T.C│COLLEGE
Dartford Grammar S	DARTFORD│O.T.C│SCHOOL
Dean Close S	DEAN CLOSE│O.T.C│SCHOOL *(1690)*
Denstone C	DENSTONE│O.T.C│COLLEGE *(1691)*
Derby S	DERBY│O.T.C│SCHOOL
Dollar Academy. Formed as Dollar Institution. Redesignated in 1921	DOLLAR│O.T.C│INSTITUTION DOLLAR│O.T.C│ACADEMY
Dorchester Grammar S	OTC│DORCHESTER *(1692)*
Dover C	OTC│DOVER COLLEGE *(1693)* in w.m.
Downside S	DOWNSIDE│OTC│SCHOOL *(1694)*
Dulwich C	DULWICH│O.T.C│COLLEGE *(1695)* also in w.m.

Durham S

Eastbourne C
Edinburgh Academy
Elizabeth C, Guernsey

Ellesmere C
Elstow S
Eltham C (Royal Naval S)
Emanuel S

Epsom C
Eton C
Exeter S
Felsted S
Fettes C
Forest S
Framlingham C
George Heriot's S
George Watson's Boys C
Giggleswick S
Glasgow Academy
Glasgow High S
Glenalmond C

Gresham's S
Grimsby Municipal C
Haberdashers' S
Haileybury C
Handsworth Grammar S
Harrow S
Hereford Cathedral S
Herne Bay C
Hertford Grammar S
Highgate S
Hillhead High S
Hulme Grammar S
Hurstpierpoint C

Hymers C
Imperial Service C. Formed as United
  Services C. Redesignated in 1912
Ipswich S
Kelly C
Kelvinside Academy
King Alfred's S. Redesignated
  Wantage S in 1923

Metal titles were not worn. The title
was embroidered into the shoulder
straps.
OTC | EASTBOURNE (*1696*)
EDINBURGH | OTC | ACADEMY (*1697*)
OTC | GUERNSEY (*1698*)
ELIZABETH | O.T.C | COLLEGE (*1699*)
ELLESMERE | O.T.C. | COLLEGE (*1700*)
ELSTOW | O.T.C | SCHOOL (*1701*)
ELTHAM | O.T.C | COLLEGE
EMANUEL | O.T.C | SCHOOL (*1702*)
OTC | EMANUEL
EPSOM | O.T.C | COLLEGE (*1703*)
ETON | OTC | COLLEGE (*1704*) in w.m.
EXETER | O.T.C. | SCHOOL (*1705*)
OTC | FELSTED (*1706*)
FETTES | O.T.C | COLLEGE
FOREST | O.T.C | SCHOOL (*1707*)
FRAMLINGHAM | O.T.C | COLLEGE (*1708*)
HERIOT'S | O.T.C | SCHOOL
WATSONS | OTC | COLLEGE (*1709*)
GIGGLESWICK | O.T.C | SCHOOL (*1710*)
GLASGOW | OTC | ACADEMY (*1711*)
HIGH SCHOOL | OTC | GLASGOW (*1712*)
O.T.C | GLENALMOND (*1713*) also in
w.m. and GLENALMOND | O.T.C (*1714*)
OTC | GRESHAM'S (*1715*)
GRIMSBY | OTC | COLLEGE (*1716*)
HABERDASHERS' | O.T.C | SCHOOL (*1717*)
O.T.C | HAILEYBURY (*1718*)
HANDSWORTH | OTC | SCHOOL (*1719*)
HARROW | OTC | SCHOOL (*1720*)
HEREFORD | OTC | SCHOOL (*1721*)
HERNE BAY | O.T.C | COLLEGE (*1722*)
OTC | HERTFORD (*1723*)
HIGHGATE | O.T.C | SCHOOL (*1724*)
HILLHEAD | OTC | SCHOOL
THE HULME | O.T.C | GRAMMAR SCHOOL
HURSTPIERPOINT | O.T.C | COLLEGE
(*1725*)
HYMERS | O.T.C | COLLEGE
IMPERIAL SERVICE | OTC | COLLEGE
(*1726*)
IPSWICH | O.T.C | SCHOOL
KELLY | O.T.C | COLLEGE (*1727*)
KELVINSIDE | O.T.C | ACADEMY
KING ALFRED'S | O.T.C | SCHOOL

King Edward VII S, Sheffield	KING EDWARD VII	O.T.C	SHEFFIELD (*1728*)
King Edward's Grammar S, Bury St Edmunds	BURY	O.T.C	ST.EDMUNDS (*1729*)
King Edward's S, Bath	KING EDWARD'S	O.T.C	SCHOOL.BATH (*1730*)
King Edward's S, Birmingham	KES	OTC	BIRMINGHAM worn in three pieces.
King William's C	KING WILLIAM'S	O.T.C	COLLEGE (*1731*)
King's Cathedral S, Worcester. Redesignated King's S in 1912	KING'S SCHOOL	O.T.C	WORCESTER (*1732*)
King's C, Taunton	KING'S	OTC	TAUNTON (*1733*)
King's C, Wimbledon	KING'S COLLEGE	O.T.C	SCHOOL (*1734*)
King's S, Bruton	KING'S SCHOOL	O.T.C	BRUTON (*1735*)
King's S, Canterbury	KING'S SCHOOL	O.T.C	CANTERBURY (*1736*)
King's S, Grantham	GRANTHAM	O.T.C	SCHOOL
King's S, Rochester	KING'S SCHOOL	O.T.C	ROCHESTER (*1737*)
King's S, Warwick	WARWICK	O.T.C	SCHOOL
Kirkcaldy High S	KIRKCALDY	O.T.C	HIGH SCHOOL
Lancing C	LANCING	O.T.C	COLLEGE
Leeds Grammar S	OTC	LEEDS (*1738*)
Leys S	LEYS	OTC	SCHOOL (*1739*)
Liverpool C	LIVERPOOL	O.T.C	COLLEGE (*1740*)
Liverpool Collegiate S	LIVERPOOL	O.T.C	COLLEGIATE
Liverpool Institute	LIVERPOOL	O.T.C	INSTITUTE (*1741*)
Llandovery C	LLANDOVERY	O.T.C	COLLEGE (*1742*)
Loretto S	LORETTO	O.T.C	SCHOOL
Louth S	LOUTH	O.T.C	SCHOOL
Magdalen C	MAGD.COLL	O.T.C	SCHOOL (*1743*)
Maidstone Grammmar S	MAIDSTONE	O.T.C	SCHOOL (*1744*)
Malvern C	MALVERN	O.T.C	COLLEGE (*1745*)
Manchester Grammar S	MANCHESTER	O.T.C	GRAMMAR SCHOOL
Mansfield S, Queen Elizabeth's	MANSFIELD	O.T.C	SCHOOL (*1746*)
Marlborough C	MARLBOROUGH	O.T.C	COLLEGE (*1747*) MARLBOROUGH	COLLEGE O.T.C (*1748*)
Merchant Taylors' S (Crosby)	MTS	OTC	CROSBY (*1749*)
Merchant Taylors' S	MERCHANT	O.T.C	TAYLORS (*1750*)
Merchiston Castle S	MERCHISTON	O.T.C	CASTLE (*1751*)
Mill Hill S	MILL HILL	OTC	SCHOOL (*1752*)
Monkton Combe S	MONKTONCOMBE	O.T.C	SCHOOL (*1753*)
Monmouth Grammar S	MONMOUTH	O.T.C	GRAMMAR SCHOOL OTC	MONMOUTH
Morrison's Academy	MORRISON'S	O.T.C	ACADEMY
Mount St Mary's C	none recorded.
Newcastle-under-Lyme High S	NEWCASTLE	O.T.C	HIGH SCHOOL (*1754*)
Newton C	NEWTON	O.T.C	COLLEGE (*1755*)

North Eastern County S.	none recorded.
Redesignated Barnard Castle S in 1924	
Northampton S	NORTHAMPTON|O.T.C|SCHOOL
Nottingham High S	NOTTINGHAM|OTC|HIGH SCHOOL (*1756*)
Oakham S	OAKHAM|O.T.C|SCHOOL (*1757*)
Oratory S	ORATORY|O.T.C|SCHOOL
Oundle S	OUNDLE|O.T.C|SCHOOL (*1758*)
Perse S	PERSE|OTC|SCHOOL (*1759*)
Peter Symond's S	PETER SYMONDS|OTC|SCHOOL (*1760*)
Plymouth C	PLYMOUTH|OTC|COLLEGE (*1761*)
Portora Royal S	PORTORA|O.T.C|SCHOOL (*1762*)
Portsmouth Grammar S	PORTSMOUTH|OTC|GR SCHOOL (*1763*)
Queen Elizabeth's S: see Mansfield S	
Queen Mary's Grammar S, Walsall	WALSALL|O.T.C|GRAMMAR SCHOOL
Quernmore and Sidcup S.	QUERNMORE & SIDCUP|O.T.C|SCHOOL
Redesignated Sidcup Hall S in 1910	
Radley C	RADLEY|O.T.C|COLLEGE (*1764*)
Reading S	READING|O.T.C|SCHOOL (*1765*)
Reigate Grammar S	REIGATE|O.T.C|SCHOOL
Repton S	OTC|REPTON (*1766*)
Rossall S	ROSSALL|O.T.C|SCHOOL (*1767*)
Royal Grammar S, High Wycombe	WYCOMBE|OTC|SCHOOL (*1768*)
Royal Grammar S, Lancaster	OTC|LANCASTER
Royal Grammar S, Newcastle-on-Tyne	NEWCASTLE ON TYNE|OTC|R.G.SCHOOL (*1769*)
Royal Grammar S, Worcester	ROYAL GRAMMAR SCHOOL|O.T.C|WORCESTER replaced by W.R.G.S|O.T.C
Royal Grammar S, Guildford	GUILDFORD|O.T.C|SCHOOL (*1770*)
Royal High S, Edinburgh	ROYAL HIGH|O.T.C|SCHOOL (*1771*)
Royal Naval S: see Eltham C	
Roysse's S. Redesignated Abingdon S in 1925	ROYSSE'S|O.T.C|SCHOOL
Rugby S	OTC|RUGBY (*1772*)
Rutlish S	RUTLISH|O.T.C|SCHOOL
Rydal S	RYDAL|O.T.C|SCHOOL
St Albans S	ST.ALBANS|O.T.C|SCHOOL (*1773*)
St Andrew's C	none recorded.
St Bees S	ST. BEES|O.T.C|SCHOOL (*1774*)
St Columba's C	ST.COLUMBA'S|O.T.C|COLLEGE (*1775*)
St Dunstan's C	O.T.C|ST.DUNSTAN. (*1776*)
St Edmund's C, Ware	ST.EDMUNDS|OTC|COLLEGE (*1777*)
St Edmund's S, Canterbury	ST.EDMUND'S|O.T.C|CANTERBURY
St Edward's S	ST.EDWARD'S|O.T.C|SCHOOL
St John's S, Leatherhead	ST.JOHN'S SCHOOL|O.T.C|LEATHERHEAD (*1778*)
St Lawrence C	ST.LAWRENCE|O.T.C|COLLEGE
St Paul's S	ST.PAUL'S|O.T.C|SCHOOL (*1779*)
St Peter's S	ST.PETER'S|O.T.C|SCHOOL (*1780*)

Sebright S	SEBRIGHT│O.T.C│SCHOOL (*1781*)
Sedbergh S	SEDBERGH│OTC│SCHOOL (*1782*)
Sherborne S	OTC│SHERBORNE (*1783*)
Shrewsbury S	SHREWSBRUY│O.T.C│SCHOOL (*1784*)
Sidcup Hall S. Formed as Quernmore and Sidcup Schools. Redesignated 1910	none recorded.
Sir Roger Manwood's S	MANWOOD'S│O.T.C│SCHOOL
Skinner's S	SKINNERS│O.T.C│SCHOOL (*1785*)
Solihull Grammar S	SOLIHULL│O.T.C│SCHOOL (*1786*)
Stamford S	STAMFORD│O.T.C│SCHOOL (*1787*)
Stonyhurst C	STONYHURST│O.T.C│COLLEGE (*1788*)
Stowe S	STOWE│OTC│SCHOOL (*1789*)
Sutton Valence S	SUTTON│OTC│VALENCE (*1790*)
Taunton S	TAUNTON│O.T.C│SCHOOL
Tonbridge S	TONBRIDGE│OTC│SCHOOL (*1791*)
Trent C	TRENT│O.T.C│COLLEGE
United Services C. Redesignated Imperial Service 1912	none recorded.
University College S	UNIV.COLL.SCHOOL│O.T.C│LONDON (*1792*)
Uppingham S	OTC│UPPINGHAM (*1793*)
Victoria C	VICT.COLL│OTC (*1794*)
Wantage S. Formed as King Alfred's S. Redesignated in 1923	WANTAGE│O.T.C│SCHOOL (*1795*)
Wellingborough Grammar S	WELLINGBOROUGH│O.T.C│SCHOOL (*1796*)
Wellington C, Berks	OTC│WELL.COLL
Wellington C, Salop. Redesignated Wrekin C in 1921	OTC│WELLINGTON (*1797*) and WELLINGTON│O.T.C│SALOP
Wellington S, Somerset. Formed as West Somerset County S. Redesignated in 1914	WELLINGTON SCHOOL│O.T.C│SOMERSET (*1798*)
Westminster S	WESTMINSTER│O.T.C│SCHOOL (*1799*)
West Somerset County S. Became Wellington S in 1914	WEST SOMERSET│O.T.C│WELLINGTON
Weymouth C	WEYMOUTH│O.T.C│COLLEGE (*1800*)
Whitgift Grammar S	WHITGIFT│O.T.C│SCHOOL (*1801*)
Wilson's S	OTC│WILSON'S
Winchester C	OTC│WINCHESTER (*1802*)
Wolverhampton Grammar S	WOLVERHAMPTON│O.T.C│SCHOOL (*1803*)
Woodbridge S	WOODBRIDGE│O.T.C│SCHOOL (*1804*)
Worksop C	WORKSOP│O.T.C│COLLEGE (*1805*)
Wrekin C. Formed as Wellington C. Redesignated in 1921	WREKIN│OTC│COLLEGE (*1806*)

Royal Military Academy (Sandhurst)

The Royal Military Academy (Woolwich) and the Royal Military College (Sandhurst) were amalgamated in 1947 as the Royal Military Academy (Sandhurst).

Shoulder titles: R.M.C (*1807*) and R.M.A which was also worn by the Royal Malta Artillery. RMAS was introduced in 1951.

Royal Military Academy (Woolwich)

See Royal Military Academy (Sandhurst).

Royal Military College (Sandhurst)

See Royal Military Academy (Sandhurst).

Royal Military School of Music

Kneller Hall in Twickenham, Middlesex, is the home of the Royal Military School of Music. The present title was adopted in 1887 after being known as the Military Music Class since 1857.

Shoulder title: RMSM (*1808*) which is worn on the greatcoat only.

13
Women's Units

Auxiliary Territorial Service
See Women's Royal Army Corps.

Green Cross
The Green Cross was a 1st World War women's volunteer medical unit. Their shoulder title was GREEN CROSS which was curved.

Queen Alexandra's Royal Army Nursing Corps
The predecessors of the above were the Queen Alexandra's Imperial Military Nursing Service, which had started life in 1897 as the Army Nursing Service, being redesignated in 1902. The present title was adopted in 1949. The only metal title so far noted is QARANC (*1809*) which was introduced in 1954 and worn on the tropical dress.

Queen Mary's Army Auxiliary Corps
Formed in 1917 as the Women's Army Auxiliary Corps with the shoulder title WAAC (*1810*), which also exists curved. Queen Mary became the Colonel-in-Chief in 1918 and the Corps was redesignated Queen Mary's Army Auxiliary Corps. The shoulder title then changed to QMAAC (*1811*) which was worn until disbandment in 1919.

Scottish Women's Hospital
One of the many women's medical units that were formed during the 1st World War, their shoulder title was S.W.H (*1812*).

Volunteer Service Legion
Formed by the Marchioness of Londonderry during the 1st World War. Their bronze shoulder title was V.S.L (*1813*).

Women's Army Auxiliary Corps
See Queen Mary's Army Auxiliary Corps.

Women's Forage Corps
The Corps was formed in 1915 and by 1917 numbered some 8,000 all ranks. Their work included hay baling, tarpaulin sheet mending, sack making and driving. A Forage Corps Guard was also formed. The shoulder title, which also served as the headdress badge, was F.C.

Women's Royal Army Corps

The forerunners of the Women's Royal Army Corps were the Auxiliary Territorial Service, formed in 1938. Their shoulder title was ATS (*1814*), the letter 'T' being larger than the other two. A much larger title with the same letters also exists but this was worn by the Army Technical School (Boys). The Corps served throughout the 2nd World War. By the beginning of 1949 the Corps had become part of the Regular Army with the designation Women's Royal Army Corps and the shoulder title WRAC (*1815*).

Women Signallers Territorial Corps

This unit existed during the 1st World War and were issued with the straight bronze title SIGNALS.

Women's Volunteer Reserve

Yet another of the many women's units that were formed by the Marchioness of Londonderry during the 1st World War. They wore the bronze shoulder title W.V.R (*1816*).

14
Miscellaneous units

Barrack Wardens
These were civilian appointments which were held by service pensioners that had a record of good conduct and held a rank of at least sergeant.
Shoulder title: BW (*1817*), which also served as both cap and collar badge.

Brompton Park Military Hospital
Formed during the Great War.
Shoulder title: BPMH | 144 | LONDON.

Channel Islands Militia

Royal Militia of the Island of Jersey
The Militia of Jersey dates from the 13th Century and at one time consisted of five battalions. The infantry, who by 1900 had been styled Light Infantry, were augmented before 1902 with Artillery and Engineer Sections. Volunteered for service in 1939 and by June, 1940, were serving as the 11th Bn, The Hampshire Regiment.
Shoulder titles: JERSEY (*1818*) was worn with the addition of a separate RA, RE or bugle horn above for Artillery, Engineers and Infantry respectively.

Royal Guernsey Militia
Also dating from the 13th Century and consisting of Artillery, Engineers and Light Infantry.
Shoulder titles: GUERNSEY (*1819*). The separate RA, RE and bugle were once again worn. Another title, ROYAL | GUERNSEY MILITIA (*1820*), was introduced just after the 1st World War for Infantry battalions. The scarcity of this title would perhaps suggest that its use was confined to officers only.

Royal Alderney Militia
Consisting of Artillery and a small Engineer Section only.
Shoulder title: ALDERNEY (*1821*), with RA or RE worn separately above.

City Imperial Volunteers
Formed during the South African War of 1899–1902 from volunteers in the London area.
Shoulder title: C.I.V (*1822*), which also served as the slouch hat badge.

Expeditionary Forces Canteen
This unit served throughout the 1st World War.
Shoulder title: EFC (*1823*).

Home Guard
Generally cloth titles were worn by the Home Guard; some units, however, wore the metal title HG (*1824*).

Irish War Hospital Supply Depot
This 1st World War unit had for its shoulder title a solid tablet inscribed with the letters I.W.H.S.D (*1825*).

Motor Volunteer Corps
Formed in 1903 and became the Army Motor Reserve in 1906. Disbanded just before 1914.
Shoulder title: M.V.C. (*1826*).

National Reserve
The National Reserve was formed in 1910 as the Veteran Reserve, being redesignated by 1913. Members were expected to maintain military efficiency and be ready to join the Colours on mobilization.
Shoulder titles: Although almost every county in the British Isles formed National Reserve units very few shoulder titles were worn. Those so far noted are: 3│NR│DEVON; NR│SUSSEX; T│WRNR (West Riding) (*1827*).

Popski's Private Army
Formed November, 1942, as No. 1 Demolition Squadron. Generally cloth titles were worn, but a photograph of LT.Col. V. Peniakoff DSO, MC who formed the unit, taken in 1946, show the metal title PPA being worn.

Royal Naval Air Service
Amalgamated with the Royal Flying Corps in April, 1918, to form the Royal Air Force.
Shoulder title: RNAS.

The Anti-Aircraft Corps of the Royal Naval Volunteer Reserve was transferred to the Royal Naval Air Service in January, 1916.
Shoulder titles: RNAS. RNAS│AAC

Ulster Volunteer Force
Formed by the Ulster Unionist Party in 1913 with the intention of preventing the passing through Parliament of the Irish Home Rule Bill. The Force, which was illegal, also included the Young Citizens' Volunteers who had been raised in September, 1912, from boys leaving the Church Lads and Boys Brigades. Another part of the U.V.F. was the Ulster Special Service Force.

On the outbreak of the 1st World War and Kitchener's call for volunteers the U.V.F. offered their services on condition that the word 'Ulster' would be included in any units formed. The offer was accepted and the volunteers soon formed service battalions of The Royal Inniskilling Fusiliers, The Royal Ulster Rifles and The Royal Irish Fusiliers and were included in the newly formed 36th (Ulster) Division.

Shoulder titles: UVF (*1828*); USSF (*1829*); YCV (*1830*) which is in w.m.; 1│YCV in w.m. also worn.

Volunteer Aid Detachments

The V.A.D. was formed in 1909 to supplement the medical elements of the Territorial Force. Personnel were supplied by the Red Cross and the Order of St John. Several detachments served overseas in the Balkan War of 1912.

To list the many thousands of units that were formed would require a book of its own. Detachments were formed and numbered within the County Territorial Force Associations, the County of Kent having some 162 alone.

It is of interest to note that even-numbered units were formed by women while those with odd numbers were made up from men.

A selection of shoulder titles are shown (*1831* to *1848*). V.A.D. titles often appear with a brooch-type fixing.

Volunteer Training Corps

The call for volunteers was once again heard in August, 1914, and by the end of that month many hundreds of units had been formed. The War Office was at first reluctant to recognize the volunteers, one reason being the fear that their existence might interfere with recruitment for the Regular Army. Recognition was, however, given in November and control vested in the Central Association of Volunteer Training Corps.

The V.T.C. was to see many changes in roll and organization during it's short existence, the final one being in August, 1918, when, with the exception of the City and County of London Regiments, volunteer regiments were linked to line regiments as volunteer battalions.

Shoulder titles worn by units formed in counties other than London have been included with those for the regiment or corps to which they were linked in 1918. Titles known to have been worn by City and County of London Regiments are listed below.

V│1│CITY OF LONDON (*1849*)	1st City of London Regiment
S.L.R.V (*1850*) in bronze	South London Regiment of Volunteers
1│C.L.R.V (*1851*)	1st County of London Regiment
C of W│VOLUNTEERS (*1852*)	City of Westminster Volunteer Regiment
LVR│VOLUNTEERS (*1853*)	London Volunteer Regiment
5│HACKNEY│N.LOND.VOL.REGT (*1854*)	5th North London Regiment
C.L.N.G│V (*1855*)	City of London National Guard

WEST LONDON REGT│V.T.C│FULHAM (*1856*), WEST LONDON REGT│V.T.C│ PADDINGTON, WEST LONDON REGT│V.T.C│ST.MARYLEBONE, and WEST LONDON│V.T.C│MOUNTED RIFLES. The bronze title V.T.C (*1857*) was issued for general use.

War Correspondents

Shoulder title: WAR│CORRESPONDENT (*1858*). Worn by War Correspondents in the 2nd World War.

Cavalry

The Life Guards

With regard to the two regiments of Life Guards wearing individual titles. A photograph of members of the 1st Regiment taken in France during 1918 shows at least four members of the party wearing titles consisting of a separate 1 over LG. Others in the group are wearing the usual LG (*8*). A one line title, 2LG, has also been noted.

The Inniskillings (6th Dragoons)

INNISKILLING, the same pattern as (*98*) but curved upwards.

15th/19th Hussars

15|19H, as (*157*) but in gold anodised.

17th/21st Lancers

12|21L, as (*172*) but in gold

Yeomanry

Queen's Own Yorkshire Dragoons

Y | YORKSHIRE DRAGOONS.

Duke of Lancaster's Own Yeomanry

T|Y|D OF LANCASTERS, as (*242*) but with non voided lower tier.

Royal East Kent Yeomanry

T|Y|E. KENT

Hampshire Carabiniers

HCY, seen in in c1910 photograph, worn on shoulder chains.

Derbyshire Yeomanry

IY | DERBYSHIRE

Royal Gloucesterhire Hussars

RGH|IY, a two piece title with letters of the same size.

Berkshire Yeomanry (Dragoons) (Hungerford)

BERKS YEO

1st County of London Yeomanry

MIY, worn prior to 1908. The oval title, MIDDLESEX | HUSSARS, was worn by members of "B" Squadron c1910. MH(*284*) was worn on the shoulder chains for a short time around 1912.

Westminster Dragoons

WESTMINSTER | DRAGOONS

3rd/4th County of London Yeomanry (Sharpshooters)
The title, SS, was worn by other ranks 1903-1908

Essex Yeomanry
EIY, the letters of this title are intertwined. E|IY, worn in three separate pieces. No less than eight sizes of the EY title have now been recorded.

Royal Wessex Yeomanry
Redesignated "Royal" in June 1979. The title now worn is, ROYAL WESSEX|YEOMANRY in gold anodised and two straight lines.

Arms and Services

Royal Army Medical Corps
Regulars
A curved version of the RAMC has been noted.

Volunteers
V|RAMC|EDINBURGH, V|RAMC LANCASHIRE FUSILIERS, V|RAMC|SEAFORTH AND CAMERON all in w.m.

Territorials
T|RAMC|NORTH MIDLAND. Under *Army Order 326* of October 1913 Clearing Hospitals were approved and added to each Territorial Division. T|NCH|RAMC was worn by the Northumbrian Clearing Hospital.

Royal Army Service Corps
Volunteers pre 1908
The three piece title already noted should in fact read, ASC|V|1. LOTHIAN
Territorials
T|ASC|GLOS & WORC

Royal Engineers
Regulars
The anodised title listed and numbered (*517*) was missed out when the photographic plates were arranged by the publishers. The missing item is the same size as (*514*).

Volunteers
L.E.V (London), curved letters. 2|RE|CHESHIRE, 2|RE|CHESIRE, EE (electrical engineers). All in white metal.

Territorials
T|RE|SCOTLAND, worn by Scottish Telegraph Companies.

Cadets
CADETS|RE|SUSSEX

Royal Artillery
The large intertwined letters RA over STAFF was worn by clerks attached to Royal Artillery Staffs.

Royal Field Artillery
Territorials
T | RFA | CARDIGANSHIRE, T | RFA | FLINTSHIRE,T | FORFAR.

Royal Garrison Artillery
Militia
The titles recorded in *Collecting Metal Shoulder Titles* for the R.G.A. Militia are those listed in *Clothing Regulations* for 1904. The following versions have also been noted, HANTS & I.OF W., LIMERICK, WATERFORD, WICKLOW.

Volunteers
1 | RA | CAITHNESS, 1 | RA | CINQUE PORTS (a three piece title), 1 | RA | KENT, 1 | RA | EDINR CITY, 1 RA | FORFAR, 2 | MA (Middlesex), 3 | MA (Middlesex), 1 | RA | MIDLOTHIAN, 1 | RA | MONMOUTH, 1 | RA | NORTHUMBERLAND, 1 | RA | NORTH YORK, 1 | RA | SUFFOLK & HARWICH. The four piece title 1 | NAV, was worn by members of the Elswick Battery of the 1st Northumberland Artillery Volunteers while serving in South Africa c 1900. The straight line title, GVA, was introduced in 1971 and worn by 266 (Gloucester Volunteer Artillery) Battery RA (V). All titles are in w.m.

Territorials
T | RGA | ARGYLL

Cadets
C1 | RA over NORFOLK (two piece w. m.), C | RFA | DURHAM, C | RFA | NORTHUMBER-LAND, C | RA worn by 1st Durham Cadet Battery (Leslies Cadet Corps). Other titles noted, RA | CITY OF LONDON, worn by City of London Territorials post 1924. The title is made from cast brass. COAST | RA also in cast brass.

Infantry Regiments

The Royal Scots (The Royal Regiment)
Regular Battalions
A large white metal RS title on a khaki drill jacket worn during the Boer War is shown in the Scottish United Services Museum. Another tunic, that of a Colour Sergeant c 1911, also has a large w.m. RS. The same title is also noted in the museum as having been worn by the 2nd Battalion on white uniform in India c 1890. The officers had a smaller version.

It has been suggested that the small w.m. title (*722*) is an item worn by Rover Scouts.

Territorial Battalions
T | 8/9 | ROYAL SCOTS This battalion was formed in 1961 by the amalgamation of the 7th/9th and 8th Battalions. T | 9 | RS | HIGHLANDERS, worn by some members of the battalion between 1908 and 1921.

The Royal Northumberland Fusiliers
Territorials Battalions
T | 5 | N grenade F

The Royal Warwickshire Regiment
Volunteer Battalions 1918
4 | VOL | WARWICKS, 5 | VOL WARWICKS

The Royal Fusiliers
Regular Battalions
ROYAL FUS, a curved title

The Royal Lincolnshire Regiment
Volunteer Battalions pre 1908
2 VB LINC, a curved title.

Cadets
STAMFORD | C | SCHOOL. This unit was affiliated to the 4th Battalion.

The Suffolk Regiment
Volunteer Battalions pre 1908
1VB | SUFFOLK, the lower tier of this title is in a straight line. Illustrations have also shown this title being worn in the slouch hat.

The Somerset Light Infantry
Regular Battalions
SOM.LI, made in a straight line from cast brass.

The East Yorkshire Regiment
Volunteer Battalions 1918
EYVB, worn by the East Yorkshire Volunteer Brigade.

Cadets
HULL | G.S | CADETS The Hull Grammar School Cadets Corps was affiliated to the 4th Bn. East Yorkshire Regiment.

The Green Howards
Volunteer Battalions 1918
The letters, NRRV with a rose placed between the two RS. Worn by the North Riding Volunteers.

The Lancashire Fusiliers
Territorial Battalions
6LF, a small cast brass title which was taken into use by the 6th Bn. while serving overseas in the First World War.

The Royal Scots Fusiliers
Regular Battalions
A grenade with a white metal thistle on the ball and scroll below inscribed 'ROYAL SCOTS FUSILIERS'. This item is the same basic design as the Royal Inniskilling Fusiliers title (*1107*) worn during the Tirah Campaign of 1897-98. the Royal Scots Fusiliers also served with the Tirah Expeditionary Force.

The Cheshire Regiment
Territorial Battalions
T | 5 | CHESHIRE

The Royal Welsh Fusiliers
Volunteer Battalions 1918
3 | CARNARVONSHIRE | V.T.C, this title is of the same design as (*970*).

The Kings Own Scottish Borderers
Volunteer Battalions pre 1908
1 | R | V | GALLOWAY, worn by retired members of the Galloway Volunteer Rifle Corps.

The Gloucester Regiment
Volunteer Battalions 1918
BVR, worn by the Bristol Volunteer Regiment.

The Border Regiment
Volunteer Battalions pre 1908
1 | V | BORDER in w.m.

The Royal Sussex Regiment
Volunteer Battalions 1918
A voided version of (*1090*) has also been noted.

The Royal Hampshire Regiment
Volunteer Battalions 1918
V | TC | PORTSMOUTH, V.T.C | RYDE

The Dorset Regiment
Regular Battalions
It has been suggested that the unidentified item, Castle | DORSET (*1130*), was worn by Boy Scouts in the Dorset area. However, no satisfactory evidence to back this claim has so far been forthcoming. It seems unlikely that the castle and key of Gibraltar, a distinction of the Dorset Regiment, would be allowed as a Boy Scout's badge.

The South Lancashire Regiment
Territorial Battalions
5 | P.W.VOLS, the lower tier of this title is curved.

Sherwood Foresters (Nottinghamshire and Derbyshire Regiment)
Cadets
C | 8 | NOTTS | AND | DERBY, the bottom section of this title is as (*1200*).

Kings Royal Rifle Corps
Cadets
14 | LONDON | C.L.B., C | KRR, worn by Durham members of the Church Lads Brigade 1917-1930.

The Durham Light Infantry
Militia Battalions
Bugle | DURHAM with silver "4" within the ribbons of the bugle. Same pattern as (*1351*).

Volunteer Battalions 1918
1 | VTC | DURHAM, 2 | VTC | DURHAM, 4 | VTC | DURHAM, 5 | VTC | DURHAM, 6 | VTC | DURHAM, 8 | VTC | DURHAM

Territorial Battalions
T | DURHAM A greatcoat title worn by all battalions.

Cadets
C | 8 | bugle | DURHAM, worn by the Chester-le-Street Parish church Cadet Company which was affiliated to the 8th Battalion.

Highland Light Infantry
Service Battalions
18 | bugle | HLI

Cadets
Bugle | BEARDMORE, worn by the Bearmore Cadet Corps which was affiliated to the 7th Bn. The lower portion of the title is solid.

Seaforth Highlanders
Territorial Battalions
T | 4/5 | SEAFORTH, a three piece title.

The Gordon Highlanders
Territorial Battalions
T | 5/7 | GORDON, a three piece title.

The Argyll and Sutherland Highlanders
Volunteer Battalions pre 1908
DRV, three separate w.m. letters one inch high. Worn by the 1st Dumbartonshire Rifle Volunteer Corps 1887-1908.

Cadets
OBAN | CC | HIGH SCHOOL, affiliated to the 8th Bn. The title is in three straight lines.

The Parachute Regiment
(1439) has also been noted in gold anodised.

Infantry Regiments Formed Since 1959

The Royal Highland Fusiliers
RHF (*1456*) is now worn in gold anodised.

The Queen's Lancashire Regiment
QUEEN'S | LANCASHIRE, gold anodised and in two straight lines. Introduced in 1983.

The Duke of Edinburgh's Royal Regiment
DERR in gold anodised is now worn by the regiment.

The Royal Regiment of Gloucestershire and Hampshire
It was intended to form the above regiment in 1970 by the amalgamation of the Gloucester and Royal Hampshire Regiments. The merger did not take place and the straight anodised title, RRGH, never used.

Territorial Army and Volunteer Reserve
Wessex Volunteers
The title, WESSEX (*1469*), with a black background is worn by the 1st Battalion. The 2nd have blue.

Territorial Regiments

The Honourable Artillery Company
The small HAC title (1478), in chromium plate was worn together with a crown over SC, also in chrome, by the Special Constabulary section of the H.A.C.

The London Regiment
8th Battalion
Two interseting titles have been discovered that were worn by "M" Company of the 24th Middlesex Rifle Volunteers. The 24th was formed from Post Office workers and in 1882 had a scheme approved for the formation of of a company of volunteers willing to undertake all postal duties connected with an army on active service overseas. The new unit was to be known as the "Army Post Office Corps" and between 1882 and 1885 adopted a bronze title consisting of two curved pieces, POST OFFICE | CORPS. the brass letters POC were offered as a shoulder title in a Regimental Order dated February 1900.

13th Battalion
The title, C | WEST END.R.PK. was worn the West End (Ravenscourt Park) Cadet Corps which was affiliated to the 13th Bn.

Royal Marines

Royal Marine Engineers
A larger version of (*1602*) has been noted.

Royal Marine Bands
A wider version of (*1604*), open at the top, has been noted.

Royal Marine Submarine Miners
Formed towards the end of 1914 from members of the Tyne Electrical Engineers. The title, RMSM, is the same pattern as that worn by the Royal Military School of Music (*1808*).

Royal Naval Division

Members of the Divisional Engineers also wore a separate "E" above the curved R.N.D. (*1616*).

Schools and Training Establishments

The Officers Training Corps

A much larger version of the Manchester Unversity title, (*1641*), has been noted. The title recorded for Southampton University should read, SOUTHAMPTON | O.T.C | UNIV.COLL. Both (*1647*) and (*1632*) are titles worn after 1922 by units of the Irish Free State. The Grimsby College title, (*1716*), has also been noted in w.m. and Buckland School was redesignated West Buckland in 1913 and not the reserve as stated. New titles to be noted are; CORK | OTC | GRAMMAR SCHOOL, MODERN | O.T.C | SCHOOL (Bedford Modern School), MSM | OTC (Mount St. Mary's College), SANDWICH | O.T.C | SCHOOL (Sir Roger Manwood's School), UNITED SERVICES | OTC | COLLEGE, ST ANDREW'S | OTC | COLLEGE.

Miscellaneous Units

The Catholic Boys Brigade
CBB

War Correspondents
FRENCH | WAR | CAMERAMAN, worn during the Second World War.

The Haverfield Mission
HAVERFIELD MISSION | SERBIA, worn by members of the mission formed during the First World War by the Hon. Evelina Haverfield.

Imperial Camel Corps
IMPERIAL | CAMEL CORPS, an oval title.

Training Reserve
TR, one inch high letters. The Training Reserve was formed in 1916 from 2nd Reserve and local reserve infantry battalions.

Volunteer Training Corps
New titles noted are: WEST LONDON REGT. | V.T.C. | KENSINGTON, WEST LONDON REGT. | V.T.C | HAMMERSMITH both these items are of the same basic design as that shown in (*1856*). VTC | CADETS, PHARMACISTS | VTC.

Cavalry Regiments

The Royal Scots Dragoon Guards (Carabiniers & Greys)
SCOTSDG – introduced in 1995. Anodised and in a straight line.

The Royal Dragoon Guards
RDG – formed in 1992 by the amalgamation of the 4th/7th Royal Dragoon Guards and 5th Royal Inniskilling Dragoon Guards. Brass for officers, anodised for soldiers.

The 5th Royal Inniskilling Dragoon Guards
5R.INNISD.GDS – post 1935 and in a straight line.

The Queen's Royal Hussars (Queen's Own and Royal Irish)
QRH – formed in 1993 by the amalgamation of the Queen's Own Hussars and Queen's Royal Irish Hussars. Brass for officers, anodised for soldiers.

The Royal Hussars
ROYAL|HUSSARS – as No.120 but in brass for officers.

The Kings Royal Hussars
KRH – formed in 1992 by the amalgamation of the Royal Hussars and 14th/20th King's Hussars. Brass for officers, anodised for soldiers.

The Light Dragoons
LIGHT/DRAGOONS – formed in 1992 by the amalgamation of the 13th/18th Royal Hussars and 15th/19th King's Royal Hussars. Brass for officers, anodised for soldiers and in two straight lines.

The Queen's Royal Lancers
QRL – formed in 1993 by the amalgamation of the 16th/5th and 17th/21st Lancers. Bronzed-brass for all ranks.

The Royal Tank Regiment
RTR – very small brass pattern worn by officers.

Yeomanry Regiments

The Scottish Yeomanry
SCOTS YEO – formed in 1992 from Lothians and Border Horse, Ayrshire, Lanarkshire and Queen's Own Royal Glasgow and Fife and Forfar/Scottish Horse Yeomanries. Anodised and in a straight line.

Royal Artillery

Volunteers c1905-1908 unless otherwise stated

1 | RA | FIFE – white metal.

2 | RA | KENT – white metal.

1 | RA | LANCASHIRE – white metal.Number is separate from the rest of the title.

2 | RA | SUSSEX – white metal.

THE | RA | TYNEMOUTH – white metal.

TAV – Tynemouth Artillery Volunteers c1900. White metal.

K.A.V – Kent Artillery Volunteers c1900. White metal.

1 | RA | WARWICKSHIRE – white metal.

RGA | V – general pattern. White metal.

Territorials

T | RFA | FIFESHIRE – Fifeshire Battery, 2nd Highland Brigade, Royal Field Artillery.

T | RFA | AYRESHIRE – Ayreshire Battery, 2nd Lowland Brigade, Royal Field Artillery.

T | RFA | NORTHAMPTONSHIRE – Northampton Battery, 4th East Anglian Brigade, Royal Field Artillery.

T | RGA | PEMBROKESHIRE

T | RGA | EAST RIDING

C | HAC and D | HAC – 12th Regiment Royal Horse Artillery (H.A.C.)(T.A.) Formed in 1939.

RA | CITY OF LONDON – 53rd (City of London) H.A.A. Regiment R.A. (T.A.). India, 1942-45. Cast brass. The letters RA have a bar running across the top and the lower line is curved. A wider version exists that has no bar across the RA and larger letters.

265 -265th L.A.A. Regiment R.A. (T.A.) 1955-1967.

Cadets

C | RFA | EAST ANGLIAN – 1st Cadet Battery, 85th (East Anglian) Field Brigade.

2 | C | RFA | N.RIDING – No.2 (North Riding) Cadet Battery. Recognised in 1916 and affiliated to 2nd Northumbrian Brigade, R.F.A.

C | RA | 1STW.LANCS – "C"(Countess of Sefton's Own) Cadet Battery. Formed 1933 and affiliated to 87th (1st West Lancashire) Field Brigade, R.A.(T.A.).

Arms and Services

Royal Army Medical Corps

V | RAMC | Welsh Border. White metal title worn by Welsh Border Brigade Company at Hereford.

The Royal Logistics Corps

RLC – formed in 1993 from postal and courier elements of the Royal

Engineers,the Royal Corps of Transport, part of the Royal Army Ordnance Corps, the Royal Pioneer Corps and the Army Catering Corps.

The Royal Army Education Corps
RAEC – as No.401 but in blackened brass. Worn by officers attached to the Gurkhas in Hong Kong during 1980s.

Infantry Regiments

The Queen's Royal Regiment (West Surrey)
CROYDON | CADETS | HIGH SCHOOL – Croydon High School Cadet Corps was recognised in October 1919 and affiliated to the 4th Battalion. Absorbed into 1st Cadet Battalion in 1919. An oval solid title, the centre line straight.

The Princess of Wales's Royal Regiment (Queen's and Royal Hampshire)
PRINCESS OF WALES'S – formed in 1992 by the amalgamation of the Queen's and Royal Hampshire Regiments. Bronzed Brass and curved.

The West Yorkshire Regiment
15 | W.YORK – 15th Battalion c1914-1918.
21 | W.YORK – 21st Battalion c1914-1918.

The Princess of Wales's Own Regiment of Yorkshire
PWO | YORKSHIRE – introduced in 1994 while serving in Bosnia. Brass for officers and anodised for soldiers.
YORKSHIRE – Yorkshire Volunteers c1991. Worn by officers and NCOs and in a straight line.

The Royal Scots Fusiliers
T | ARDEER | RSF | COMPANY – similiar to No.952. RSF in the centre of the oval.

The Cheshire Regiment
LHS | 4 | CHESHIRE – Liscard High School cadets. Recognised in 1914 and affiliated to 4th Battalion, Cheshire Regiment.

The Royal Irish Regiment
ROYAL IRISH – formed in 1992 by the almalgamation of the Royal Irish Rangers and Ulster Defence Regiment. As No.917 but in blackened-brass.

The Royal Gloucestershire, Berkshire and Wiltshire Regiment
RGBW – formed in 1994 by the amalgamtion of the Gloucestershire and duke of Edinburgh's Royal Regiments. Brass for officers and anodised for soldiers.

The Royal Hampshire Regiment
R.HAMPSHIRE – As No.1101 but in gold anodised.

The Dorset Regiment
DORSET – in a straight line.

The South Lancashire Regiment
SOUTH | LANCASHIRE – top line straight, bottom curved.

The Essex Regiment
C | 5 | ESSEX – 5th (Schools) Cadet Battalion. Recognised in 1916 with headquarters at South Woodford.

The Loyal North Lancashire Regiment
BSCC – Bolton School Cadet Corps. Recognised in 1915 as Bolton Grammar School Cadet Corps and affiliated to 5th Battalion, Loyal North Lancashire Regiment. Redesignated 1919.

The Highland Light Infantry
GLASGOW | C.C | ACADEMY – affiliated to 1st Volunteer Battalion. Became Glasgow Academy O.T.C. after 1908. See No.1711.

The Gordon Highlanders
LONDON | SCOTTISH | GORDONS – top and bottom lines curved, centre straight.

The Highlanders (Seaforth, Gordons and Camerons)
THE | HIGHLANDERS – formed in1994 by the amalgamation of the Queen's Own and Gordon Highlanders. Brass for officers, anodised for soldiers. When the new regiment was first formed, soldiers were instructed to remove the "QO" from thier existing titles – QO | HIGHLANDERS. Thus leaving the deeply curved HIGHLANDERS. The style of the new title is as the previous pattern but with "THE" replacing "QO".

The Queen's Division Band
QUEEN'S | DIVISION – introduced in 1994. Anodised and in two straight lines.

The King's Division Band
KING'S DIVISION – introduced in 1994. Anodised and in two straight lines.

The London Regiment
C | 10 | LONDON – 10th Battalion, London Regiment Cadet Corps. Recognised in 1914.
LIR – London Irish Rifles officer's and senior N.C.O's title worn c1939-45. Blackened brass.
ARTISTS – a curved title worn by the Artists Rifles. Blackened brass.

LONDON | REGIMENT – formed in 1993 from companies of 8th Queen's Fusiliers, London Scottish and London Irish. Anodised and in straight lines.

The Hertfordshire Regiment
T | HARTS – this wording was submitted in 1908 but rejected by the War Office.

Women's Units

Territorial Army Nursing Service
TANS – in a straight line and worn after 1921.

Queen Alexandra's Imperial Military Nursing Service
QAIMNS – in straight line.
QAIMNSR – (Reserve). Also straight as above but longer and larger letters.

Volunteer Service League
V.S.L – as shown at No.1816. The correct designation of the units as above. Not Volunteer Service Legion as shown.

Schools and Training Establishments

ETON | OTC | COLLEGE – as No.1704 but in brass.
OTC | RUGBY – as No.1772 but in two pieces.
W.R.G.S | J.T.C. – Royal Grammar School, Worcester Junior Training Corps. The Junior Division, Officers Training Corps was redesignated as Junior Training Corps in September, 1940. Top line curved, bottom straight.

Miscellaneous Units

T | 86 | KVAD – 86th Kent Volunteer Aid Detachment. This unit was raised in 1912 at Beckenham. the title has been constructed from three separate items, the "T" and "6" from a 16th London Regiment title. Lower line is curved.

Volunteer Training Corps

MT | CC | ROYAL BERKS – Maidenhead Town Cadet Company. Recognised in May, 1918 and affiliated to 1st Battalion, Berkshire Volunteer Regiment. Disbanded 1921.

BIBLIOGRAPHY

Shoulder-belt Plates and Buttons, Major H.G. Parkyn OBE
Military Insignia of Cornwall, D. Endean Ivall and Charles Thomas
Regimental Badges (6 Editions), Major T. J. Edwards MBE
Military Badge Collecting, John Gaylor
His Majesty's Territorial Army, W. Richards
A Register of the Regiments and Corps of the British Army, A. Swinson
The Uniforms of the London-Scottish 1859–1959, J. O. Robson
Rank and Badges in Her Majesty's Army and Navy, O. L. Perry
Lineage Book of the British Army, J. B. M. Fredrick
British Infantry Regiments 1914–18, Brigadier E. A. James OBE,TD
The Shropshire Yeomanry, G. A. Parfitt
Dress of the Royal Artillery 1898–1959, Major D. A. Cambell
The Highland Light Infantry Uniforms 1881–1914, J. B. McKay & D. N. Anderson
Head-dress Badges of the British Army, A. L. Kipling & H. L. King
Hertfordshire Soldiers, Major J. D. Sainsbury TD
Records of the Scottish Volunteer Force 1859–1908, Lieut-General Sir J. Grierson
Bulletins of the Military Historical Society
Journals of the Society of Army Historical Research
Army Lists
Army Orders
Dress Regulations
Clothing Regulations
Priced Vocabulary of Clothing and Necessaries
Generally Regimental Histories have not been of much help in dating shoulder titles. One exception, however, is *The King's Own, The Story of a Royal Regiment*, Vol. 11 by Colonel L. I. Cowper OBE.

D

1

H

2

L

3

DG

4

D-G

5

D-G

6

D-G

7

LG

8

LG

9

LG

10

RHG

11

RHG

12

BLUES & ROYALS

13

14

HB

15

16

K
D-G

17

18

19

1 D G

20

Plate 1

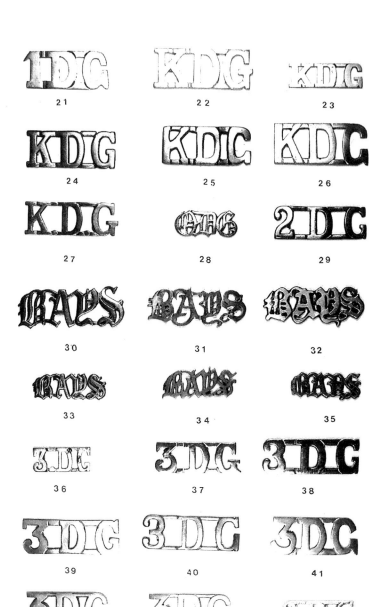

2 1

2 2

2 3

2 4

2 5

2 6

2 7

2 8

2 9

3 0

3 1

3 2

3 3

3 4

3 5

3 6

3 7

3 8

3 9

4 0

4 1

4 2

4 3

4 4

Plate 2

45

46

47

48

49

50

51

52

53

54

55

56

57

58

59

60

61

62

63

64

65

Plate 3

66

67

68

69

70

71

72

73

74

75

76

77

78

79

80

81

82

83

84

85

86

Plate 4

87

88

89

90

91

92

93

94

95

96

97

98

99

100

101

102

103

104

105

106

107

108

Plate 5

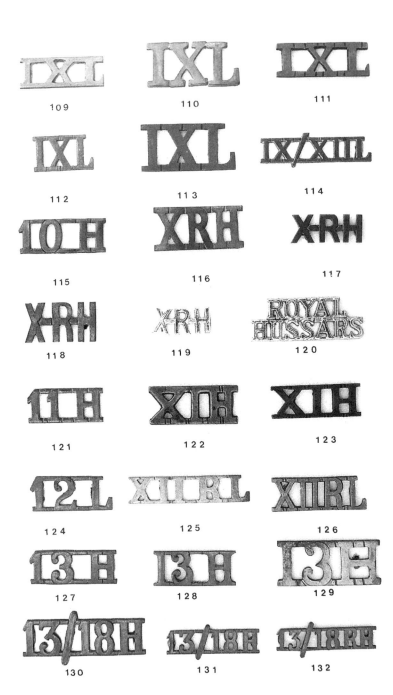

109

110

111

112

113

114

115

116

117

118

119

120

121

122

123

124

125

126

127

128

129

130

131

132

Plate 6

133

134

135

136

137

138

139

140

141

142

143

144

145

146

147

148

149

150

151

152

153

154

155

156

157

Plate 7

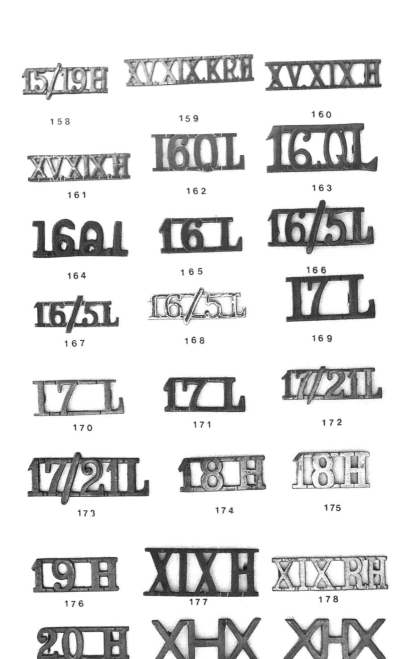

158

159

160

161

162

163

164

165

166

167

168

169

170

171

172

173

174

175

176

177

178

179

180

181

Plate 8

182

183

184

185

186

187

188

189

190

191

192

193

194

195

196

197

198

199

200

201

Plate 9

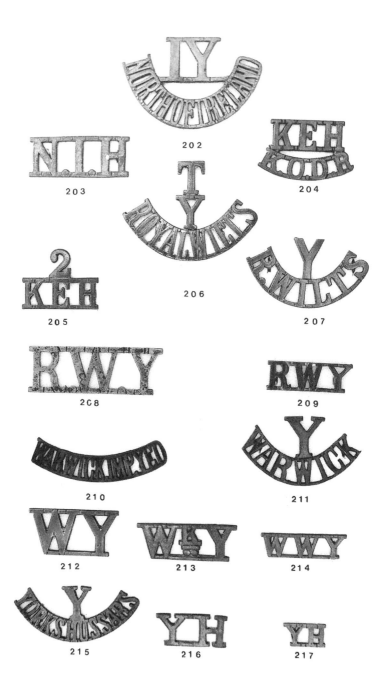

Plate 10

218

219

220

221

222 SRY

223 SRY

224

225

226

227

228 ATY

229

230

231 AY

Plate 11

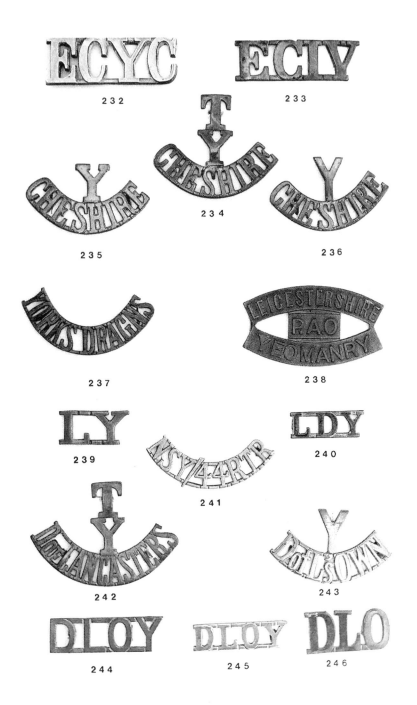

232

233

234

235

236

237

238

239

240

241

242

243

244

245

246

Plate 12

247

248

249

250

251

252

253

254

255

256

257

258

259

260

261

Plate 13

262

263

264

265

266

268

267

269

270

271

272

273

274

275

Plate 14

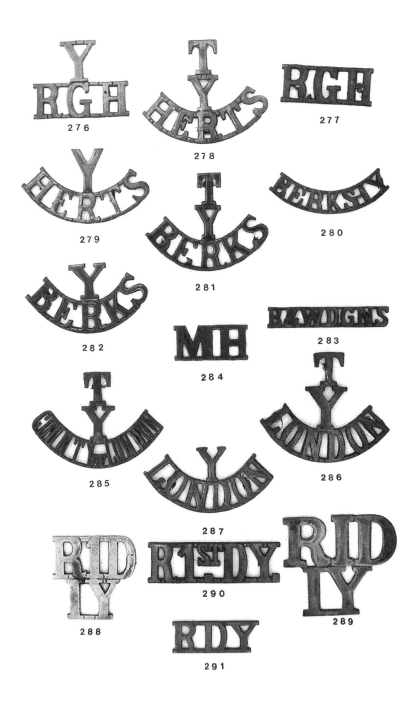

276

277

278

279

280

281

282

283

284

285

286

287

288

289

290

291

Plate 15

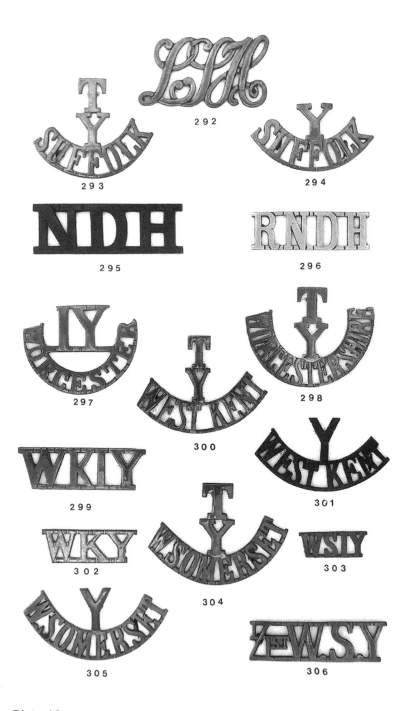

Plate 16

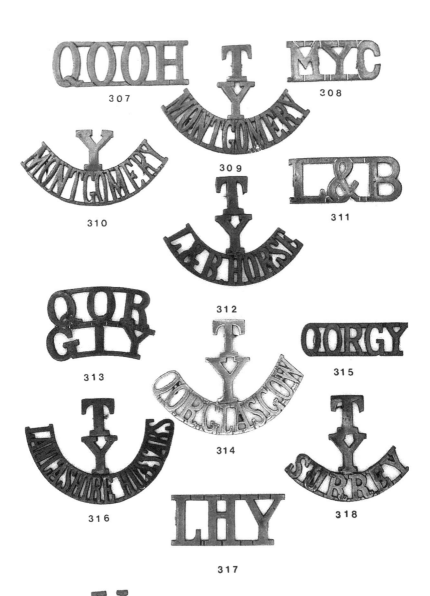

307

T
Y
MONTGOMERY
309

308

Y
MONTGOMERY
310

L&B
311

T
Y
L.&B.HORSE
312

QOR
GLY
313

T
Y
QORGTASICOY
314

QORGY
315

T
Y
LANCASHIRE HUSSARS
316

LHY
317

T
Y
SURREY
318

Y
SURREY
319

S.&S.YEO
320

Plate 17

321

322

323

324

325

326

327

328

330

329

331

332

333

334

335

336

Plate 18

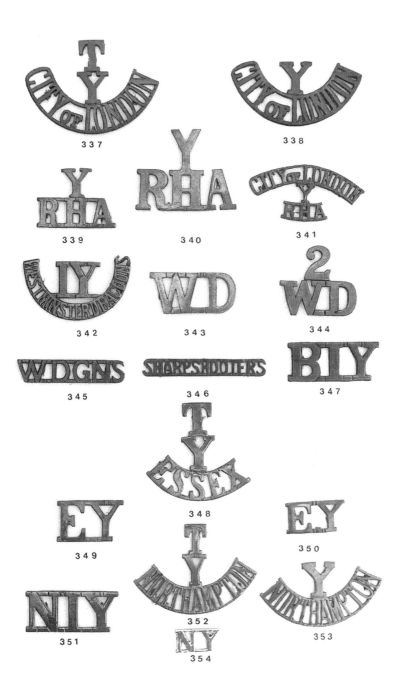

337

338

339

340

341

342

343

344

345

346

347

348

349

350

351

352

NY
354

353

Plate 19

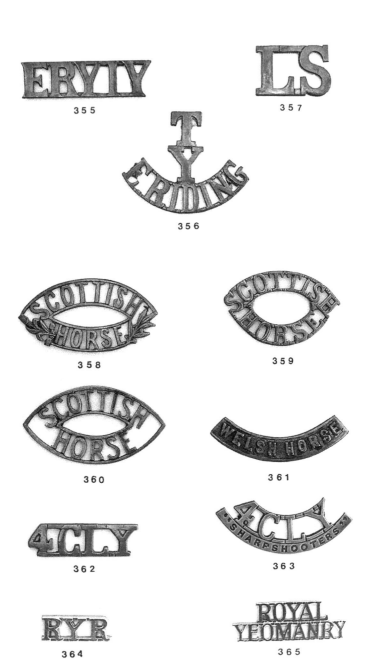

355

357

356

358

359

360

361

362

363

364

365

Plate 20

365

367

368

369

370

371

372

373

374

375

376

377

379

378

380

381

382 383 384 385

386

387

388

389

390

Plate 21

Plate 21

391

392

393

394

396

395

397

398

399

400

401

402

403

404

405

406

407

408

409

410

411

Plate 22

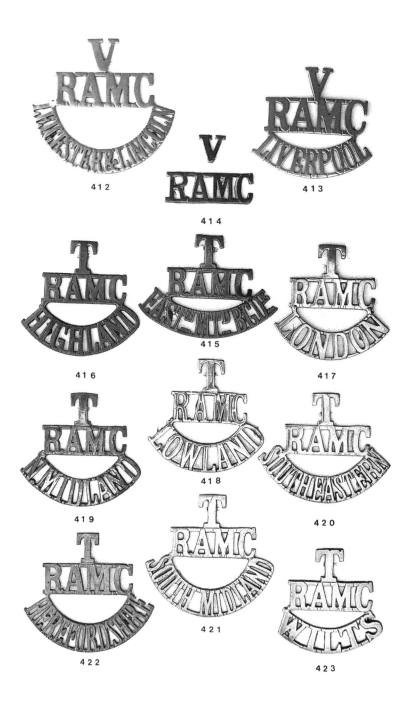

412

413

414

415

416

417

418

419

420

421

422

423

Plate 23

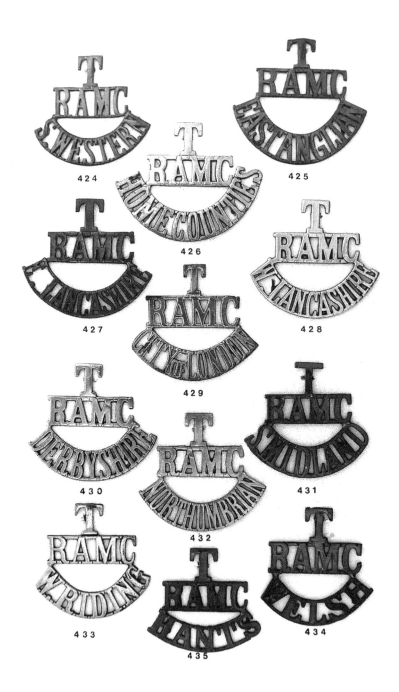

424

425

426

427

428

429

430

431

432

433

434

435

Plate 24

436

437

438

439

440   441   442

443   444   445

446   447

449   448   450

Plate 25

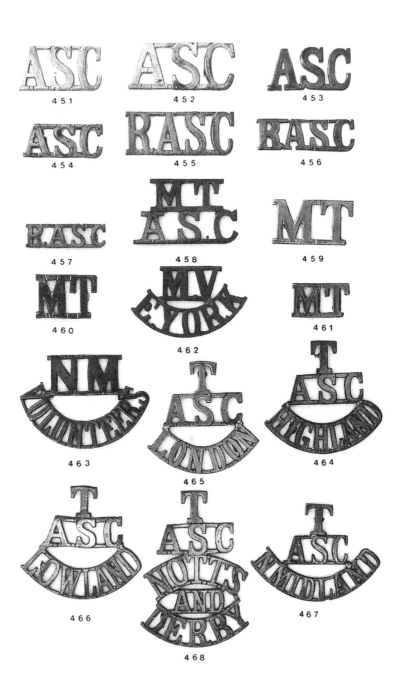

451 452 453

454 455 456

457 458 459

460 462 461

463 465 464

466 468 467

Plate 26

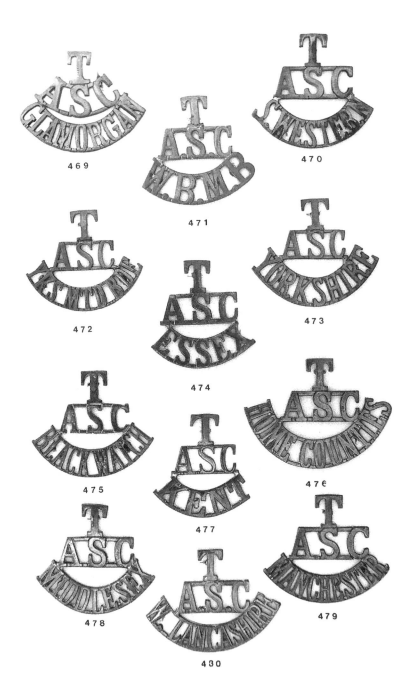

469

471

470

472

474

473

475

477

476

478

480

479

Plate 27

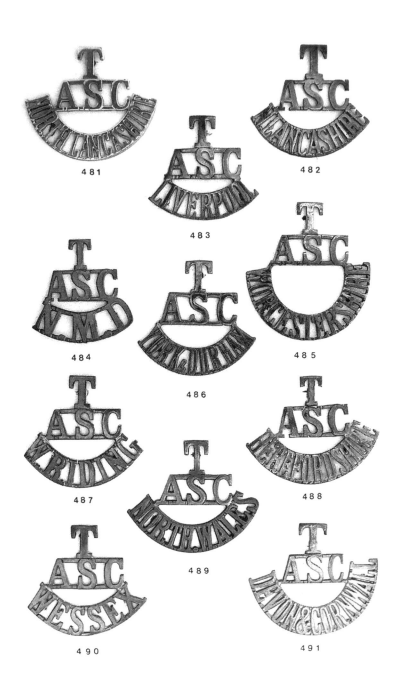

481

483

482

484

486

485

487

488

489

490

491

Plate 28

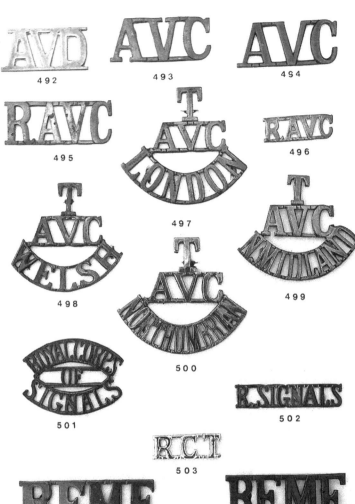

492

493

494

495

497

496

498

500

499

501

R.SIGNALS

502

R.C.T

503

REME

504

REME

505

REME

506

REME

507

508

REME

509

Plate 29

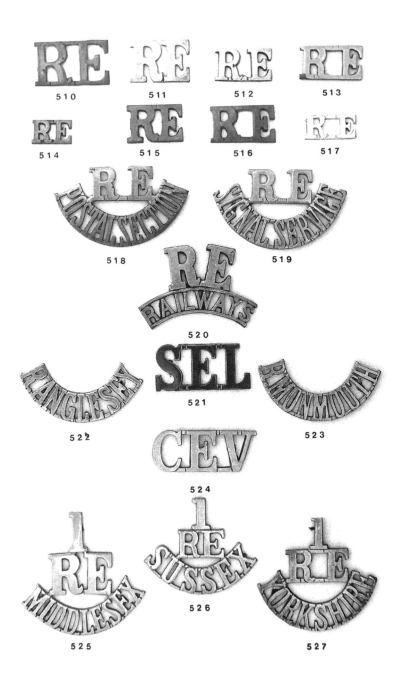

Plate 30

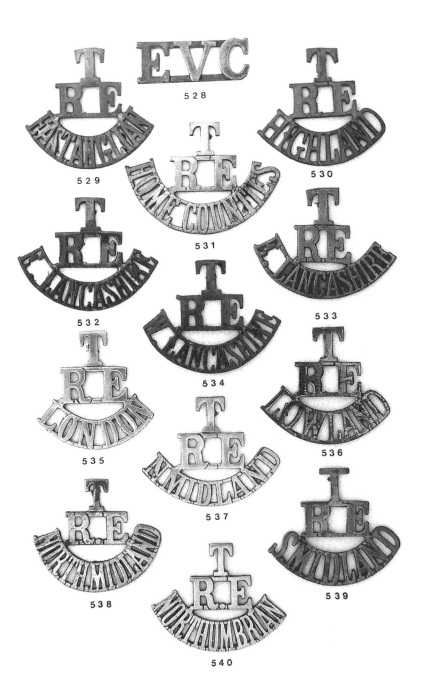

T / R.E / EAST ANGLIAN
529

E.V.C
528

T / R.E / HIGHLAND
530

T / R.E / HOME COUNTIES
531

T / R.E / E. LANCASHIRE
532

T / R.E / E. LANCASHIRE
533

T / R.E / W. LANCASHIRE
534

T / R.E / LONDON
535

T / R.E / N. MIDLAND
537

T / R.E / LOWLAND
536

T / R.E / NORTH MIDLAND
538

T / R.E / NORTHUMBRIAN
540

T / R.E / S. MIDLAND
539

Plate 31

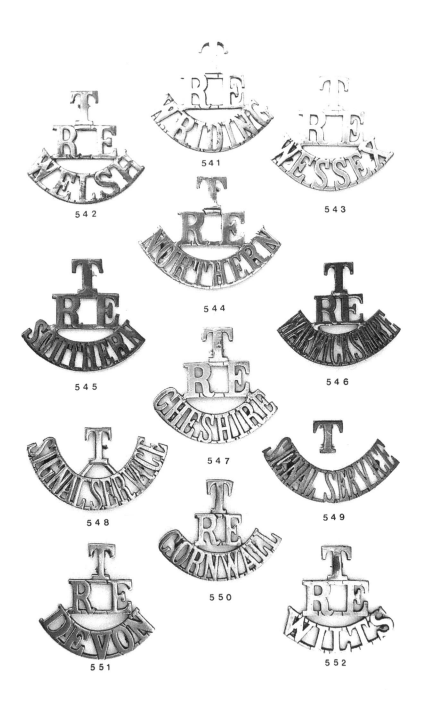

542

541

543

544

545

546

547

548

549

550

551

552

Plate 32

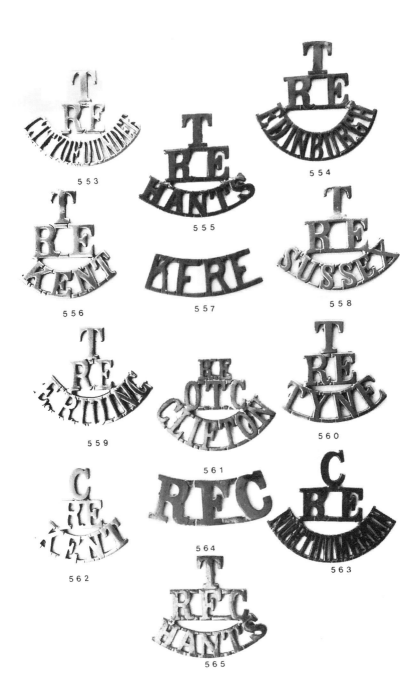

553

554

555

556

557

558

559

560

561

562

563

564

565

Plate 33

566

567

568

569

570

571.

572

573

574

575

576

577

578

579

580

581

582

583

584

585

586

Plate 34

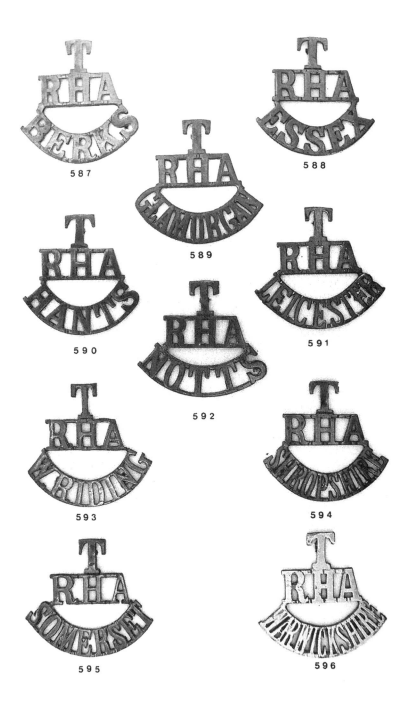

587

588

589

590

591

592

593

594

595

596

Plate 35

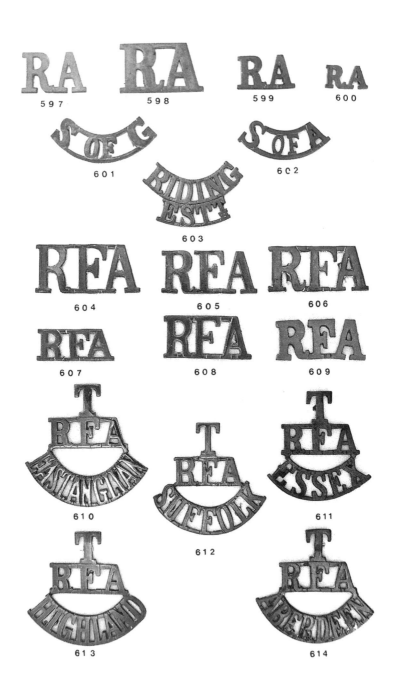

597 598 599 600

601 602

603

604 605 606

607 608 609

610 612 611

613 614

Plate 36

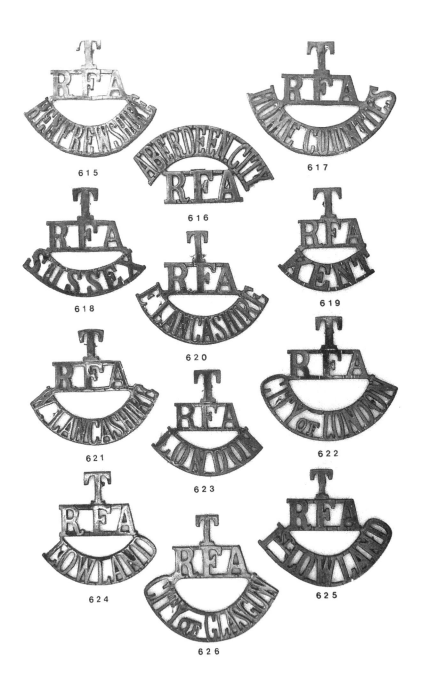

615

616

617

618

619

620

621

622

623

624

625

626

Plate 37

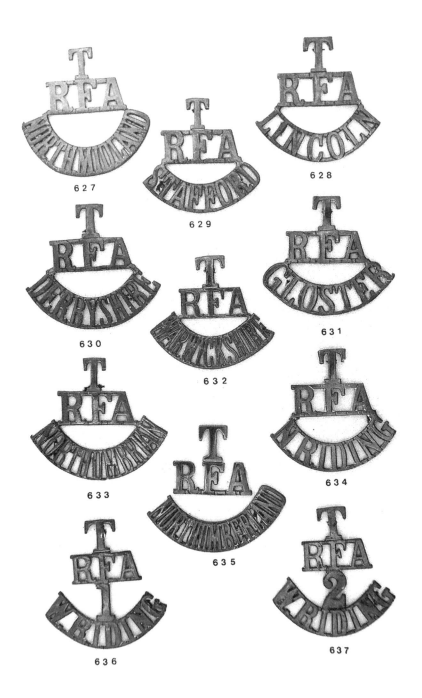

627

628

629

630

631

632

633

634

635

636

637

Plate 38

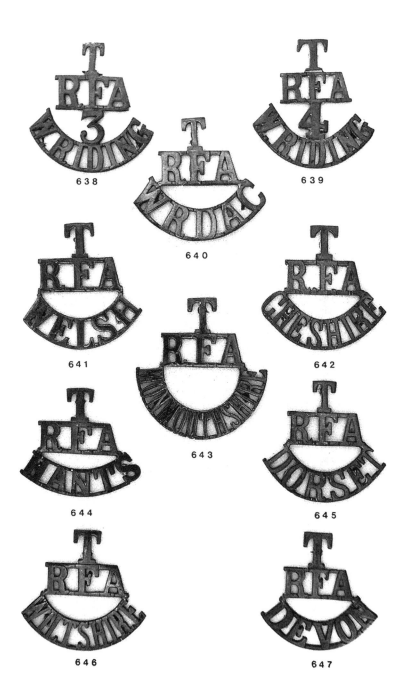

638

639

640

641

642

643

644

645

646

647

Plate 39

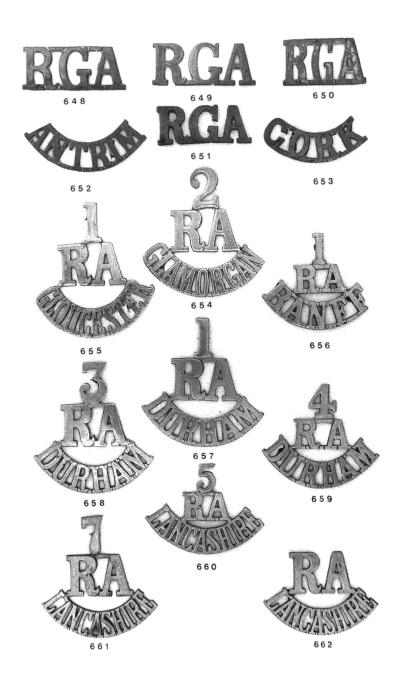

648
649
650
651
652
653
654
655
656
657
658
659
660
661
662

Plate 40

664

663

665

666

667

668

669

670

671

672

673

674

Plate 41

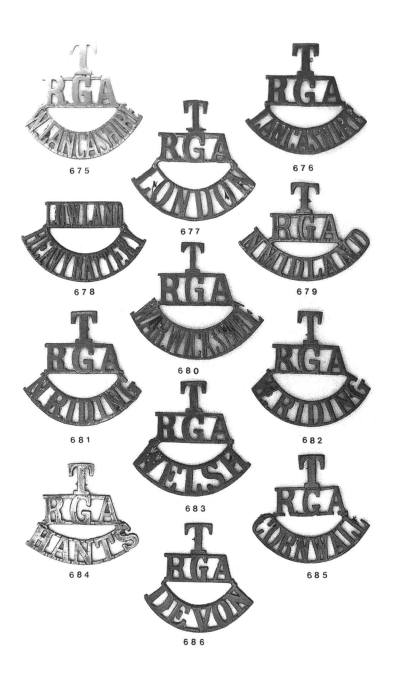

675

676

677

678

679

680

681

682

683

684

685

686

Plate 42

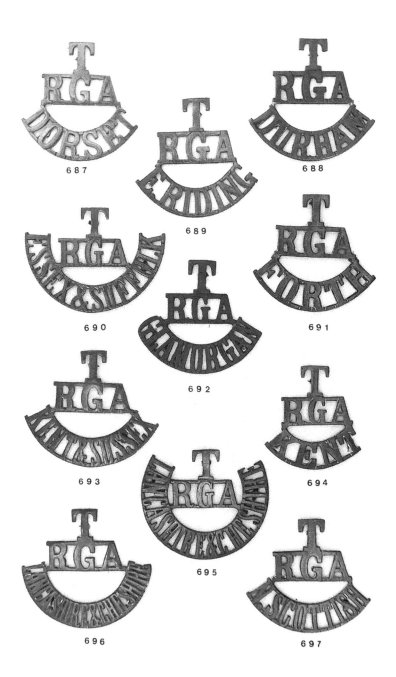

687

688

689

690

691

692

693

694

695

696

697

Plate 43

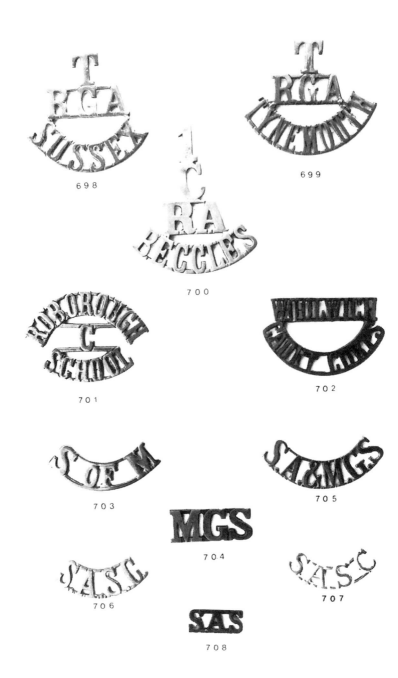

698

699

700

701

702

703

705

704

706

707

708

Plate 44

709

710

711

712

713

714

715

716

Plate 45

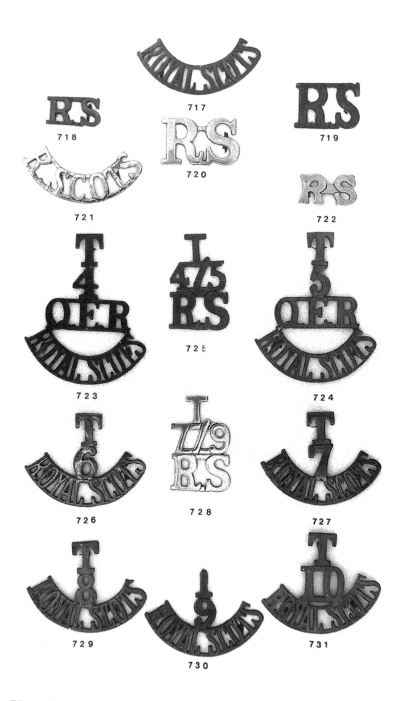

717

718

719

720

721

722

723

725

724

726

728

727

729

730

731

Plate 46

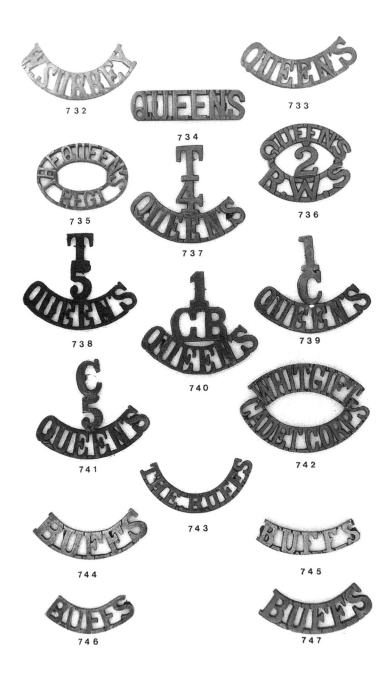

732

733

734

735

736

737

738

739

740

741

742

743

744

745

746

747

Plate 47

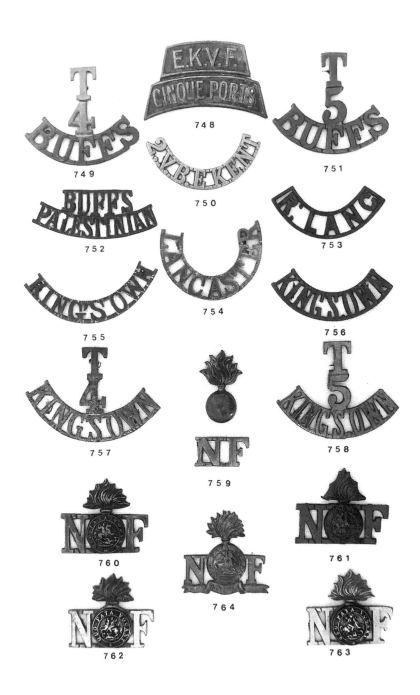

Plate 48

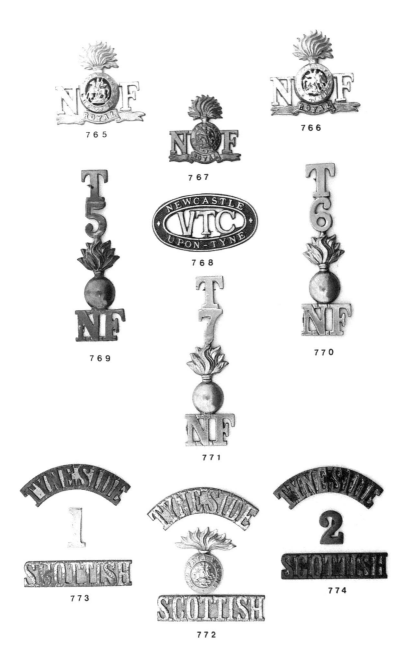

765

767

766

768

769

770

771

773

772

774

Plate 49

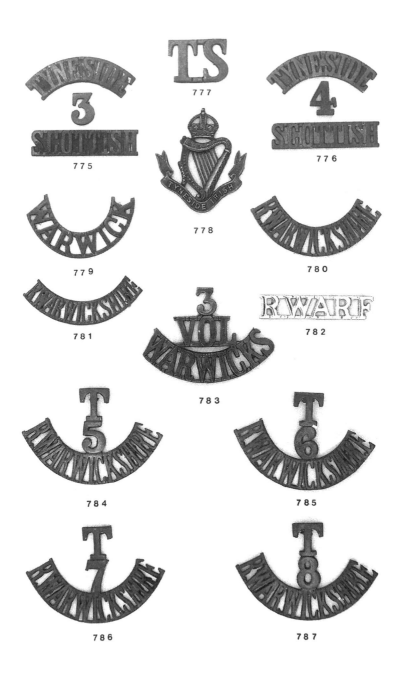

777

775

776

778

779

780

781

782

783

784

785

786

787

Plate 50

788

790

789

791

792

793

794

795

796

797

23

800

798

1 SPORTSMANS RF

799

2 SPORTSMANS RF

801

Plate 51

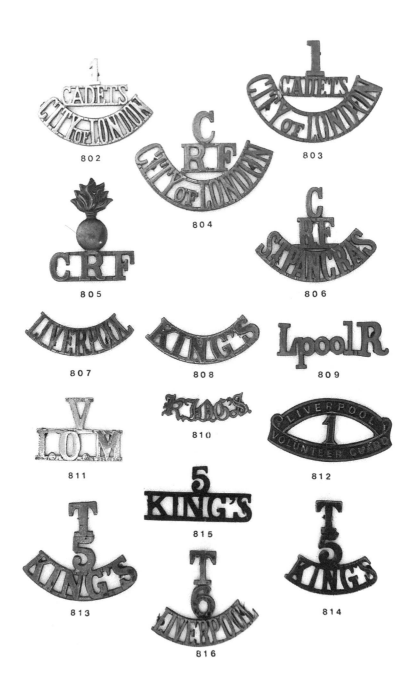

802

803

804

805

806

807

808

809

810

811

812

813

814

815

816

Plate 52

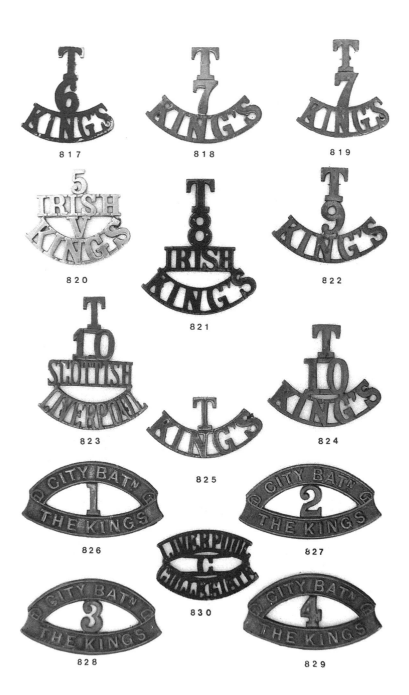

817

818

819

820

821

822

823

825

824

826

827

828

830

829

Plate 53

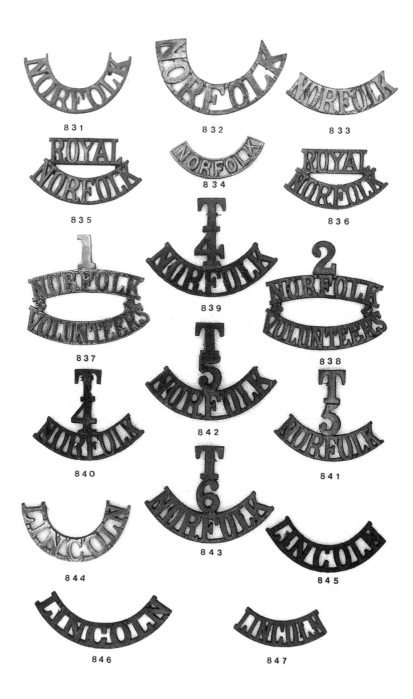

831

832

833

835

834

836

837

839

838

840

842

841

843

844

845

846

847

Plate 54

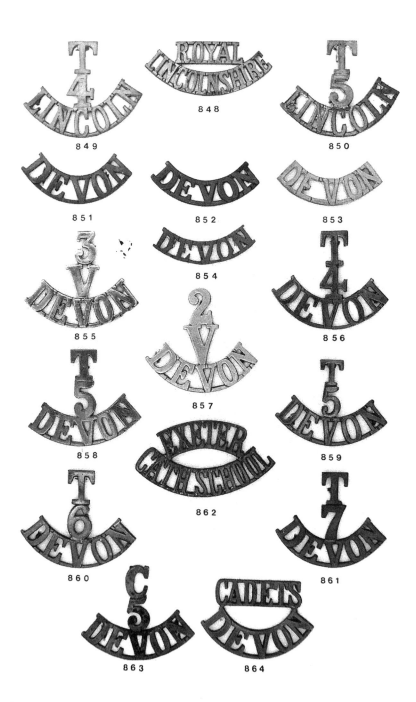

849

848

850

851

852

853

855

854

856

858

857

859

860

862

861

863

864

Plate 55

865

866

867

868

869

870

871

872

873

874

875

876

877

878

879

880

Plate 56

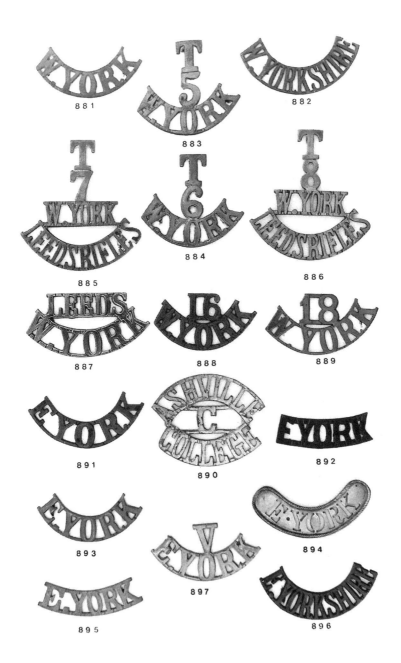

881

883

882

885

884

886

887

888

889

891

890

892

893

897

894

895

896

Plate 57

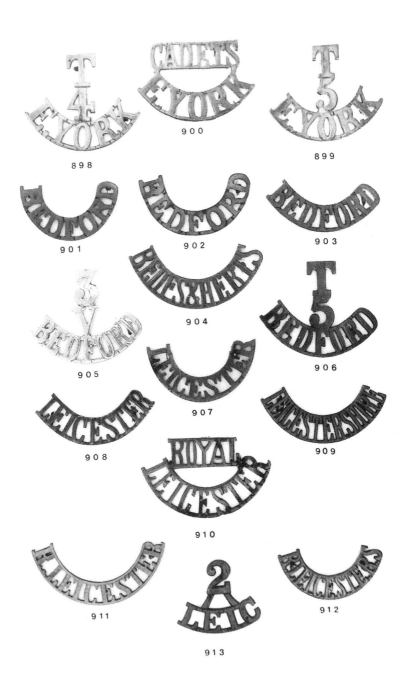

898

900

899

901

902

903

904

905

906

907

908

909

910

911

913

912

Plate 58

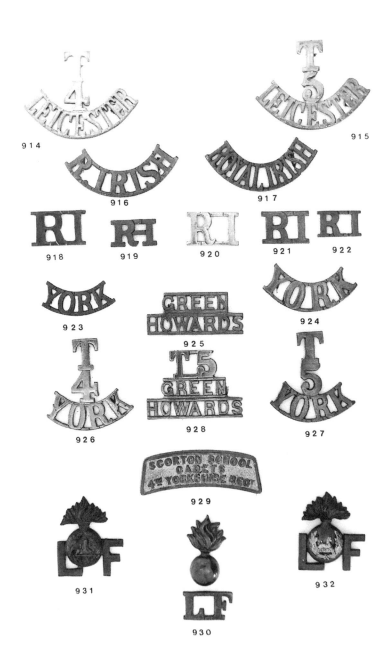

914

915

916

917

918 919 920 921 922

923 924

925

926 928 927

929

931 932

930

Plate 59

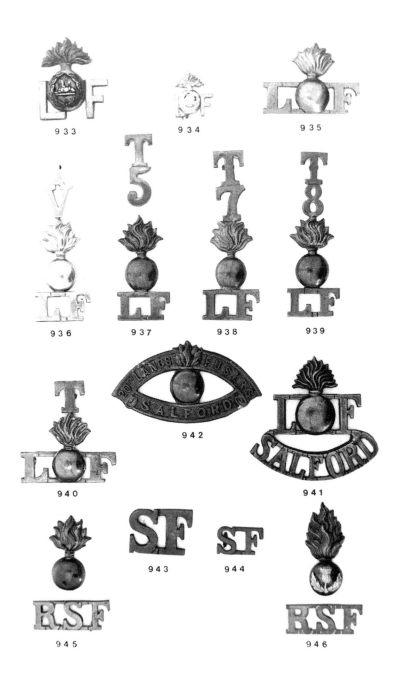

933

934

935

936

937

938

939

940

942

941

943

944

945

946

Plate 60

947

948

949

952

950

953

951

954

955

956

957

959

958

960

961

Plate 61

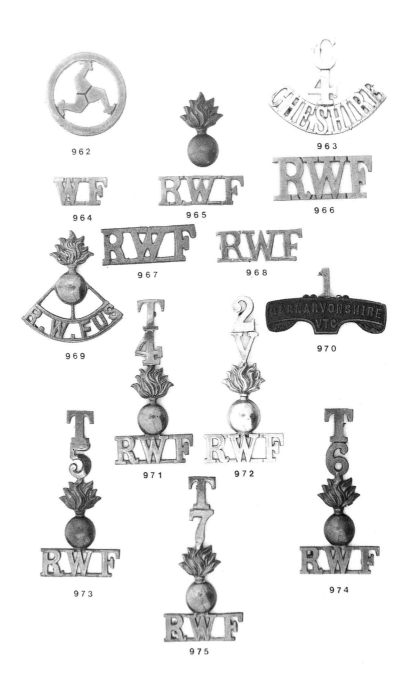

962   963

964   965   966

967   968

969   970

971   972

973   974

975

Plate 62

976

977

978

979

980

981

982

983

984

985

986

987

988

989

990

991

992

993

994

995

996

997

Plate 63

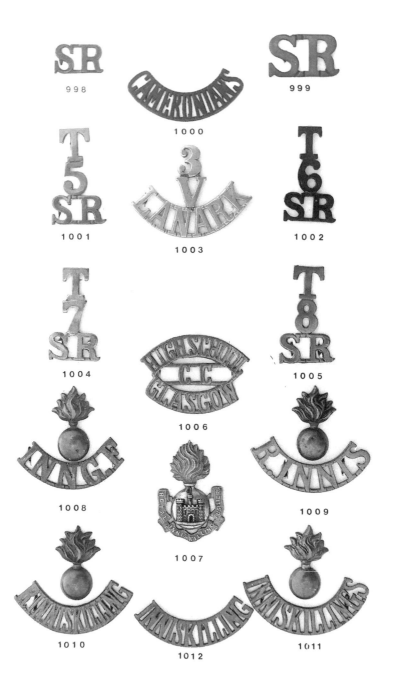

998

1000

999

1001

1003

1002

1004

1006

1005

1008

1007

1009

1010

1012

1011

Plate 64

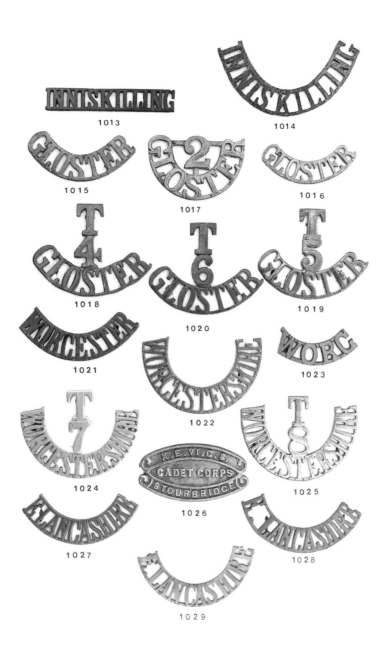

1013

1014

1015

1017

1016

1018

1020

1019

1021

1022

1023

1024

1026

1025

1027

1028

1029

Plate 65

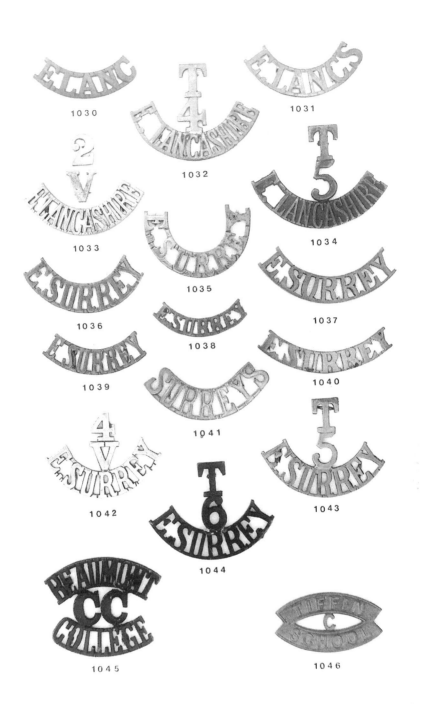

1030

1031

1032

1033

1034

1035

1036

1037

1038

1039

1040

1041

1042

1043

1044

1045

1046

Plate 66

1047

1048

1049

1050

1051

1052

1053

1054

1055

1056

1057

1058

1059

1060

Plate 67

1062

1061

1063

1065

1066

1064

1068

1069

1067

1071

1072

1070

1074

1075

1073

1077

1078

1079

1076

1080

Plate 68

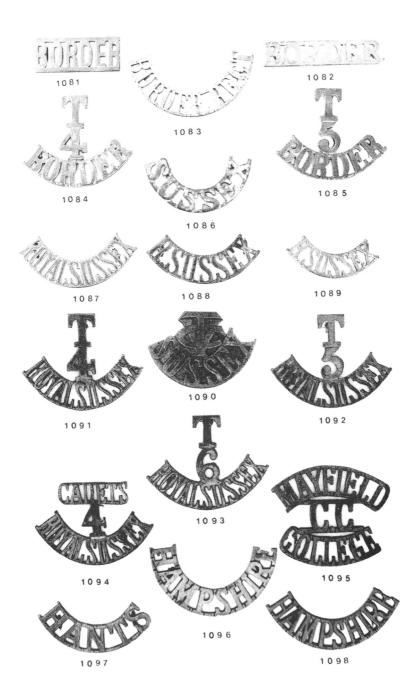

BORDER
1081

BORDERSHIRE
1083

BORDER
1082

T 4 BORDER
1084

SUSSEX
1086

T 5 BORDER
1085

ROYAL SUSSEX
1087

R. SUSSEX
1088

R. SUSSEX
1089

T 4 ROYAL SUSSEX
1091

SUSSEX
1090

T 5 ROYAL SUSSEX
1092

CADETS 4 ROYAL SUSSEX
1094

T 6 ROYAL SUSSEX
1093

MAYFIELD C.C. COLLEGE
1095

HANTS
1097

HAMPSHIRE
1096

HAMPSHIRE
1098

Plate 69

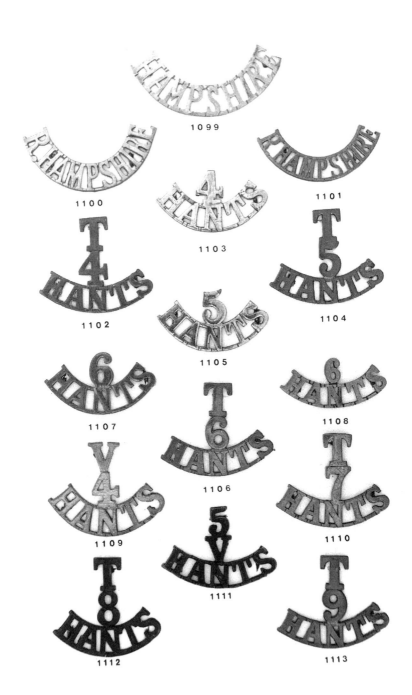

1099

1100

1101

1103

1102

1104

1105

1107

1106

1108

1109

1110

1112

1111

1113

Plate 70

1114

1116

1115

1117

1119

1118

1120

1121

1122

1126

1123

1124

1127

1125

1128

1129

Plate 71

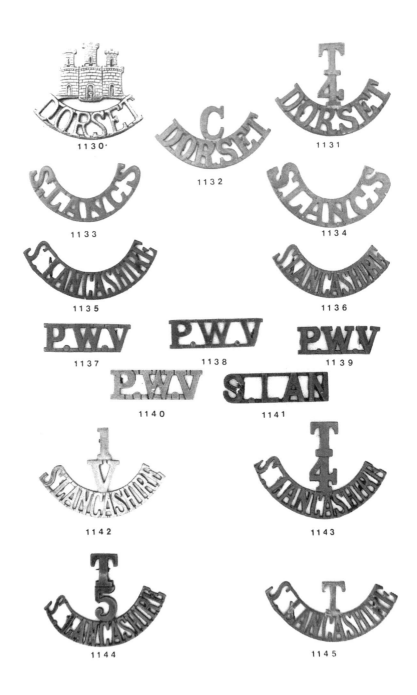

1130

1132

1131

1133

1134

1135

1136

1137

1138

1139

1140

1141

1142

1143

1144

1145

Plate 72

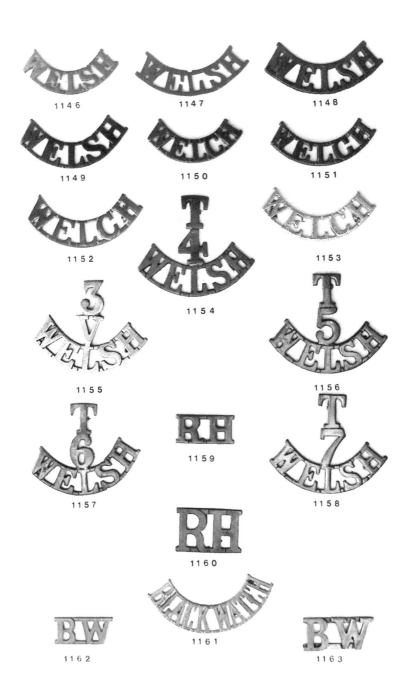

1146 1147 1148 1149 1150 1151 1152 1154 1153 1155 1156 1157 1159 1158 1160 1161 1162 1163

Plate 73

1164   1165   1166   1167   1168

1169   1170   1171

1172   1174   1173

1176   1175   1177

1180

1178   1181   1179

Plate 74

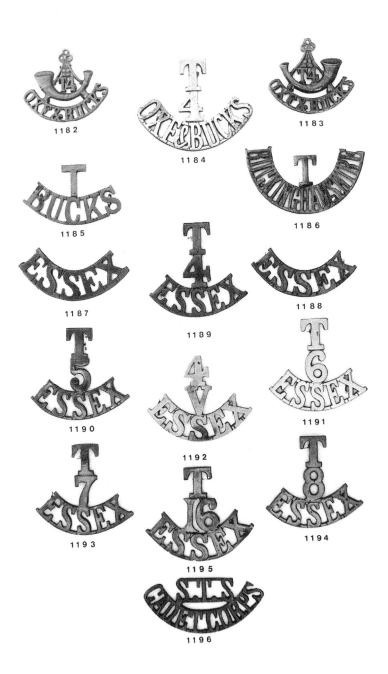

1182

1184

1183

1185

1186

1187

1189

1188

1190

1192

1191

1193

1195

1194

1196

Plate 75

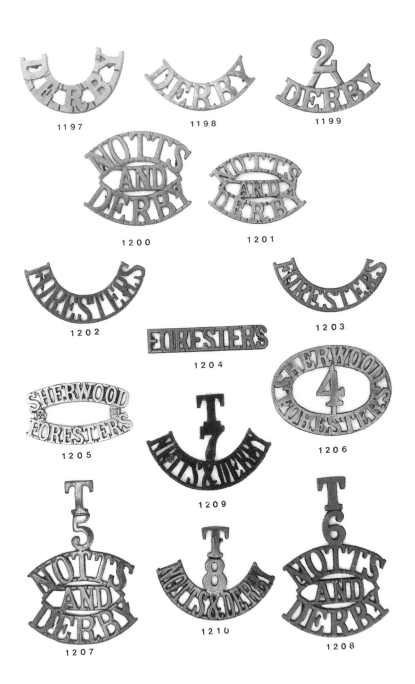

1197

1198

1199

1200

1201

1202

1204

1203

1205

1209

1206

1207

1210

1208

Plate 76

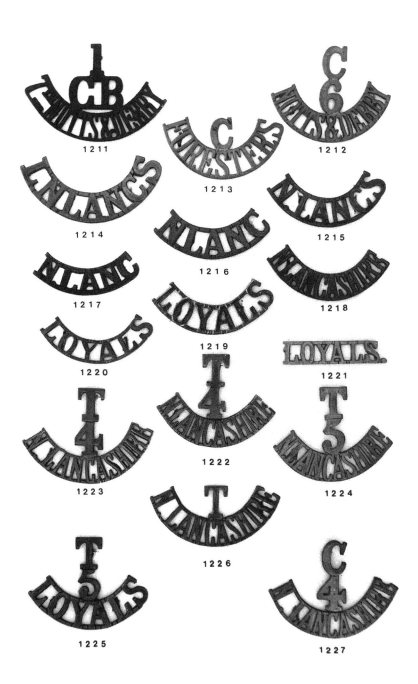

1211

1213

1212

1214

1215

1216

1217

1218

1219

1221

1220

1223

1222

1224

1226

1225

1227

Plate 77

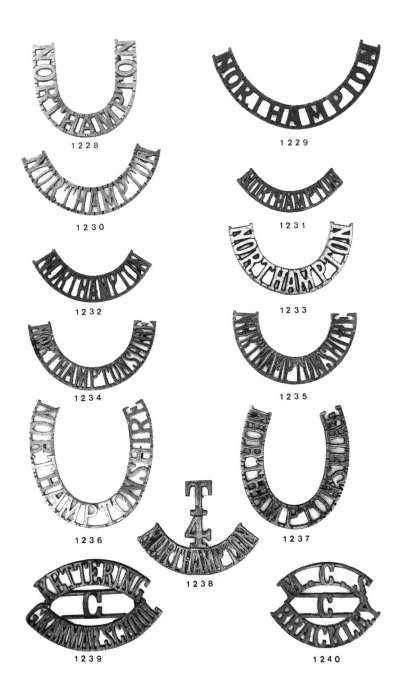

1228

1229

1230

1231

1232

1233

1234

1235

1236

1237

1238

1239

1240

Plate 78

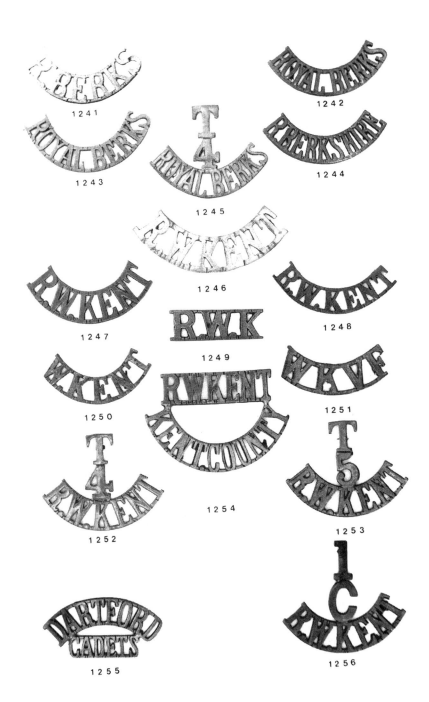

1241

1242

1243

1245

1244

1246

1247

1249

1248

1250

1251

1252

1254

1253

1255

1256

Plate 79

1257

1258

1259

1260

1262

1261

1263

1264

1266

1267

1268

1265

1269

1270

1271

Plate 80

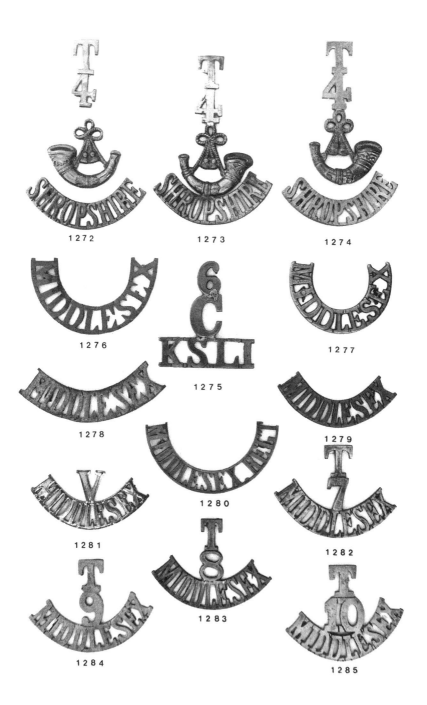

1272

1273

1274

1276

1275

1277

1278

1279

1281

1280

1282

1284

1283

1285

Plate 81

1286

1287

1288

1289

1290

1291

1292

1293

1294

1295

1296

1297

1298

1299

1300

1301

1302

1303

1304

Plate 82

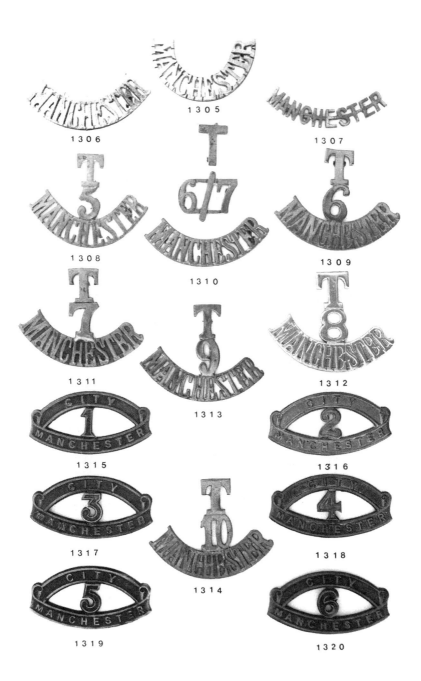

1 3 0 6
1 3 0 5
1 3 0 7
1 3 0 8
1 3 1 0
1 3 0 9
1 3 1 1
1 3 1 3
1 3 1 2
1 3 1 5
1 3 1 6
1 3 1 7
1 3 1 4
1 3 1 8
1 3 1 9
1 3 2 0

Plate 83

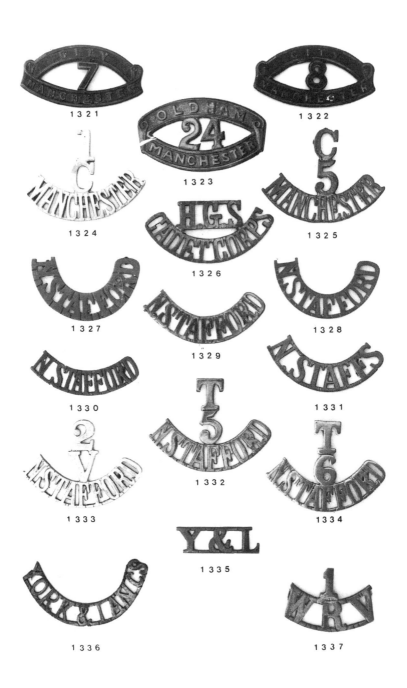

1321

1322

1323

1324

1325

1326

1327

1328

1329

1330

1331

1332

1333

1334

1335

1336

1337

Plate 84

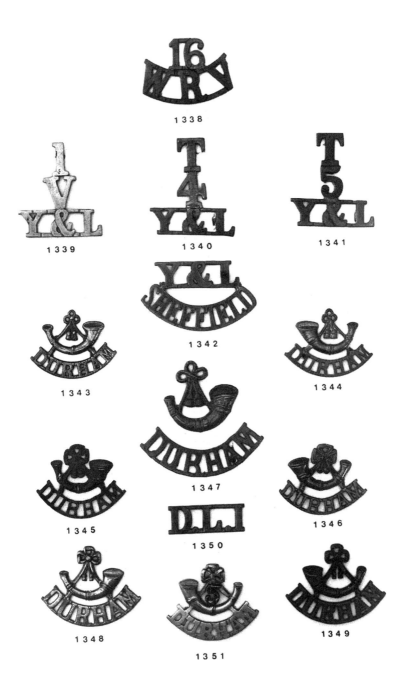

1338

1339

1340

1341

1342

1343

1344

1347

1345

1350

1346

1348

1351

1349

Plate 85

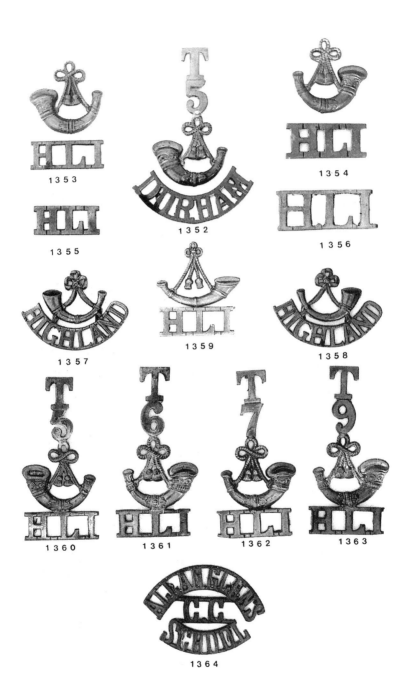

1 3 5 3

1 3 5 5

1 3 5 2

1 3 5 4

1 3 5 6

1 3 5 7

1 3 5 9

1 3 5 8

1 3 6 0

1 3 6 1

1 3 6 2

1 3 6 3

1 3 6 4

Plate 86

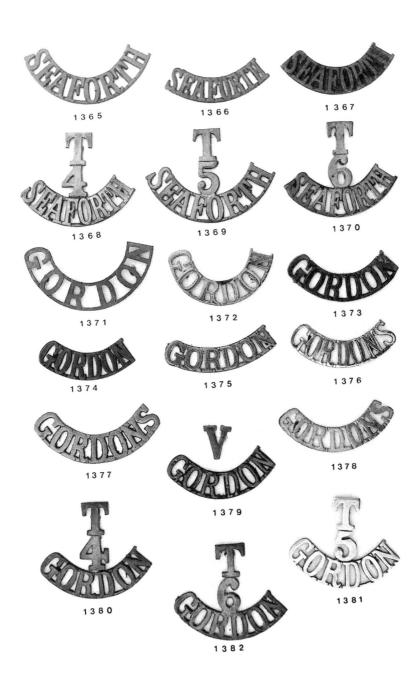

1 3 6 5

1 3 6 6

1 3 6 7

1 3 6 8

1 3 6 9

1 3 7 0

1 3 7 1

1 3 7 2

1 3 7 3

1 3 7 4

1 3 7 5

1 3 7 6

1 3 7 7

1 3 7 9

1 3 7 8

1 3 8 0

1 3 8 2

1 3 8 1

Plate 87

1383   1384   1385

1386   1387   1388

1389

1390   1392   1391

1393   1394   1395   1396

1397   1399   1400   1398

1403

1401   1402

Plate 88

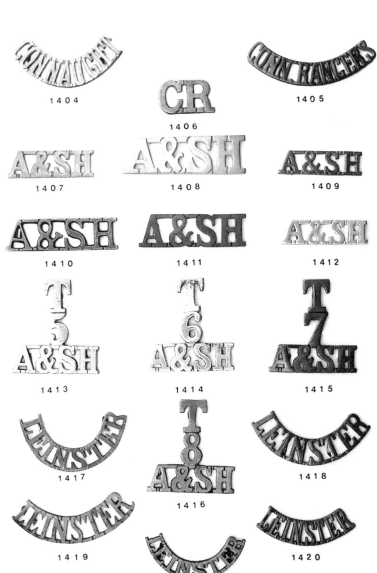

1404

1405

1406

1407

1408

1409

1410

1411

1412

1413

1414

1415

1417

1416

1418

1419

1421

1420

1422

Plate 89

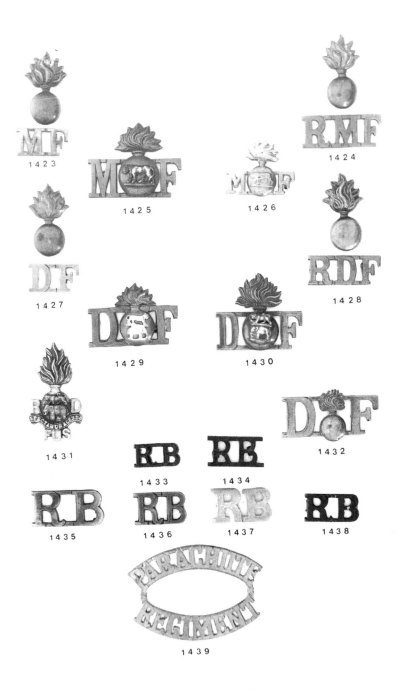

1 4 2 3

1 4 2 5

1 4 2 6

1 4 2 4

1 4 2 7

1 4 2 9

1 4 3 0

1 4 2 8

1 4 3 1

1 4 3 3

1 4 3 4

1 4 3 2

1 4 3 5

1 4 3 6

1 4 3 7

1 4 3 8

1 4 3 9

Plate 90

1 4 4 0

1 4 4 1

1 4 4 2

1 4 4 3

1 4 4 4

1 4 4 5

1 4 4 6

1 4 4 7

1 4 4 8

1 4 5 1

1 4 4 9

1 4 5 0

1 4 5 2

1 4 5 3

1 4 5 5

1 4 5 4

1 4 5 6

Plate 91

1457

1458

1459

1460

1461

1462

1463

1464

1465

1466

1468

1467

1469

Plate 92

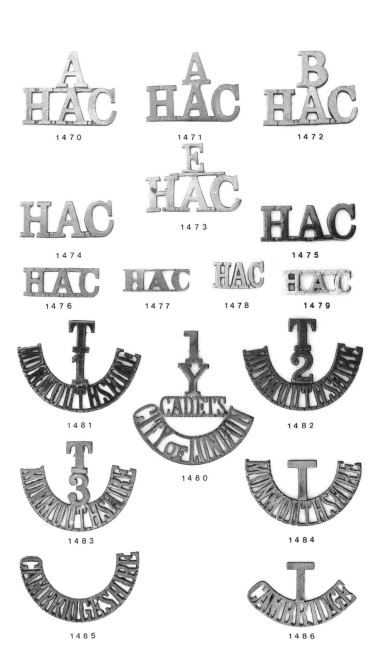

1470

1471

1472

1473

1474

1475

1476

1477

1478

1479

1481

1480

1482

1483

1484

1485

1486

Plate 93

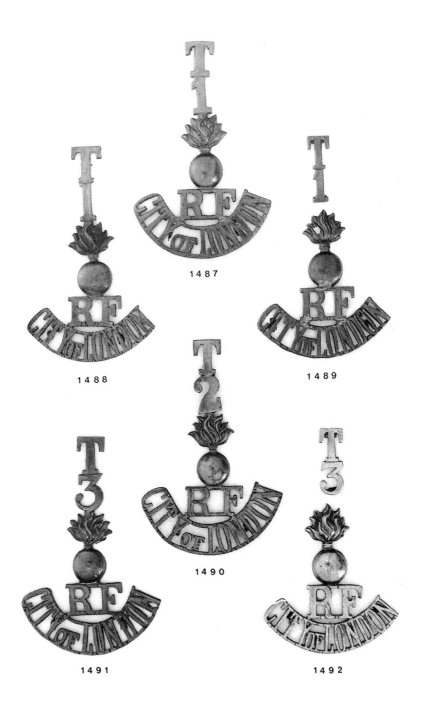

1487

1488

1489

1490

1491

1492

Plate 94

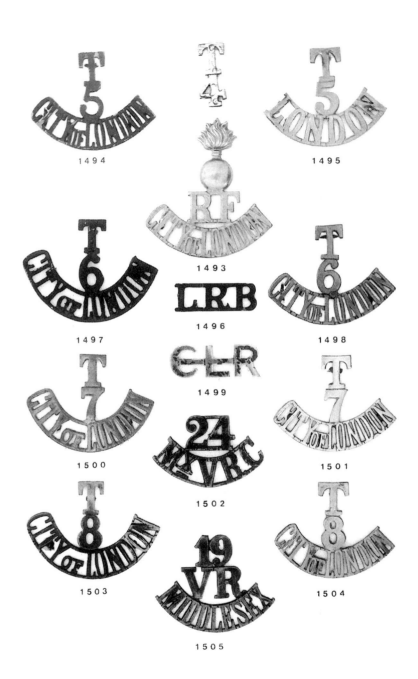

1494

1495

1493

1496

1497

1498

1499

1500

1501

1502

1503

1504

1505

Plate 95

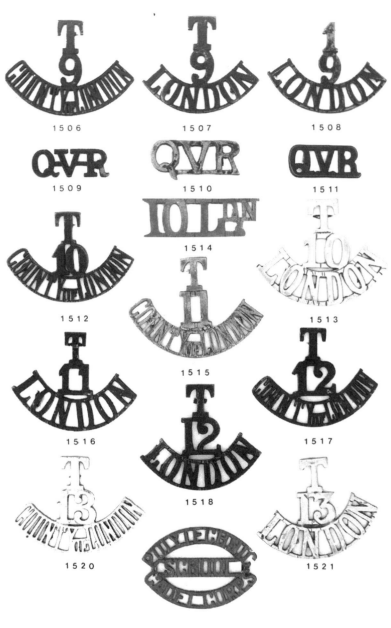

1506

1507

1508

1509

1510

1511

1512

1514

1513

1515

1516

1517

1518

1520

1519

1521

Plate 96

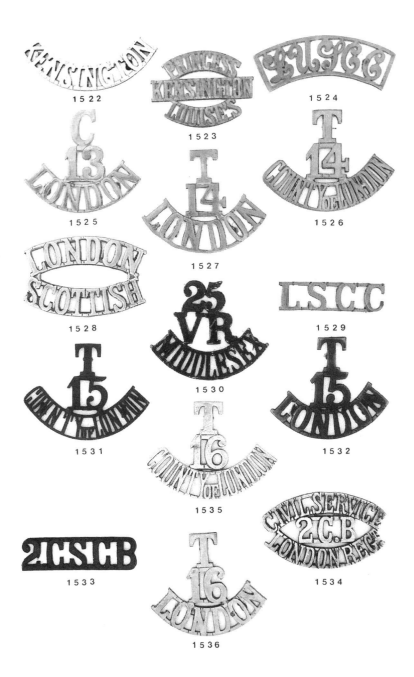

1522

1523

1524

1525

1526

1527

1528

1529

1530

1531

1532

1535

1533

1534

1536

Plate 97

Plate 98

1552

1553

1555

1554

1556

1558

1557

1559

1560

1561

1565

1562

1563

1564

Plate 99

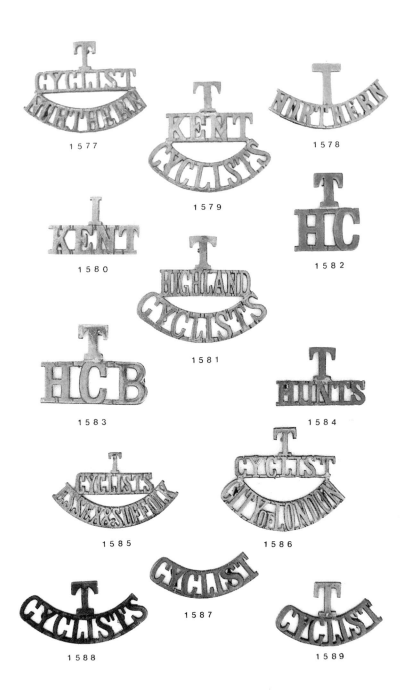

1577

1578

1579

1580

1582

1581

1583

1584

1585

1586

1587

1588

1589

Plate 100

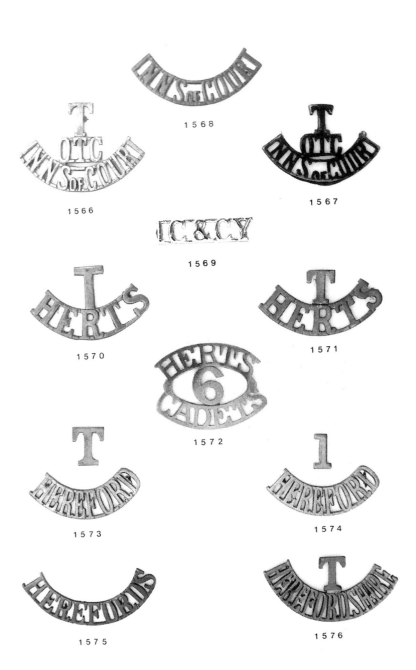

1568

1566

1567

IC & CY

1569

1570

1571

1572

1573

1574

1575

1576

Plate 101

1590

1591

1592

1593

1594

Plate 102

1595

1597

1596

1598

1599

1600

1601

1602

1603

1604

1605

1606

1607

Plate 103

1 6 0 8

1 6 0 9

1 6 1 0

1 6 1 1

1 6 1 2

1 6 1 3

1 6 1 4

1 6 1 5

1 6 1 6

1 6 1 7

Plate 104

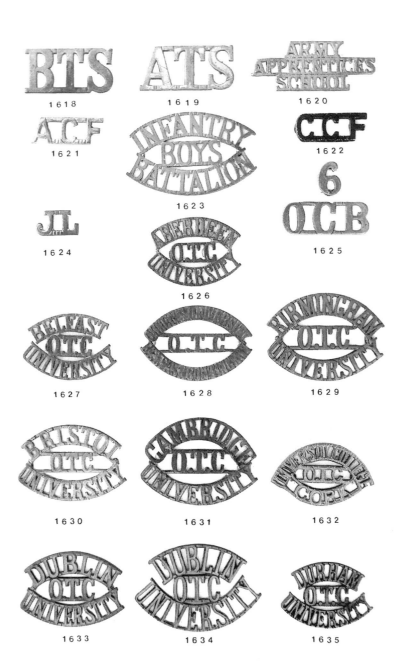

1618

1619

1620

1621

1622

1623

1624

1625

1626

1627

1628

1629

1630

1631

1632

1633

1634

1635

Plate 105

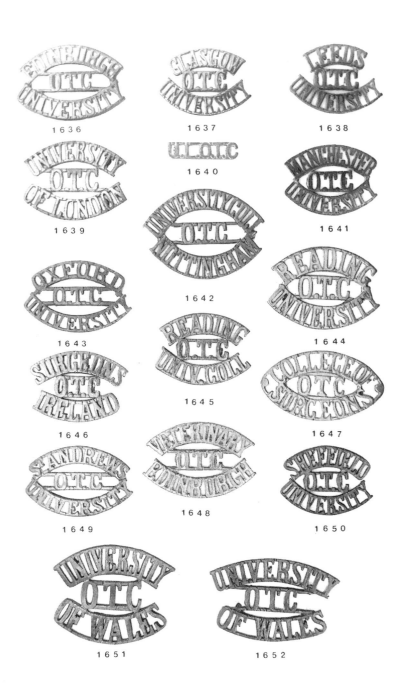

1636

1637

1638

1639

1640

1641

1642

1643

1644

1645

1646

1647

1648

1649

1650

1651

1652

Plate 106

ABINGDON / O.T.C.
1653

ALDENHAM / O.T.C. / SCHOOL
1654

O.T.C. / ALLEYN'S
1655

ALL HALLOWS / O.T.C. / SCHOOL
1656

AMPLEFORTH / O.T.C. / COLLEGE
1657

BARNARD / O.T.C. / CASTLE
1659

ARDINGLY / O.T.C. / COLLEGE
1658

BEDFORD / O.T.C. / GRAMMAR SCHOOL
1662

BATH / O.T.C. / COLLEGE
1660

BEAUMONT / O.T.C. / COLLEGE
1661

BEDFORD / O.T.C. / MODERN SCHOOL
1664

BEDFORD / O.T.C. / SCHOOL
1663

BERKHAMSTED / O.T.C. / SCHOOL
1665

BLOXHAM / O.T.C. / SCHOOL
1667

BISHOP VESEYS / O.T.C. / GRAMMAR SCHOOL
1666

Plate 107

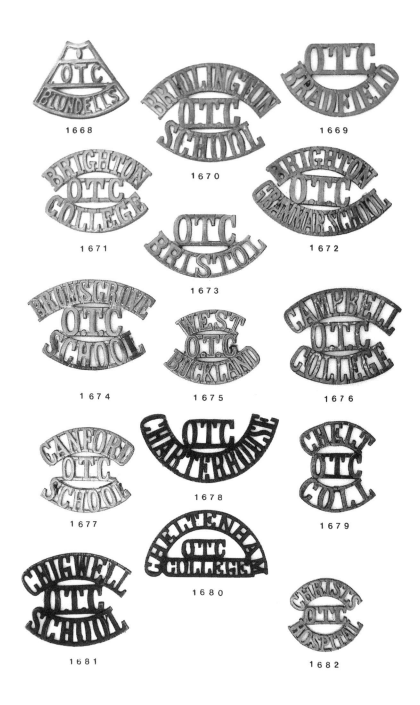

1668

1670

1669

1671

1672

1673

1674

1675

1676

1677

1678

1679

1680

1681

1682

Plate 108

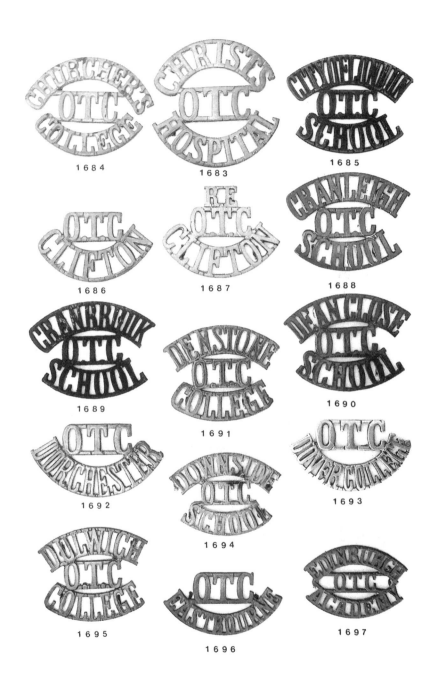

CHURCHER'S / OTC / COLLEGE
1684

CHRIST'S / OTC / HOSPITAL
1683

CITY OF LONDON / OTC / SCHOOL
1685

OTC / CLIFTON
1686

RE / OTC / CLIFTON
1687

CRANLEIGH / OTC / SCHOOL
1688

CRANBROOK / OTC / SCHOOL
1689

DENSTONE / OTC / COLLEGE
1691

DEANCLOSE / OTC / SCHOOL
1690

OTC / DORCHESTER
1692

DOWNSIDE / OTC / SCHOOL
1694

OTC / DOVER COLLEGE
1693

DULWICH / OTC / COLLEGE
1695

OTC / EASTBOURNE
1696

EDINBURGH / OTC / ACADEMY
1697

Plate 109

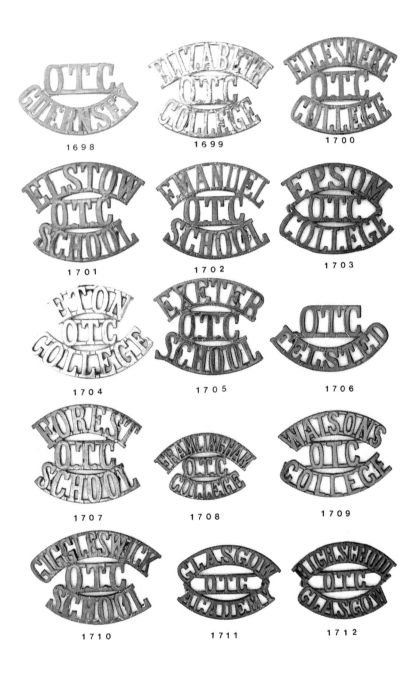

1698

1699

1700

1701

1702

1703

1704

1705

1706

1707

1708

1709

1710

1711

1712

Plate 110

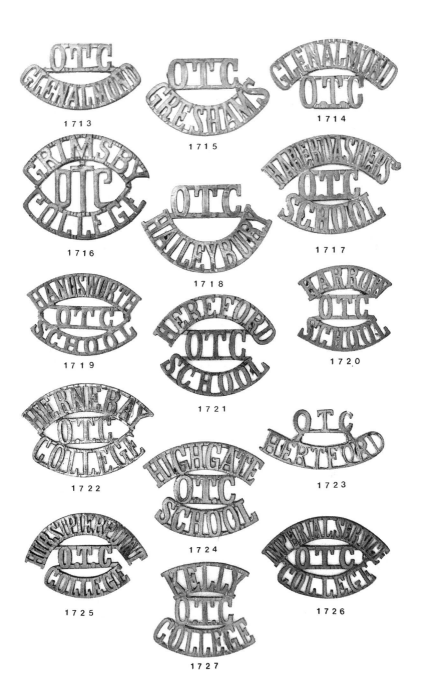

1713

1715

1714

1716

1718

1717

1719

1721

1720

1722

1724

1723

1725

1727

1726

Plate 111

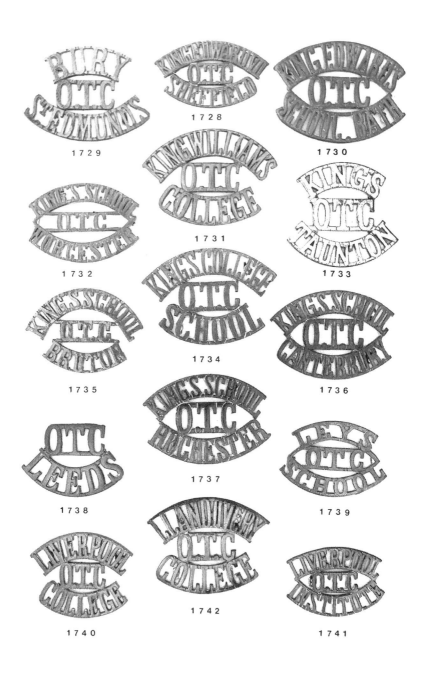

1729

1728

1730

1732

1731

1733

1735

1734

1736

1738

1737

1739

1740

1742

1741

Plate 112

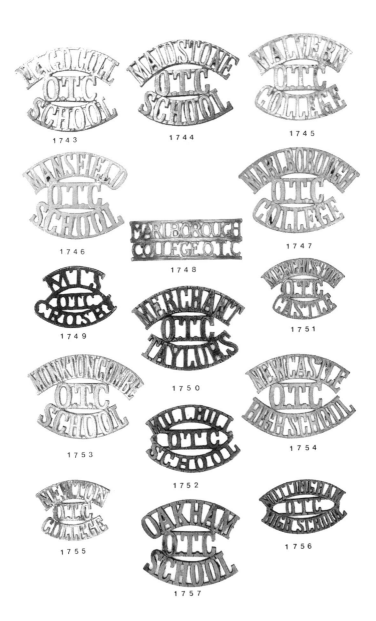

1743

1744

1745

1746

1747

1748

1749

1750

1751

1752

1753

1754

1755

1756

1757

Plate 113

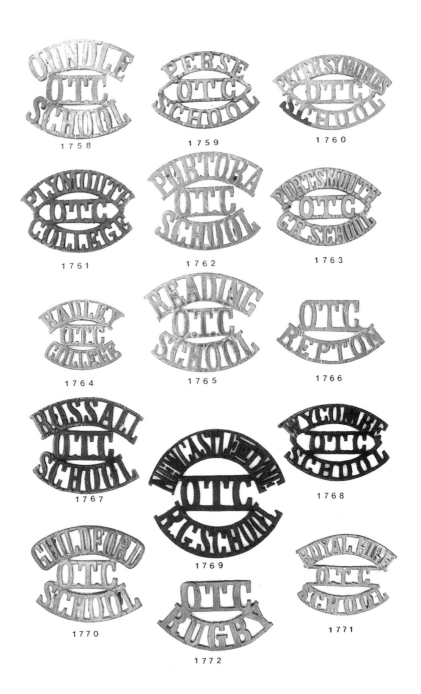

1758

1759

1760

1761

1762

1763

1764

1765

1766

1767

1768

1769

1770

1771

1772

Plate 114

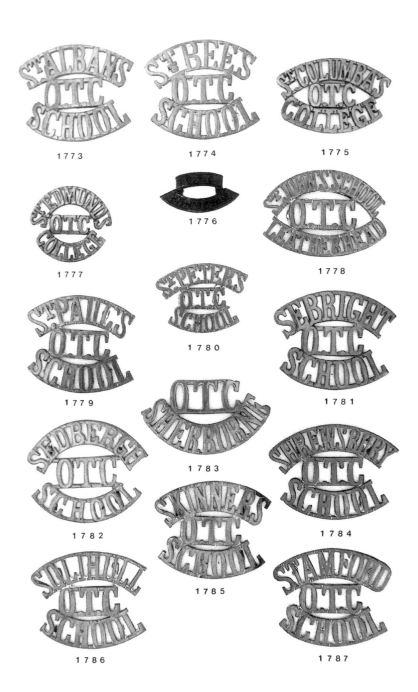

1773

1774

1775

1777

1776

1778

1779

1780

1781

1782

1783

1784

1786

1785

1787

Plate 115

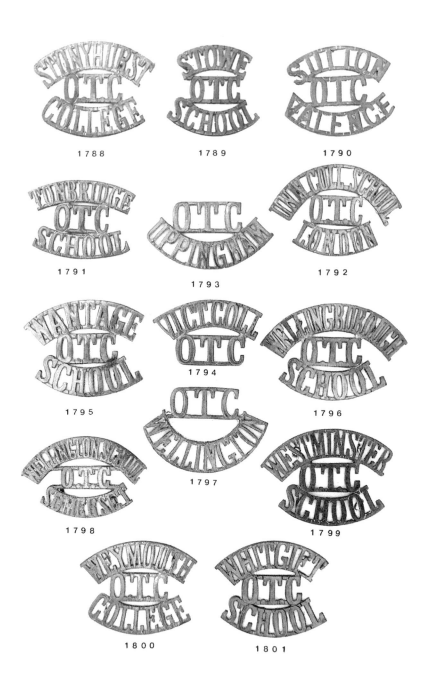

1788

1789

1790

1791

1793

1792

1795

1794

1796

1797

1798

1799

1800

1801

Plate 116

1 8 0 2

1 8 0 3

1 8 0 4

1 8 0 5

1 8 0 6

1 8 0 7

1 8 0 8

1 8 0 9

1 8 1 0

1 8 1 2

1 8 1 1

1 8 1 3

1 8 1 5

1 8 1 4

1 8 1 6

Plate 117

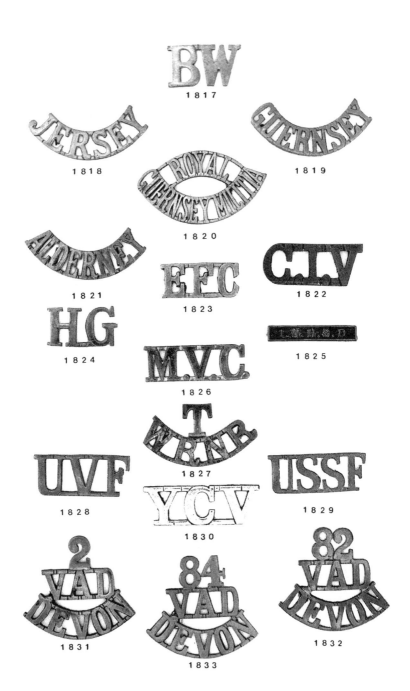

Plate 118

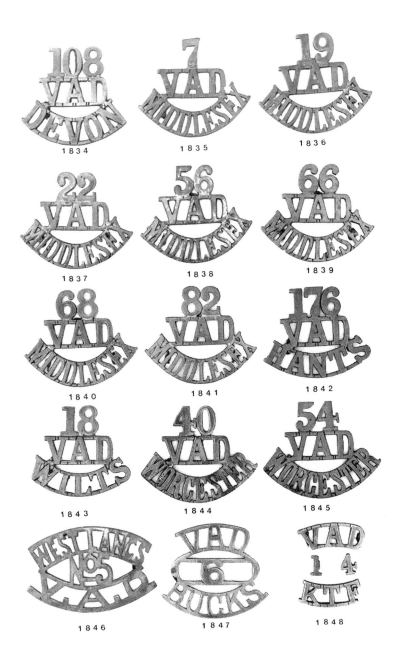

108
V.A.D
DEVON
1 8 3 4

7
V.A.D
MIDDLESEX
1 8 3 5

19
V.A.D
MIDDLESEX
1 8 3 6

22
V.A.D
MIDDLESEX
1 8 3 7

56
V.A.D
MIDDLESEX
1 8 3 8

66
V.A.D
MIDDLESEX
1 8 3 9

68
V.A.D
MIDDLESEX
1 8 4 0

82
V.A.D
MIDDLESEX
1 8 4 1

176
V.A.D
HANTS
1 8 4 2

18
V.A.D
WILTS
1 8 4 3

40
V.A.D
WORCESTER
1 8 4 4

54
V.A.D
WORCESTER
1 8 4 5

WEST LANCS
No 5
V.A.D
1 8 4 6

V.A.D
6
BUCKS
1 8 4 7

V.A.D
1   4
K.T.F
1 8 4 8

Plate 119

1849

1851

1850

1852

1853

1854

1856

1855

VTC

1857

1858

Plate 120

Index